Better Homes and Gardens®

NEW diabetic COOKBOOK

Better Homes and Gardens₀ Books
An imprint of Meredith₀ Books

New Diabetic Cookbook
Editor: Kristi M. Fuller, R.D.
Associate Design Director: Ken Carlson
Photographer: Studio Central
Contributing Writers: Diane Quagliani, R.D.; David Feder, R.D.; Donna Shields, R.D.
Contributing Editors: Margaret Agnew, Jan Miller, R.D.; Kathy Rethman, R.D., C.D.E.; Marcia Stanley, R.D.;
Recipe Development: Deanne Hrabak, R.D., Debbie Maugans, Carol Munson
Copy Chief: Catherine Hamrick
Copy and Production Editor: Terri Fredrickson
Contributing Copy Editor: Marcia Gilmer
Contributing Proofreaders: Susie Kling, Sheila Mauck, Beth Popplewell
Electronic Production Coordinator: Paula Forest
Editorial and Design Assistants: Judy Bailey, Karen Schirm
Test Kitchen Director: Sharon Stilwell
Test Kitchen Product Supervisor: Marilyn Cornelius
Production Director: Douglas M. Johnston
Production Manager: Pam Kvitne
Assistant Prepress Manager: Marjorie J. Schenkelberg

Meredith₀ Books
Editor in Chief: James D. Blume
Design Director: Matt Strelecki
Managing Editor: Gregory H. Kayko
Executive Food Editor: Lisa Holderness

Director, Sales & Marketing, Retail: Michael A. Peterson
Director, Sales & Marketing, Special Markets: Rita McMullen
Director, Sales & Marketing, Home & Garden Center Channel: Ray Wolf
Director, Operations: George A. Susral

Vice President, General Manager: Jamie L. Martin

Better Homes and Gardens₀ Magazine
Editor in Chief: Jean LemMon
Executive Food Editor: Nancy Byal

Meredith Publishing Group
President, Publishing Group: Christopher M. Little
Vice President, Consumer Marketing & Development: Hal Oringer

Meredith Corporation
Chairman and Chief Executive Officer: William T. Kerr

Chairman of the Executive Committee: E. T. Meredith III

All of us at Better Homes and Gardens₀ Books are dedicated to providing you with the information and ideas you need to create delicious foods. We welcome your comments and suggestions. Write to us at: Better Homes and Gardens₀ Books, Cookbook Editorial Department, 1716 Locust St., Des Moines, IA 50309-3023.

If you would like to purchase any of our books, please check wherever books are sold.

Our seal assures you that every recipe in *New Diabetic Cookbook* has been tested in the Better Homes and Gardens₀ Test Kitchen. This means that each recipe is practical and reliable, and meets our high standards of taste appeal. We guarantee your satisfaction with this book for as long as you own it.

contents

snacks
& SIPPERS

Small snacks throughout the day fit nicely into a well-balanced diabetic meal plan—but an ordinary snack of cheese and crackers can become monotonous. Here is a variety of snacks to look forward to. From Minty Cocoa to Crispy Parmesan Chips, snacking just got more exciting!

Mango Yogurt Pops, *recipe page 10*

minty COCOA

Chocolate and mint have always been a great flavor duo. The combination in this beverage is no exception; getting your daily calcium never tasted so good. The Mocha Cooler variation is a must for coffee fans.

Start to Finish: 15 minutes

½ **cup unsweetened cocoa powder**

Heat-stable sugar substitute equal to ¼ cup sugar, or ¼ cup sugar

10 **striped round peppermint candies, finely crushed**

6 **cups fat-free milk**

Exchanges: 1½ Milk

1 In a large saucepan stir together the cocoa powder, sugar substitute or sugar, crushed candies, and ¾ cup of the milk. Cook and stir over medium heat until mixture just comes to boiling. Stir in the remaining milk; heat through. Do not boil. Remove from heat. If desired, beat with a rotary beater until frothy. Makes six 1-cup servings.

Nutrition facts per serving: 134 calories, **1 g** total fat (**0 g** saturated fat), **4 mg** cholesterol, **128 mg** sodium, **21 g** carbohydrate, **0 g** fiber, **10 g** protein
Daily values: 15% vit. A, **3%** vit. C, **31%** calcium, **7%** iron

If using ¼ cup sugar option: 167 calories and **28 g** carbohydrate

Mocha Cooler: Prepare as above, except omit the peppermint candies; increase the heat-stable sugar substitute to equal ⅓ cup sugar or increase the sugar to ⅓ cup. Add 2 to 3 teaspoons instant coffee crystals with the ¾ cup milk. Cook and stir over medium heat until mixture just comes to boiling. Remove from heat; stir in the remaining milk. Serve immediately over ice. (Or, cover and chill. Stir before serving over ice.)

Nutrition facts per serving: 117 calories, **1 g** total fat (**0 g** saturated fat), **4 mg** cholesterol, **126 mg** sodium, **17 g** carbohydrate, **0 g** fiber, **10 g** protein
Daily values: 15% vit. A, **3%** vit. C, **31%** calcium, **7%** iron

If using ⅓ cup sugar option: 160 calories and **26 g** carbohydrate

pineapple ginger SPRITZER

You'll find crystallized ginger (candied ginger), the key ingredient in this fruit flavored drink, in the supermarket spice aisle or stocked with the dried fruits. Or, look for it in a specialty food store.

Prep: 10 minutes
Chill: 2 to 24 hours

4   **cups unsweetened pineapple juice**

1   **tablespoon chopped crystallized ginger**

    Ice cubes

2   **cups carbonated water, chilled**

    Pineapple spears (optional)

Exchanges: 1½ Fruit

❶ In a pitcher combine pineapple juice and ginger. Cover and chill for 2 to 24 hours. Strain juice mixture, discarding ginger.

❷ For each serving, pour pineapple juice into a tall glass over ice, filling each glass about three-fourths full. Add enough carbonated water to each glass to fill. If desired, garnish with pineapple spears. Makes six 1-cup servings.

Nutrition facts per serving: 101 calories, **0 g** total fat (**0 g** saturated fat), **0 mg** cholesterol, **19 mg** sodium, **25 g** carbohydrate, **0 g** fiber, **1 g** protein
Daily values: 0% vit. A, **31%** vit. C, **3%** calcium, **6%** iron

Sweets for the Sweet

At one time, sugar was strictly forbidden for someone with diabetes. That's no longer true. Research has shown that sugar doesn't affect blood sugar levels any more than other carbohydrates, such as rice, potatoes, or fruit. However, high-sugar foods can be high in fat and calories and low in nutrition. The bottom line: Use sugar in moderation and count sugary foods as part of your meal plan—not in addition to it. Choose snacks and treats that have nutrition pluses, such as calcium-rich hot chocolate (see recipe, page 6) or a vitamin-packed fruit juice spritzer (see recipe, above).

fruit KABOBS

Kabobs are a fun way to serve fruit for parties, and a cool dip adds extra pizzazz. Seasonal substitutes, such as fresh peaches, nectarines, and plums or mangoes, add flavorful variety.

Prep: 20 minutes
Chill: 30 to 60 minutes

¾ **cup cantaloupe chunks**

¾ **cup honeydew melon chunks**

¾ **cup small strawberries**

¾ **cup pineapple chunks**

2 **small bananas, peeled and cut into 1-inch slices**

1 **cup orange juice**

¼ **cup lime juice**

1 **8-ounce carton vanilla low-fat or fat-free yogurt**

2 **tablespoons frozen orange juice concentrate, thawed**

Ground nutmeg or ground cinnamon (optional)

Exchanges: 1½ Fruit

❶ On eight 6-inch or four 10-inch skewers alternately thread the cantaloupe, honeydew melon, strawberries, pineapple, and bananas. Place kabobs in a glass baking dish. Combine orange juice and lime juice; pour evenly over kabobs. Cover; chill kabobs for 30 to 60 minutes, turning occasionally.

❷ Meanwhile, for dip, in a small bowl stir together the yogurt and orange juice concentrate. Cover and chill until ready to serve.

❸ To serve, arrange the kabobs on a serving platter; discard juice mixture. If desired, sprinkle nutmeg or cinnamon over dip. Serve dip with kabobs. Makes 8 servings.

Nutrition facts per serving (1 kabob and 2 tablespoons dip): 91 calories, **1 g** total fat (**0 g** saturated fat), **2 mg** cholesterol, **20 mg** sodium, **21 g** carbohydrate, **1 g** fiber, **2 g** protein **Daily values: 6%** vit. A, **78%** vit. C, **4%** calcium, **2%** iron

mango YOGURT POPS

Made with real fruit and fat-free yogurt, these pops are a healthful low-calorie treat. On a hot summer day, the tropical taste of this refreshing snack will hit the spot—for kids and adults alike. (See photograph, page 5.)

Prep: 15 minutes
Freeze: 4 to 6 hours

- **1 teaspoon unflavored gelatin**
- **⅓ cup peach nectar or apricot nectar**
- **2 6- or 8-ounce cartons vanilla or peach fat-free yogurt with sweetener**
- **⅓ of a 26-ounce jar refrigerated mango slices, drained, or one 8-ounce can peach slices, drained**

Exchanges: ½ Milk

1 In a small saucepan combine the unflavored gelatin and peach or apricot nectar. Let stand for 5 minutes. Cook and stir over medium heat until gelatin is dissolved.

2 In a blender container combine gelatin mixture, yogurt, and drained mango or peach slices. Cover and blend until smooth. Spoon mixture into eight 3-ounce paper cups. Cover each cup with foil. Cut a small slit in the center of each foil cover and insert a rounded wooden stick into each. Freeze pops for 4 to 6 hours or until firm.

3 To serve, remove the foil and tear paper cups away from pops. Makes 8 pops.

Nutrition facts per pop: 49 calories, **0 g** total fat (**0 g** saturated fat), **1 mg** cholesterol, **28 mg** sodium, **10 g** carbohydrate, **0 g** fiber, **2 g** protein
Daily values: 5% vit. A, **6%** vit. C, **6%** calcium, **0%** iron

Snack Sense

Snacking is important to any balanced diet. It helps your body go with the flow during the day and keeps your energy expenditure on an even keel, with fewer peaks and valleys. When you keep the edge off of your appetite, you tend to eat less during mealtimes. Some of the best snacks to enjoy are those high in protein. Yogurt fits that role very well. Keep a variety of flavored fat-free yogurts in the fridge. If a savory snack is what you're after, stir some chopped fresh vegetables into plain yogurt (a dash or two of garlic powder or a snippet of fresh herbs are other possible additions). But don't forget: It's important to keep track of snacks and stay within your total calorie allowance for the day.

crispy PARMESAN CHIPS

These homemade chips require no dip or spread since the cheese is baked right in. Look for wonton wrappers in the refrigerated area of the produce section.

Start to Finish: 30 minutes

30 **wonton wrappers**
    Nonstick spray coating
2   **tablespoons olive oil**
1   **clove garlic, minced**
½   **teaspoon dried basil, crushed**
¼   **cup grated Parmesan or Romano cheese**

Exchanges: ½ Starch ½ Fat

1 Use a sharp knife to cut wonton wrappers diagonally in half to form 60 triangles. Spray a baking sheet with nonstick coating. Arrange one-third of the triangles in a single layer on prepared baking sheet.

2 In a small bowl stir together the olive oil, garlic, and basil. Brush the wonton triangles lightly with some of the oil mixture; sprinkle with some of the Parmesan or Romano cheese.

3 Bake in a 350° oven about 8 minutes or until golden brown. Cool completely on a wire rack. Repeat with the remaining wonton triangles, oil mixture, and Parmesan or Romano cheese. Makes 60 chips (15 servings).

Nutrition facts per serving (4 chips): 70 calories, **3 g** total fat (**1 g** saturated fat), **3 mg** cholesterol, **123 mg** sodium, **9 g** carbohydrate, **0 g** fiber, **2 g** protein
Daily values: 0% vit. A, **0%** vit. C, **2%** calcium, **3%** iron

chèvre & TOMATO SPREAD

Goat cheese, with its intense tangy flavor, is a delightful complement to dried tomatoes. Together, they make an ideal spread for entertaining or everyday snacking.

Prep: 20 minutes
Chill: 2 to 4 hours

⅓ cup dried tomatoes (not oil-packed)

4 ounces soft goat cheese (chèvre)

½ of an 8-ounce package reduced-fat cream cheese (Neufchâtel), softened

¼ cup snipped fresh basil or 2 teaspoons dried basil, crushed

3 cloves garlic, minced

⅛ teaspoon black pepper

1 to 2 tablespoons fat-free milk

10 slices party rye bread or 20 assorted reduced-fat crackers

Assorted garnishes, such as quartered cherry tomatoes, broccoli flowerets, chopped yellow sweet pepper, and/or small fresh basil leaves (optional)

Exchanges: ½ Starch 1 Fat

1 In a small bowl cover dried tomatoes with boiling water. Let stand for 10 minutes. Drain tomatoes, discarding liquid. Finely snip tomatoes.

2 In a bowl stir together the snipped tomatoes, goat cheese, cream cheese, basil, garlic, and black pepper. Stir in enough milk to make the mixture of spreading consistency. Cover and chill for 2 to 4 hours. Serve with rye bread or crackers. If desired, top with assorted garnishes. Makes 1¼ cups spread (10 servings).

Nutrition facts per serving (2 slices party rye and 2 tablespoons spread):
94 calories, **6 g** total fat (**3 g** saturated fat), **19 mg** cholesterol, **202 mg** sodium, **6 g** carbohydrate, **0 g** fiber, **4 g** protein **Daily values: 5%** vit. A, **1%** vit. C, **2%** calcium, **2%** iron

creamy SPINACH DIP

Dips typically are loaded with fat, but by combining fat-free cottage cheese and light mayo, you get all the creaminess of a traditional dip without the unwanted extra calories and fat.

snacks & sippers

Prep: 15 minutes
Chill: 1 to 4 hours

1½ **cups fat-free cottage cheese**

⅓ **cup light mayonnaise dressing or salad dressing**

1 **tablespoon lemon juice**

1 **tablespoon fat-free milk**

1 **clove garlic, minced**

½ **teaspoon dried Italian seasoning, crushed**

Dash pepper

1 **cup finely chopped fresh spinach**

Assorted vegetable dippers, such as carrot, celery, zucchini, or sweet pepper sticks; cucumber slices; and/or cauliflower or broccoli flowerets

Exchanges: 2 Vegetable ½ Fat

1 In a blender container or food processor bowl combine the cottage cheese, mayonnaise dressing or salad dressing, lemon juice, milk, garlic, Italian seasoning, and pepper. Cover and blend or process until smooth. Stir in spinach. Cover and chill for 1 to 4 hours or overnight.

2 Stir dip before serving. Serve with vegetable dippers. Makes about 1¾ cups dip (8 servings).

Nutrition facts per serving (1 carrot and 3 tablespoons dip): 98 calories, **4 g** total fat (**1 g** saturated fat), **2 mg** cholesterol, **281 mg** sodium, **11 g** carbohydrate, **2 g** fiber, **6 g** protein **Daily values: 207%** vit. A, **16%** vit. C, **11%** calcium, **4%** iron

Skinnier Dairy Products

Fat-free milk (previously called skim) and reduced-fat milk (previously called low fat) have been around for years, but now almost every dairy-based product has a low-fat or fat-free version. Great news, since a low-fat diet is essential to controlling weight and minimizing health risks. Fat-free versions of yogurt, cottage cheese, and ice cream are readily available, and the majority of these dairy products have the full flavor we've come to expect. The next time you buy a dairy product, try the reduced-fat version or the fat-free version. You may be pleasantly surprised.

salmon CUCUMBER DIP

Cucumbers provide just the right amount of crunchy texture to this dip, which also can be used as a spread for making dainty tea sandwiches. The salmon makes this snack elegant enough to serve to party guests.

Prep: 20 minutes
Chill: 1 to 4 hours

- 1 **8-ounce carton fat-free dairy sour cream**
- 2 **tablespoons catsup or chili sauce**
- 1 **tablespoon finely chopped onion**
- ¼ **teaspoon salt**
- ½ **cup flaked, cooked salmon or canned salmon, drained, flaked, and skin and bones removed**
- ½ **cup finely chopped, seeded cucumber**
- 1 **plum tomato, seeded and finely chopped**
- 1 **tablespoon snipped fresh dill or parsley**

   Whole grain crackers or assorted vegetable dippers

Exchanges: 1 Starch

1 In a medium mixing bowl combine sour cream, catsup or chili sauce, onion, and salt. Stir in the salmon, cucumber, tomato, and dill or parsley. Cover and chill for 1 to 4 hours.

2 Serve dip with assorted crackers or vegetable dippers. Makes about 2 cups dip (16 servings).

Nutrition facts per serving (4 crackers and 2 tablespoons dip): 86 calories, **3 g** total fat (**0 g** saturated fat), **2 mg** cholesterol, **167 mg** sodium, **11 g** carbohydrate, **3 g** fiber, **3 g** protein **Daily values: 2%** vit. A, **2%** vit. C, **3%** calcium, **12%** iron

roasted pepper ROLL-UPS

The spinach and roasted red peppers combine for a bright, colorful filling. The high-fiber and high-protein beans create a very nutritious snack.

Prep: 20 minutes
Chill: 2 to 24 hours

1   **15-ounce can white kidney beans, rinsed and drained**

½   **of an 8-ounce package reduced-fat cream cheese (Neufchâtel), softened**

¼   **cup packed fresh basil**

1   **tablespoon fat-free milk**

2   **small cloves garlic, quartered**

⅛   **teaspoon freshly ground black pepper**

⅓   **cup roasted red sweet peppers, drained and finely chopped**

6   **6-inch flour tortillas**

1   **cup packed spinach leaves**

Exchanges: 1½ Starch 1 Fat

❶ For the filling, in a blender container or food processor bowl combine the beans, cream cheese, basil, milk, garlic, and black pepper. Cover and blend or process until smooth. Stir in roasted sweet peppers.

❷ To assemble, spread about ⅓ cup of the filling evenly over each tortilla to within ½ inch of the edges. Arrange spinach leaves over filling to cover. Carefully roll tortillas up tightly. Cover and chill roll-ups for 2 hours to 24 hours.

❸ To serve, use a sharp knife to cut roll-ups crosswise into 1½-inch slices. Serve immediately. Makes 6 servings.

Nutrition facts per serving: 173 calories, **7 g** total fat (**3 g** saturated fat), **15 mg** cholesterol, **289 mg** sodium, **24 g** carbohydrate, **4 g** fiber, **8 g** protein
Daily values: 10% vit. A, **38%** vit. C, **5%** calcium, **11%** iron

snacks & sippers

breads
& ROLLS

Breads (or starches) comprise a large proportion of a diabetic meal plan. You'll enjoy filling your quota with these recipes that go beyond a simple slice of bread. Choose from favorites such as scones, focaccia, muffins, popovers, and more.

Rosemary-Citrus Scones, *recipe page 24*

apple-cheddar MUFFINS

Applesauce and dried fruit keep these muffins moist. Spicy and aromatic, they're good for breakfast, brunch, tea, or snacks—especially when served with a cup of tea, cold milk, or hot cider.

breads & rolls

Prep: 20 minutes
Bake: 20 minutes

Nonstick spray coating

1¼ cups unprocessed wheat bran (Miller's Bran)

1 cup all-purpose flour

½ cup shredded reduced-fat sharp cheddar cheese (2 ounces)

2 teaspoons baking powder

½ teaspoon ground cinnamon

¼ teaspoon baking soda

¼ teaspoon salt

¾ cup unsweetened applesauce

½ cup fat-free milk

3 tablespoons honey plus 2 packets heat-stable sugar substitute, or ⅓ cup honey

¼ cup refrigerated or frozen egg product, thawed

1 tablespoon cooking oil

½ cup finely snipped dried apples or raisins

Exchanges: 1½ Starch

1 Spray twelve 2½-inch muffin cups with nonstick coating; set aside. In a medium bowl combine wheat bran, flour, cheese, baking powder, cinnamon, baking soda, and salt. Make a well in the center of the flour mixture; set aside.

2 In another bowl combine applesauce, milk, honey plus sugar substitute or honey, egg product, and oil. Add applesauce mixture all at once to flour mixture. Stir just until moistened (batter should be lumpy). Fold in dried apples or raisins.

3 Spoon the batter into prepared muffin cups, filling each three-fourths full. Bake in a 400° oven about 20 minutes or until golden. Cool in muffin cups on a wire rack for 5 minutes. Remove from muffin cups; serve warm. Makes 12 muffins.

Nutrition facts per muffin: 114 calories, **3 g** total fat (**1 g** saturated fat), **4 mg** cholesterol, **184 mg** sodium, **21 g** carbohydrate, **2 g** fiber, **4 g** protein
Daily values: **2%** vit. A, **0%** vit. C, **9%** calcium, **9%** iron

Using honey only option: **126** calories and **24 g** carbohydrate

High-Five for Fiber

Fiber is important in helping regulate blood sugar levels. And, you need lots of it—about 35 grams a day. Why all the fiber? Fiber helps you eat less, lose weight, and feel better. It fills you up without filling you out, keeps your digestive system regulated, and helps lower your body's level of the "bad" cholesterol—LDL cholesterol. The best sources are whole grains and fruits and vegetables (especially with the peel on). Also, include whole-grain breads, pastas, beans, and legumes in your menu plans. If you're not used to eating a high-fiber diet, remember to gradually incorporate fiber-rich foods into your diet and drink lots of water.

apricot-filled MUFFINS

Discover the extraordinary flavor of these muffins bursting with fruit. Tucked inside each muffin is a sweet pocket of your choice of fruit spread.

Prep: 20 minutes
Bake: 18 minutes

Nonstick spray coating

1½ **cups all-purpose flour**

3 **tablespoons sugar plus
    3 packets heat-stable sugar
    substitute, or ⅓ cup sugar**

1 **teaspoon baking powder**

1 **teaspoon ground cinnamon**

¼ **teaspoon baking soda**

⅛ **teaspoon salt**

⅔ **cup buttermilk**

¼ **cup refrigerated or frozen
    egg product, thawed**

3 **tablespoons cooking oil**

¼ **cup sugar-free apricot, peach,
    or raspberry spread**

Exchanges: 1½ Starch ½ Fat

❶ Spray twelve 2½-inch muffin cups with nonstick coating; set aside. In a medium bowl stir together flour, sugar plus sugar substitute or the sugar, baking powder, cinnamon, baking soda, and salt. Make a well in the center of the flour mixture; set aside.

❷ In another bowl stir together buttermilk, egg product, and oil. Add buttermilk mixture all at once to flour mixture. Stir just until moistened (batter should be lumpy).

❸ Spoon batter into prepared muffins cups, filling each about one-fourth full. Place about 1 teaspoon of the spreadable fruit in center of each. Top with remaining batter. Bake in a 400° oven for 18 to 20 minutes or until golden. Cool in muffin cups on a wire rack for 5 minutes. Remove from muffin cups; serve warm. Makes 12 muffins.

Nutrition facts per muffin: 109 calories, **4 g** total fat (**1 g** saturated fat),
1 mg cholesterol, **103 mg** sodium, **18 g** carbohydrate, **0 g** fiber, **3 g** protein
Daily values: 1% vit. A, **0%** vit. C, **4%** calcium, **6%** iron

Using the ⅓ cup sugar option: 121 calories and **21 g** carbohydrate

pumpkin MUFFINS

The secret to these enticing muffins is a combination of moist, rich pumpkin and flavorful buckwheat. Though buckwheat is often thought of as a cereal, it actually is made from the seeds of the buckwheat herb.

Prep: 20 minutes
Bake: 15 minutes

Nonstick spray coating

1⅓ **cups all-purpose flour**

¾ **cup buckwheat flour**

¼ **cup sugar plus 2 packets heat-stable sugar substitute, or ⅓ cup sugar**

1½ **teaspoons baking powder**

1 **teaspoon ground cinnamon**

½ **teaspoon baking soda**

½ **teaspoon salt**

2 **slightly beaten eggs**

1 **cup canned pumpkin**

½ **cup fat-free milk**

2 **tablespoons cooking oil**

½ **teaspoon finely shredded orange peel**

¼ **cup orange juice**

Exchanges: 1½ Starch ½ Fat

❶ Spray twelve 2½-inch muffin cups with nonstick coating; set pan aside. In a medium bowl combine the all-purpose flour, buckwheat flour, sugar plus sugar substitute or the sugar, baking powder, cinnamon, baking soda, and salt. Make a well in the center of flour mixture; set aside.

❷ In another bowl combine the eggs, pumpkin, milk, oil, orange peel, and orange juice. Add the egg mixture all at once to the flour mixture. Stir just until moistened (batter should be lumpy).

❸ Spoon batter into the prepared muffin cups, dividing the batter evenly. Bake in a 400° oven for 15 to 20 minutes or until the muffins are light brown. Cool in muffin cups on a wire rack for 5 minutes. Remove from muffin cups; serve warm. Makes 12 muffins.

Nutrition facts per muffin: 134 calories, **4 g** total fat (**1 g** saturated fat), **36 mg** cholesterol, **204 mg** sodium, **22 g** carbohydrate, **2 g** fiber, **4 g** protein
Daily values: 47% vit. A, **6%** vit. C, **6%** calcium, **9%** iron

Using the ⅓ cup sugar option: 141 calories and **24 g** carbohydrate

rosemary-citrus SCONES

According to legend, scones are named for the Stone of Scone, the place where Scottish kings were crowned. With only 3 tablespoons of oil, these scones are fit for fit royalty. (See photograph, page 19.)

(See photograph, page 19.)

Prep: 20 minutes
Bake: 15 minutes

Nonstick spray coating
1¾ **cups all-purpose flour**
1 **cup rolled oats**
¼ **cup sugar**
1 **tablespoon baking powder**
1 **tablespoon finely shredded orange peel**
1½ **teaspoons dried rosemary, crushed**
¼ **teaspoon salt**
½ **cup evaporated fat-free milk**
3 **tablespoons cooking oil**
3 **tablespoons refrigerated or frozen egg product, thawed**

Exchanges: 1½ Starch ½ Fat

① Spray a baking sheet with nonstick coating; set aside. In a large bowl combine flour, oats, sugar, baking powder, orange peel, rosemary, and salt. In another bowl stir together milk, oil, and egg product. Add milk mixture all at once to flour mixture. Stir just until moistened.

② On a lightly floured surface knead dough 10 times. Lightly roll or pat dough to an 8-inch circle, about ¾ inch thick. Cut dough into 12 wedges. Carefully transfer wedges to prepared baking sheet. Bake in a 400° oven for 15 to 18 minutes or until golden brown. Remove from baking sheet and cool on a wire rack for 5 minutes; serve warm. Makes 12 scones.

Nutrition facts per scone: 145 calories, **4 g** total fat (**1 g** saturated fat), **0 mg** cholesterol, **153 mg** sodium, **23 g** carbohydrate, **1 g** fiber, **4 g** protein
Daily values: **3%** vit. A, **1%** vit. C, **10%** calcium, **8%** iron

A Meal Fit For A King

Oatmeal has always been a wise choice for breakfast. Because it's naturally high in fiber, oatmeal is a powerful player in helping prevent heart disease. It also has been credited with helping to reduce blood pressure, regulating blood glucose levels, and reducing the risk of certain cancers, such as stomach and colon cancer. Add variety to your daily bowl of hot oatmeal by stirring in fresh fruit slices, dried fruits—such as tart cherries or blueberries—or an occasional spoonful of chopped toasted nuts. Or, for a new twist, try it in baked goods, as in these delicious scones (see recipe, above).

caramelized ONION ROLLS

Roll up the flavor of onions! Cooked until caramelized and brown, onions are baked into the simplest of yeast breads—a convenient hot roll mix. Serve these spiral rolls with soup or salad.

Prep: 30 minutes
Rise: 30 minutes
Bake: 20 minutes

- **2 large onions, chopped**
- **2 teaspoons oil**
- **1 tablespoon margarine or butter**
- **2 tablespoons brown sugar**
   Nonstick spray coating
- **1 16-ounce package hot roll mix**

Exchanges: 2 Starch ½ Fat

1 In a large nonstick skillet cook onions in oil and margarine or butter over medium-low heat about 10 minutes, stirring frequently, until tender and golden brown. Stir in brown sugar; continue cooking until sugar melts. Set aside.

2 Spray a 13×9×2-inch baking pan with nonstick coating; set aside. Prepare hot roll mix according to package directions. On a lightly floured surface, roll the dough into a 15×10-inch rectangle. Spread caramelized onions evenly over dough. Roll up dough, jelly-roll style, starting from a long side; seal seam. Cut crosswise into 12 slices. Arrange rolls, cut sides down, in prepared baking pan. Cover and let rise in a warm place until double (about 30 minutes).

3 Bake in a 375° oven for 20 to 30 minutes or until golden brown. Remove from pan; serve warm or cool. Makes 12 rolls.

Nutrition facts per roll: 194 calories, **5 g** total fat (**1 g** saturated fat), **18 mg** cholesterol, **261 mg** sodium, **33 g** carbohydrate, **0 g** fiber, **6 g** protein
Daily values: 4% vit. A, **1%** vit. C, **0%** calcium, **7%** iron

breads & rolls

easy herb FOCACCIA

Focaccia (foh-KAH-chee-ah) is an Italian yeast bread usually topped with onions, herbs, olive oil, or cheese. Our easy version is made with a hot roll mix. Serve it with pasta or enjoy a slice as a midafternoon snack.

Prep: 20 minutes
Rise: 30 minutes
Bake: 15 minutes

Nonstick spray coating

1 **16-ounce package hot roll mix**

1 **egg**

2 **tablespoons olive oil**

⅔ **cup finely chopped onion**

1 **teaspoon dried rosemary, crushed**

2 **teaspoons olive oil**

Exchanges: 1 Starch

① Spray a 15×10×1-inch baking pan or a 12- to 14-inch pizza pan with nonstick coating; set aside.

② Prepare the hot roll mix according to package directions for the basic dough, using the 1 egg and substituting the 2 tablespoons olive oil for the margarine. Knead dough; allow to rest as directed. If using the large baking pan, roll dough into a 15×10-inch rectangle and carefully transfer to prepared pan. If using the pizza pan, roll dough into a 12-inch circle and carefully transfer to prepared pan.

③ In a skillet cook onion and rosemary in the 2 teaspoons hot olive oil until tender. With fingertips, press indentations every inch or so in dough. Top dough evenly with onion mixture. Cover and let rise in a warm place until nearly double (about 30 minutes).

④ Bake in a 375° oven for 15 to 20 minutes or until golden. Cool 10 minutes on a wire rack. Remove focaccia from pan; cool completely. Makes 24 servings.

Nutrition facts per serving: 88 calories, **2 g** total fat (**0 g** saturated fat), **9 mg** cholesterol, **113 mg** sodium, **15 g** carbohydrate, **0 g** fiber, **3 g** protein
Daily values: 0% vit. A, **0%** vit. C, **0%** calcium, **3%** iron

Parmesan and Pine Nut Focaccia: Prepare focaccia as above, except omit the onion, rosemary, and 2 teaspoons olive oil. Make the indentations, then brush the dough with mixture of 1 egg white and 2 tablespoon water. Sprinkle with ¼ cup pine nuts, pressing lightly into dough. Sprinkle with 2 tablespoons fresh grated Parmesan cheese. Bake as directed.

Nutrition facts per serving: 95 calories, **3 g** total fat (**0 g** saturated fat), **9 mg** cholesterol, **122 mg** sodium, **15 g** carbohydrate, **0 g** fiber, **4 g** protein
Daily values: 0% vit. A, **0%** vit. C, **0%** calcium, **4%** iron

tomato-basil CORNBREAD

Enjoy old-fashioned cornbread with a new twist! This updated classic has fewer calories and less fat than the original, but the flavor is better than ever due to the addition of basil and zesty dried tomatoes.

Prep: 20 minutes
Bake: 15 minutes

Nonstick spray coating

1 **cup all-purpose flour**

1 **cup cornmeal**

2 **tablespoons sugar**

2 **tablespoons snipped fresh basil or 1 teaspoon dried basil, crushed**

1 **tablespoon baking powder**

¼ **teaspoon salt**

1 **cup fat-free milk**

½ **cup egg product**

3 **tablespoon cooking oil**

½ **cup dried tomato pieces (not oil-packed)**

Exchanges: 1½ Starch ½ Fat

❶ Spray a 9×1½-inch round baking pan with nonstick coating; set aside. In a large bowl combine flour, cornmeal, sugar, basil, baking powder, and salt. In small bowl combine the milk, egg product, and oil. Add the milk mixture all at once to flour mixture. Stir just until moistened (batter should be lumpy). Fold the tomato pieces into the batter. Spoon the batter into prepared pan.

❷ Bake in a 425° oven for 15 to 20 minutes or until a wooden toothpick inserted into center comes out clean. Cool on a wire rack. Cut into wedges to serve. Makes 12 servings.

Nutrition facts per serving: 138 calories, **4 g** total fat (**1 g** saturated fat), **0 mg** cholesterol, **212 mg** sodium, **21 g** carbohydrate, **1 g** fiber, **4 g** protein
Daily values: 4% vit. A, **1%** vit. C, **10%** calcium, **8%** iron

chile & cheese CORNBREAD

Want to be hailed as the hero of the kitchen? Just serve chunks of this pepper-, corn-, and onion-laced cornbread. It's the ideal accompaniment for hot soup, grilled meat, or baked chicken.

Prep: 25 minutes
Bake: 20 minutes

Nonstick spray coating

1   **tablespoon margarine or butter**

⅓   **cup finely chopped red sweet pepper**

¼   **cup finely chopped red onion**

⅔   **cup whole kernel corn**

3   **tablespoons canned diced green chile peppers, drained**

1⅓ **cups yellow cornmeal**

1¼ **cups all-purpose flour**

2   **teaspoons baking powder**

1   **teaspoon sugar**

½   **teaspoon baking soda**

¼   **teaspoon salt**

1¼ **cups buttermilk**

2   **eggs, slightly beaten**

2   **tablespoons margarine or butter, melted and cooled**

½   **cup shredded, reduced-fat cheddar cheese**

Exchanges: 1 Starch **½** Fat

1 Spray an 11×7×2-inch baking pan with nonstick coating; set aside. In a medium skillet heat the 1 tablespoon margarine or butter over medium-high heat. Cook and stir sweet pepper and onion for 3 minutes. Add corn and chile peppers; cook and stir for 2 more minutes. Remove from heat; cool slightly.

2 Meanwhile, in a large bowl stir together cornmeal, flour, baking powder, sugar, baking soda, and salt. In another bowl stir together the buttermilk, eggs, and the 2 tablespoons melted margarine or butter. Add the buttermilk mixture all at once to flour mixture. Stir just until moistened (batter should be lumpy). Fold in the corn mixture and cheese. Spoon batter into prepared pan. Bake in a 425° oven for 20 to 25 minutes or until golden. Serve warm. Makes 18 servings.

Chile & Cheese Corn Muffins: Prepare as above, except spoon batter into 18 greased or paper-lined 2½-inch muffin cups. Bake in a 425° oven about 20 minutes or until muffins are golden. Cool in muffin cups on a wire rack for 5 minutes. Remove the muffins from the muffin cups; serve warm. If desired, place muffins in an airtight freezer container and freeze for up to 3 months.

Nutrition facts per serving: 119 calories, **4 g** total fat (**1 g** saturated fat), **27 mg** cholesterol, **182 mg** sodium, **17 g** carbohydrate, **1 g** fiber, **4 g** protein
Daily values: 6% vit. A, **7%** vit. C, **7%** calcium, **6%** iron

breads & rolls

apricot LADDER LOAF

Don't tell! There's no need for everyone to know how easy it is to make this impressive yeast bread. It only takes three main ingredients—frozen bread dough, light preserves, and chopped fruit.

Prep: 30 minutes
Rise: 40 minutes
Bake: 20 minutes

Nonstick spray coating

1 **16-ounce loaf frozen white or whole wheat bread dough, thawed***

½ **cup sugar-free apricot, strawberry, or red raspberry spread**

½ **cup chopped apricots; chopped, peeled peaches; blueberries; or raspberries**

Exchanges: ½ Starch

① Spray 2 baking sheets with nonstick coating; set aside. Transfer thawed bread dough onto a lightly floured surface. Divide the dough in half. Roll each half of the dough into a 12×7-inch rectangle. Carefully transfer each rectangle to a prepared baking sheet.

② Cut up any large pieces of fruit in the preserves. For each loaf, spoon about ¼ cup of the preserves down the center third of the dough rectangle to within 1 inch of the ends. Sprinkle ¼ cup of the fruit over the preserves. On the long sides, make 2-inch-long cuts from the edges toward the center at 1-inch intervals. Starting at one end, alternately fold opposite strips of dough, at an angle, across filling. Slightly press the ends together in the center to seal. Cover and let rise in a warm place until nearly double (about 40 minutes).

③ Bake in a 350° oven about 20 minutes or until golden brown. Remove from baking sheets. Cool slightly on wire racks; serve warm. Makes 2 loaves (24 servings).

*Note: To quick-thaw frozen bread dough in your microwave oven, remove from wrapper and place dough in a microwave-safe bowl. Cover and cook on 10% power (low) for 15 to 17 minutes or until thawed, rotating dough frequently.

Nutrition facts per serving: 54 calories, **0 g** total fat (**0 g** saturated fat), **0 mg** cholesterol, **6 mg** sodium, **10 g** carbohydrate, **0 g** fiber, **1 g** protein
Daily values: 0% vit. A, **1%** vit. C, **1%** calcium, **0%** iron

wheat & oat BREAD

Even a novice bread baker can succeed with this quick bread. The loaf has a crunchy wheat germ-topped crust and a pleasing nutty flavor. Warm from the oven, this bread is irresistible.

Prep: 20 minutes
Bake: 35 minutes

Nonstick spray coating
1¾ **cups all-purpose flour**
¾ **cup whole wheat flour**
½ **cup regular rolled oats, toasted***
3 **tablespoons toasted wheat germ**
3 **tablespoons sugar**
2½ **teaspoons baking powder**
¼ **teaspoon salt**
1⅓ **cups fat-free milk**
¼ **cup refrigerated or frozen egg product, thawed**
2 **tablespoons cooking oil**
1 **tablespoon toasted wheat germ**

Exchanges: 1½ Starch

① Spray the bottom and sides of an 8×1½-inch round baking pan with nonstick coating; set aside.

② In a large bowl stir together the all-purpose flour, whole wheat flour, toasted oats, the 3 tablespoons wheat germ, sugar, baking powder, and salt. In another bowl combine milk, egg product, and oil. Add milk mixture all at once to dry mixture. Stir just until moistened (batter should be lumpy). Spread batter in prepared pan. Sprinkle with the 1 tablespoon wheat germ.

③ Bake in a 375° oven for 35 to 40 minutes or until golden brown and a toothpick inserted near the center comes out clean. Cool bread in pan on a wire rack for 10 minutes. Remove from pan; serve warm. Makes 16 servings.

***Note:** To toast rolled oats, place in a shallow baking pan. Bake rolled oats in a 350° oven for 5 to 8 minutes or until oats are lightly browned, shaking pan once.

Nutrition facts per serving: 116 calories, **3 g** total fat (**0 g** saturated fat), **0 mg** cholesterol, **108 mg** sodium, **20 g** carbohydrate, **1 g** fiber, **4 g** protein
Daily values: 2% vit. A, **0%** vit. C, **7%** calcium, **8%** iron

A Germ to Behold

Wheat germ—the toasted and ground "germ" of the wheat kernel—is concentrated in protein and minerals. Toasted wheat germ perks up cereals or soups and brings texture to baked goods. It even can bring its nutlike flavor to sandwich spreads—try folding a teaspoon or two into chicken or tuna salad. Look for toasted wheat germ in health food stores and most supermarkets.

whole wheat POPOVERS

Steam causes the batter to rise and "pop over" the sides of the baking cups. For moist popovers, remove from the oven immediately after baking; for crisper results, turn off the oven and let "bake" a few more minutes.

Prep: 20 minutes
Bake: 40 minutes

Nonstick spray coating

2   **beaten eggs**

1   **cup fat-free milk**

1   **teaspoon cooking oil**

¾   **cup all-purpose flour**

¼   **cup whole wheat flour**

¼   **teaspoon salt**

Exchanges: 1½ Starch

❶ Spray bottoms and sides of six 6-ounce custard cups or cups of a popover pan with nonstick coating. Set aside.

❷ In a mixing bowl use a wire whisk or rotary beater to beat eggs, milk, and oil until combined. Add all-purpose flour, whole wheat flour, and salt; beat until smooth. Fill prepared cups half full with batter.

❸ Bake in a 400° oven about 40 minutes or until very firm. Immediately after removing from oven, prick each popover to allow the steam to escape. (For crisper popovers, turn off the oven; return the popovers to the oven for 5 to 10 minutes or until desired crispness is reached.) Remove popovers from cups; serve immediately. Makes 6 popovers.

Nutrition facts per popover: 119 calories, **3 g** total fat (**1 g** saturated fat), **73 mg** cholesterol, **131 mg** sodium, **17 g** carbohydrate, **1 g** fiber, **6 g** protein **Daily values: 5%** vit. A, **0%** vit. C, **5%** calcium, **7%** iron

breads & rolls

breakfast
& BRUNCH

Skipping breakfast isn't wise for people who have diabetes. And you won't want to miss this meal when you have so many delicious choices! Pancakes, cereals, egg dishes, homemade sausage, fruit shakes, and even coffee cakes—the selection is inspiring, varied, and anything but ordinary. Many are special enough for weekend company.

Apricot Coffee Cake, *recipe page 51*

honey granola WITH YOGURT

Fruits, nuts, grains, and yogurt blend to make a nutritionally powerful breakfast, rich in vitamins A and C, calcium, and iron. The smooth yogurt contrasted with crunchy granola will wake up everyone's taste buds.

Prep: 15 minutes
Bake: 30 minutes

Nonstick spray coating

2½ **cups regular rolled oats**

1 **cup wheat flakes**

⅓ **cup toasted wheat germ**

⅓ **cup sliced almonds or pecan pieces**

⅓ **cup unsweetened pineapple juice or apple juice**

⅓ **cup honey**

¼ **teaspoon ground allspice**

¼ **teaspoon ground cinnamon**

6 **cups desired fat-free yogurt**

4 **cups fruit, such as blueberries; raspberries; sliced strawberries; and/or peeled, seeded, and chopped peaches**

Exchanges: 1½ Starch ½ Fruit ½ Milk

1 Spray a 15×10×1-inch baking pan with nonstick coating; set aside. In a large bowl stir together the oats, wheat flakes, wheat germ, and almonds or pecans. In a small saucepan stir together juice, honey, allspice, and cinnamon. Cook and stir just until boiling. Remove from heat. Pour over oat mixture, tossing just until coated.

2 Spread the oat mixture evenly in prepared pan. Bake in a 325° oven for 30 to 35 minutes or until oats are lightly browned, stirring twice. Remove from oven. Immediately turn out onto a large piece of foil; cool completely.

3 Cover and chill for up to 2 weeks. For longer storage, seal in freezer bags and freeze for up to 3 months.

4 For each serving, spoon ½ cup of the yogurt into a bowl. Top with ⅓ cup of the oat mixture and ⅓ cup desired fruit. Makes twelve ⅓-cup servings.

Nutrition facts per serving: 220 calories, **4 g** total fat (**0 g** saturated fat), **3 mg** cholesterol, **122 mg** sodium, **40 g** carbohydrate, **2 g** fiber, **10 g** protein
Daily values: 3% vit. A, **14%** vit. C, **11%** calcium, **11%** iron

A Nutty Note

Nuts are plucky little packets of nutrition power. True, a lot of calories are packed into each bite, but most of those calories come from monounsaturated fats—the heart-healthy fats that keep cholesterol in check. Besides providing energy, nuts contain important trace minerals, such as calcium, zinc, and the antioxidant mineral selenium. One of the best sources of vitamin E, nuts also are rich in folate and other B vitamins. Because of their high calorie content, limit your intake to only a few—only occasionally.

breakfast & brunch

36

pineapple-CRANBERRY MUESLI

Muesli, the German word for "mixture," typically includes raw or toasted cereals, dried fruits, nuts, and wheat germ or bran. Usually eaten with milk, fruit juice, or yogurt, it's a hot cereal with real staying power.

Start to Finish: 35 minutes

- 2 **cups water**
- ½ **cup wheat berries**
- 1 **15¼-ounce can crushed pineapple (juice pack), undrained**
- 1⅔ **cups unsweetened pineapple juice**
- 1½ **cups regular rolled oats**
- ½ **cup dried cranberries**
- 1 **8-ounce carton plain fat-free yogurt**
- ¼ **cup toasted wheat germ**
- 3 **tablespoons toasted slivered almonds**
- 2 **tablespoons honey**

Exchanges: 2½ Starch 2 Fruit

① In a medium saucepan bring water to boiling. Add wheat berries. Return to boiling; cook for 15 minutes. Drain; return to saucepan.

② Meanwhile, drain crushed pineapple, reserving juice (you should have about ¾ cup juice). Set the pineapple aside. Stir the reserved pineapple juice, unsweetened pineapple juice, oats, and cranberries into the cooked wheat berries. Bring to boiling, stirring constantly; reduce heat. Simmer, uncovered, for 3 minutes, stirring constantly.

③ Remove saucepan from heat; stir in the pineapple, yogurt, wheat germ, almonds, and honey. Serve warm. Makes six 1-cup servings.

Nutrition facts per serving: 323 calories, **4 g** total fat (**1 g** saturated fat), **1 mg** cholesterol, **34 mg** sodium, **65 g** carbohydrate, **2 g** fiber, **10 g** protein **Daily values: 0%** vit. A, **24%** vit. C, **10%** calcium, **18%** iron

breakfast & brunch

streusel FRENCH TOAST

Crushed, shredded wheat biscuits add a slightly crunchy topping to this make-ahead, nutrition-packed breakfast. Fresh strawberries make it even more special.

Prep: 20 minutes
Chill: 2 to 24 hours
Bake: 30 minutes

Nonstick spray coating

¾ **cup refrigerated or frozen egg product, thawed, or 3 eggs, slightly beaten**

1 **cup evaporated fat-free milk**

3 **tablespoons sugar**

2 **teaspoons vanilla**

½ **teaspoon ground cinnamon**

¼ **teaspoon ground nutmeg**

6 **1-inch slices Italian bread (3 to 4 inches in diameter)**

1 **large shredded wheat biscuit, crushed (⅔ cup)**

1 **tablespoon butter or margarine, melted**

2 **cups sliced strawberries**

3 **tablespoons sugar, or sugar substitute equal to 3 tablespoons sugar**

½ **teaspoon ground cinnamon**

Exchanges: 2 Starch ½ Lean Meat ½ Fruit ½ Milk

1 Spray a 2-quart rectangular baking dish with nonstick coating; set aside. In a medium bowl beat together the egg product or eggs, evaporated milk, 3 tablespoons sugar, vanilla, ½ teaspoon cinnamon, and nutmeg. Arrange the bread slices in a single layer in prepared baking dish. Pour egg mixture evenly over slices. Cover and chill for 2 to 24 hours, turning bread slices once with a wide spatula.

2 Combine crushed biscuit and melted butter or margarine; sprinkle evenly over the bread slices. Bake, uncovered, in a 375° oven about 30 minutes until lightly browned.

3 Meanwhile, in a small bowl combine the strawberries, 3 tablespoons sugar or sugar substitute, and ½ teaspoon cinnamon. Serve with French toast. Makes 6 servings.

Nutrition facts per serving: 244 calories, **5 g** total fat (**2 g** saturated fat), **7 mg** cholesterol, **300 mg** sodium, **41 g** carbohydrate, **1 g** fiber, **10 g** protein
Daily values: 14% vit. A, **48%** vit. C, **15%** calcium, **14%** iron

Using sugar substitute option: 220 calories and **35 g** carbohydrate

breakfast & brunch

stuffed FRENCH TOAST

The cream cheese-and-fruit stuffing creates a delicious surprise with every bite. To save time in the morning, fill the pockets the night before, covering the bread tightly with plastic wrap and storing it in the refrigerator.

Prep: 15 minutes
Bake: 8 minutes

4 **1-inch-thick diagonally cut slices French bread**

¼ **of an 8-ounce tub light cream cheese**

½ **cup finely chopped fruit, such as nectarines or peeled peaches, pears, or apricots**

1 **teaspoon sugar-free apricot, apricot-pineapple, orange marmalade, or peach spread**

Nonstick spray coating

¼ **cup refrigerated or frozen egg product, thawed**

¼ **cup fat-free milk**

⅛ **teaspoon ground cinnamon**

½ **cup sugar-free apricot, apricot-pineapple, orange marmalade, or peach spread**

Exchanges: 1½ Starch ½ Fruit 1 Fat

❶ Cut a pocket in the top of each bread slice; set aside. In a small bowl stir together the cream cheese, chopped fruit, and the 1 teaspoon fruit spread. Fill each pocket with a rounded tablespoon of the cream cheese mixture.

❷ Spray a foil-lined baking sheet with nonstick coating; set aside. In a shallow bowl stir together the egg product, milk, and cinnamon. Dip the stuffed slices into the egg mixture, coating both sides.

❸ Arrange bread slices on the prepared baking sheet. Bake in a 450° oven for 8 to 10 minutes or until heated through.

❹ Meanwhile, in a small saucepan heat the remaining ½ cup fruit spread over medium heat just until melted. Invert the French toast onto serving plates. Top with melted spread. Makes 4 servings.

Nutrition facts per serving: 196 calories, **6 g** total fat (**1 g** saturated fat), **18 mg** cholesterol, **355 mg** sodium, **28 g** carbohydrate, **0 g** fiber, **6 g** protein
Daily values: 13% vit. A, **1%** vit. C, **5%** calcium, **8%** iron

oat PANCAKES

Pancakes always are a treat for a leisurely weekend breakfast or brunch. But these wheat and oat pancakes are exceptionally good. The pear sauce with a hint of maple adds the crowning touch.

Prep: 30 minutes
Stand: 15 to 30 minutes
Cook: 4 minutes per batch

1¼ **cups regular rolled oats**
¾ **cup all-purpose flour**
½ **cup whole wheat flour**
1 **tablespoon baking powder**
¼ **teaspoon salt**
3 **slightly beaten egg whites**
2¼ **cups buttermilk**
2 **tablespoons cooking oil**
2 **tablespoons honey (optional)**
1 **teaspoon vanilla**
1 **recipe Maple-Pear Sauce**
   Nonstick spray coating

Exchanges: 1½ Starch 1 Fruit ½ Milk

1 In a large bowl combine the oats, all-purpose flour, whole wheat flour, baking powder, and salt. Make a well in the center of mixture; set aside. In a medium bowl combine the egg whites, buttermilk, oil, honey (if desired), and vanilla. Add egg white mixture all at once to flour mixture. Stir just until moistened (batter should be lumpy). Cover batter; allow to stand at room temperature for 15 to 30 minutes. Meanwhile, prepare Maple-Pear Sauce; keep warm.

2 Spray a griddle or heavy skillet with nonstick coating. Preheat over medium-high heat. For each pancake, pour about ¼ cup of the batter onto the hot griddle or skillet. Spread batter into a circle about 4 inches in diameter. Cook over medium heat about 2 minutes on each side or until the pancakes are golden, turning to cook second sides when pancakes have bubbly surfaces and edges are slightly dry. Serve with Maple-Pear Sauce. Makes 8 servings (16 pancakes).

Maple-Pear Sauce: Peel and core 4 large pears; cut pears into ¼-inch slices. Toss with 1 tablespoon lemon juice; set aside. In a large heavy saucepan combine ½ cup unsweetened apple juice, ½ cup sugar-free pancake and waffle syrup product, and 3 inches stick cinnamon. Bring to boiling. Add pear slices; reduce heat. Simmer, uncovered, for 3 to 5 minutes or until the pears are tender. Stir together 2 tablespoons unsweetened apple juice and 1 tablespoon cornstarch; stir into pear mixture along with ¼ cup dried cranberries. Cook and stir until bubbly. Cook and stir for 2 minutes more. Remove from heat; discard cinnamon. Makes about 2½ cups (eight ¼-cup servings).

Nutrition facts per serving: 257 calories, **5 g** total fat (**1 g** saturated fat), **3 mg** cholesterol, **320 mg** sodium, **46 g** carbohydrate, **3 g** fiber, **8 g** protein
Daily values: 0% vit. A, **6%** vit. C, **18%** calcium, **12%** iron

breakfast & brunch

cranberry-WHEAT PANCAKES

A helpful trick in low-fat cooking is to use small amounts of intensely flavored ingredients to boost taste without adding a lot of fat or calories. Orange peel adds the flavor punch for these pancakes.

Prep: 30 minutes
Cook: 4 minutes per batch

- 1 recipe Orange Sauce
- 1 cup whole wheat flour
- ½ cup all-purpose flour
- 1 tablespoon sugar
- 1 tablespoon baking powder
- ½ teaspoon salt
- 1½ cups evaporated fat-free milk
- ¼ cup refrigerated or frozen egg product, thawed
- 2 tablespoons margarine or butter, melted
- 1 teaspoon vanilla
- ½ cup dried cranberries, snipped
- 1 tablespoon finely shredded orange peel
  Nonstick spray coating

Exchanges: 1½ Starch 1 Fruit ½ Milk ½ Fat

1 Prepare Orange Sauce; keep warm.

2 In a large bowl combine the whole wheat flour, all-purpose flour, sugar, baking powder, and salt. Make a well in the center of mixture; set aside. In another bowl combine evaporated milk, egg product, melted margarine or butter, and vanilla; add all at once to flour mixture. Stir just until moistened (batter should be slightly lumpy). Fold in the cranberries and orange peel.

3 Spray a griddle or heavy skillet with nonstick coating. Preheat over medium-high heat. For each pancake, pour about ¼ cup batter onto hot griddle or skillet. Spread batter into a circle about 4 inches in diameter. Cook over medium heat about 2 minutes on each side or until pancakes are golden brown, turning to cook second sides when pancakes have bubbly surfaces and edges are slightly dry. Serve the pancakes with Orange Sauce. Makes 6 servings (12 pancakes).

Orange Sauce: In a small saucepan combine 1 teaspoon finely shredded orange peel, ¾ cup orange juice, ⅓ cup water, 3 packets heat-stable low-calorie sweetener or 2 tablespoons sugar, 2 tablespoons snipped dried cranberries (if desired), and 1 tablespoon cornstarch. Cook and stir over medium heat until thickened and bubbly. Cook and stir for 2 minutes more. Makes about 1 cup sauce.

Nutrition facts per 2 pancakes with about 3 tablespoons sauce: 250 calories, **5 g** total fat (**1 g** saturated fat), **2 mg** cholesterol, **500 mg** sodium, **44 g** carbohydrate, **4 g** fiber, **10 g** protein **Daily values: 15%** vit. A, **30%** vit. C, **31%** calcium, **13%** iron

breakfast & brunch

42

toasted walnut WAFFLES

Why go out for waffles when you can make these great-tasting ones at home? Ground walnuts provide a light crunch and nutty flavor to make these waffles more special.

Exchanges: 1½ Starch   ½ Fruit   ½ Milk   ½ Fat

Prep: 25 minutes
Cook: per waffle iron directions

1 recipe Blueberry Sauce
1 cup all-purpose flour
1 cup whole wheat flour
¼ cup toasted coarsely ground walnuts
2 teaspoons baking powder
1 teaspoon baking soda
4 egg whites
2¼ cups buttermilk
2 tablespoons cooking oil

① Prepare Blueberry Sauce. Set aside.

② For waffles, stir together all-purpose flour, whole wheat flour, walnuts, baking powder, and baking soda. In a large bowl beat the egg whites with an electric mixer on medium speed until very foamy. Stir in buttermilk and oil. Gradually add flour mixture, beating by hand until smooth.

③ Pour 1 cup of the batter onto grids of a preheated, lightly greased waffle iron. Close lid quickly; do not open lid until waffle is done. Bake according to manufacturer's directions. When done, use a fork to lift waffle off grid. Repeat with remaining batter. Serve waffles with Blueberry Sauce. Makes 8 servings (16 waffles).

Blueberry Sauce: In a saucepan combine 1 cup blueberries, ¼ cup white grape juice, and 1 tablespoon honey. Heat just until bubbles form around edges. Let cool for 1 to 2 minutes. Transfer to a blender container. Cover and blend until smooth. Transfer sauce to a serving bowl. Stir in 1 cup blueberries. Makes 1⅔ cups sauce.

Nutrition facts per 2 waffles with about 3 tablespoons sauce: 227 calories, **7 g** total fat (**1 g** saturated fat), **3 mg** cholesterol, **352 mg** sodium, **35 g** carbohydrate, **3 g** fiber, **8 g** protein **Daily values: 0%** vit. A, **8%** vit. C, **14%** calcium, **10%** iron

breakfast & brunch

mushroom-FONTINA STRATA

Using mostly egg whites—rather than whole eggs—helps lighten up this strata. If fontina cheese is unavailable, the dish tastes great using part-skim mozzarella cheese or Swiss cheese.

Prep: 25 minutes
Chill: 4 to 24 hours
Bake: 35 minutes

Nonstick spray coating

3 cups assorted sliced fresh mushrooms, such as shiitake, button, white, and/or cremini

½ cup chopped onion

1 clove garlic, minced

2 ounces Canadian-style bacon, finely chopped

8 ½-inch-thick slices French bread

½ cup shredded fontina cheese

2 tablespoons assorted snipped fresh herbs (such as basil, oregano, marjoram, or thyme) or 2 teaspoons assorted dried herbs, crushed

1 cup fat-free cottage cheese

1 cup evaporated fat-free milk

3 egg whites

1 egg

1 tablespoon Dijon-style mustard

⅛ teaspoon pepper

1 small tomato, seeded and chopped

Exchanges: 1½ Starch 2 Lean Meat

1 Spray a medium skillet with nonstick coating. Cook the mushrooms, onion, and garlic in skillet until tender. Drain off any liquid. Stir in Canadian-style bacon.

2 Spray a 2-quart rectangular baking dish with nonstick coating. Arrange the bread slices in the prepared baking dish, cutting as necessary to fit. Sprinkle mushroom mixture over bread. In a small bowl toss together fontina cheese and desired herbs. Sprinkle over mushroom mixture.

3 In a blender container or food processor bowl combine cottage cheese, evaporated milk, egg whites, egg, mustard, and pepper. Cover and blend or process until smooth; pour evenly over ingredients in baking dish. Lightly press bread down with the back of a spoon. Cover; chill for 4 to 24 hours.

4 Bake, uncovered, in a 350° oven about 35 minutes or until a knife inserted near the center comes out clean. Sprinkle with chopped tomato. Let stand for 5 minutes before serving. Makes 6 servings.

Nutrition facts per serving: 227 calories, **6 g** total fat (**2 g** saturated fat), **56 mg** cholesterol, **543 mg** sodium, **24 g** carbohydrate, **1 g** fiber, **20 g** protein
Daily values: 12% vit. A, **11%** vit. C, **18%** calcium, **11%** iron

breakfast & brunch

45

cheddar-POLENTA PUFF

With an airy, soufflé like texture, this side dish works as well for dinner as it does for brunch. Extra-sharp cheddar cheese gives an extra-rich flavor to this puff.

Prep: 40 minutes
Bake: 25 minutes

4 **egg whites**

1½ **cups fat-free milk**

2 **tablespoons finely chopped red sweet pepper**

1 **tablespoon thinly sliced green onion**

¼ **teaspoon salt**

⅛ **teaspoon ground red pepper**

⅓ **cup cornmeal**

1 **egg yolk, slightly beaten**

¼ **cup grated Parmesan cheese**

¼ **cup shredded extra-sharp cheddar cheese (1 ounce)***

Nonstick spray coating

Exchanges: ½ Starch **1** Lean Meat ½ Milk

1 Allow egg whites to stand at room temperature for 30 minutes. Meanwhile, in a large heavy saucepan combine milk, sweet pepper, green onion, salt, and red pepper. Cook and stir over medium heat until mixture just begins to bubble. Slowly add cornmeal, stirring constantly. Cook and stir over medium heat about 5 minutes or until mixture begins to thicken. Remove from heat. Stir half of the cornmeal mixture into the egg yolk. Return mixture to the saucepan. Stir in Parmesan cheese and cheddar cheese until melted.

2 Lightly spray a 1½-quart soufflé dish with nonstick coating; set aside. In a large mixing bowl beat egg whites with an electric mixer on medium to high speed until stiff peaks form (tips stand straight). Gently fold about half of the beaten egg whites into the cheese mixture. Gradually pour cheese mixture over remaining beaten egg whites, folding to combine. Pour into prepared soufflé dish.

3 Bake in a 375° oven about 25 minutes or until a knife inserted in center comes out clean and top is golden brown. Serve immediately. Makes 4 servings.

***Note:** This recipe calls for regular cheddar cheese—not reduced-fat cheddar. The baking time may cause reduced-fat cheese to toughen.

Nutrition facts per serving: **168** calories, **6 g** total fat (**4 g** saturated fat), **69 mg** cholesterol, **397 mg** sodium, **14 g** carbohydrate, **1 g** fiber, **13 g** protein
Daily values: **20%** vit. A, **10%** vit. C, **21%** calcium, **5%** iron

breakfast & brunch

spring-fresh FRITTATA

Spring is prime time for fresh asparagus and new potatoes. Both are showcased here in a frittata, the classic Italian omelet. Use a broiler-proof skillet, as the frittata finishes cooking under the broiler.

Start to Finish: 25 minutes

¼ **pound whole tiny new potatoes, coarsely chopped (about 1 cup)**

1 **cup water**

¼ **pound asparagus spears, trimmed and cut into 1-inch lengths (about ½ cup)**

1½ **cups refrigerated or frozen egg product, thawed***

¼ **cup fat-free milk**

1 **tablespoon snipped fresh rosemary or 1 teaspoon dried rosemary, crushed**

⅛ **teaspoon pepper**
  Dash salt

2 **teaspoons olive oil**

1 **small onion, thinly sliced and separated into rings**

1 **clove garlic, minced**

⅓ **cup crumbled basil-and-tomato feta cheese**

1 **small tomato, seeded and chopped**

Exchanges: ½ Starch **2** Lean Meat **1** Vegetable ½ Fat

1 In a medium saucepan combine potatoes and water. Bring to boiling; reduce heat. Simmer, covered, for 10 minutes. Add the asparagus; return to simmering. Simmer, covered, for 4 to 6 minutes more or until vegetables are just tender. Drain the vegetables well.

2 Meanwhile, beat together the egg product, milk, rosemary, pepper, and salt; set aside. In a 10-inch broiler-proof skillet heat olive oil; cook onion and garlic in hot oil until tender. Stir in potatoes and asparagus.

3 Pour egg mixture into skillet over vegetables. Cook over medium heat. As mixture sets, run a spatula around edge of skillet, lifting egg mixture so the uncooked portion flows underneath. Continue cooking and lifting edges until egg mixture is almost set (surface will be moist). Sprinkle with the feta cheese.

4 Place broiler-proof skillet under the broiler 4 to 5 inches from the heat. Broil about 1 minute or until the top is just set. Sprinkle with tomato. Cut into wedges. Makes 4 servings.

*Note: If desired, omit egg product; use 4 whole eggs and 3 egg whites.

Nutrition facts per serving: 191 calories, **9 g** total fat (**3 g** saturated fat), **15 mg** cholesterol, **393 mg** sodium, **12 g** carbohydrate, **1 g** fiber, **16 g** protein
Daily values: 26% vit. A, **24%** vit. C, **13%** calcium, **19%** iron

breakfast CASSEROLE

To make ahead, cook the potatoes and leeks. Layer the cooked mixture, ham, and cheese in the baking dish.
Cover and refrigerate. In the morning, combine the remaining ingredients, pour over the casserole, and bake.

Prep: 25 minutes
Bake: 35 minutes

- 1 **pound whole tiny new potatoes, cut into ¼-inch slices**
- ⅓ **cup thinly sliced leek**
  Nonstick spray coating
- ¾ **cup chopped lower-fat and lower-sodium cooked ham**
- 3 **ounces reduced-fat Swiss cheese, cut into small pieces**
- 1¼ **cups fat-free milk**
- 1 **tablespoon all-purpose flour**
- ¾ **cup refrigerated or frozen egg product, thawed**
- 2 **teaspoons snipped fresh thyme or ½ teaspoon dried thyme, crushed**
- ¼ **teaspoon pepper**

Exchanges: 1½ Starch 1 Lean Meat

1 In a large saucepan cook sliced potatoes in a small amount of lightly salted boiling water about 10 minutes or just until tender, adding leeks during the last 5 minutes of cooking. Drain potato and leek mixture.

2 Spray a 2-quart rectangular baking dish with nonstick coating. Layer cooked potatoes and leeks in bottom of dish. Sprinkle ham and Swiss cheese over potatoes.

3 In a medium bowl stir the milk into the flour until smooth. Stir in the egg product, thyme, and pepper. Pour the egg mixture over the potatoes.

4 Bake, uncovered, in a 350° oven for 35 to 40 minutes or until a knife inserted near center comes out clean. Serve immediately. Makes 6 servings.

Nutrition facts per serving: **180** calories, **4 g** total fat (**1 g** saturated fat), **16 mg** cholesterol, **445 mg** sodium, **23 g** carbohydrate, **1 g** fiber, **13 g** protein
Daily values: **10%** vit. A, **26%** vit. C, **14%** calcium, **16%** iron

breakfast & brunch

Eggonomics

Many recipes that call for eggs require the binding property found in the egg white. The white, made primarily of protein and water, is the main ingredient in most egg substitutes, or "egg product." The yolk is omitted, along with most of the fat and cholesterol. Egg product can be used in many recipes that call for whole eggs. Or, prepare your own substitute by using 2 egg whites for each whole egg called for in a recipe. If the recipe requires several eggs or needs a little richness or color, use 2 egg whites and 1 whole egg for every 2 whole eggs.

turkey-APPLE SAUSAGE

A nice change of pace from pork sausage, these turkey patties have a hint of apple. If you like, try the Mexican-style version, which substitutes green chile peppers for the apple.

Prep: 15 minutes
Broil: 10 minutes

½ **cup shredded peeled apple**

2 **tablespoons soft bread crumbs**

1½ **teaspoons snipped fresh sage or ½ teaspoon dried sage, crushed**

¼ **teaspoon black pepper**

⅛ **teaspoon salt**

⅛ **teaspoon paprika**

⅛ **teaspoon ground red pepper**

Dash ground nutmeg

8 **ounces ground raw turkey**

Nonstick spray coating

Exchanges: 1 Medium-Fat Meat

1 In a large bowl combine the shredded apple, bread crumbs, sage, black pepper, salt, paprika, red pepper, and nutmeg. Add the turkey; mix well. Shape mixture into four ½-inch-thick patties.

2 Spray the unheated rack of a broiler pan with nonstick coating. Arrange patties on rack. Broil 4 to 5 inches from the heat about 10 minutes or until no longer pink, turning once. (Or, spray large skillet with nonstick coating. Preheat over medium heat. Add sausage and cook for 8 to 10 minutes or until no longer pink.) Makes 4 servings.

Nutrition facts per serving: 89 calories, **5** grams total fat (**1 g** saturated fat), **21 mg** cholesterol, **99 mg** sodium, **4 g** carbohydrate, **0 g** fiber, **8 g** protein
Daily values: 0% vit. A, **2%** vit. C, **1%** calcium, **4%** iron

Mexican-Style Turkey Sausage: Prepare as directed above, except substitute one 4½-ounce can diced green chile peppers for the apple, and omit the sage, paprika, and nutmeg. Add 1 large clove garlic, minced; ¼ teaspoon ground cumin; and ¼ teaspoon dried oregano, crushed, to the turkey mixture. Continue as directed.

Nutrition facts per serving: 83 calories, **5 g** total fat (**1 g** saturated fat), **21 mg** cholesterol, **179 mg** sodium, **2 g** carbohydrate, **0 g** fiber, **8 g** protein
Daily values: 0% vit. A, **15%** vit. C, **4%** calcium, **6%** iron

The Turkey Grind

You can purchase ground turkey at the supermarket, but you may want to check whether the meat also includes the skin (which adds a considerable amount of fat). If you like, purchase skinless, boneless turkey breasts and grind them in your food processor. This ensures that the turkey has the lowest possible fat content and, therefore, is more healthful.

apricot COFFEE CAKE

A member of the ginger family, cardamom is an aromatic spice used in Scandinavian and Indian cooking. It has a sweet-spicy flavor that pairs nicely with fruits, such as apricots, pears, or peaches. (See photograph, page 35.)

Prep: 20 minutes
Rise: 50 minutes
Bake: 30 minutes

Nonstick spray coating

2 **cups all-purpose flour**

1 **package active dry yeast**

½ **teaspoon ground cardamom or nutmeg**

½ **cup water**

2 **tablespoons sugar**

2 **tablespoons butter or margarine**

¼ **teaspoon salt**

⅓ **cup refrigerated or frozen egg product, thawed**

⅓ **cup finely snipped dried apricots**

Sugar-free apricot spread (optional)

Exchanges: 1 Starch ½ Fruit

❶ Generously spray a 1-quart casserole or soufflé dish with nonstick coating; set aside. In a large bowl combine 1 cup of the flour, the yeast, and cardamom or nutmeg. In a saucepan heat and stir the water, sugar, butter or margarine, and salt just until warm (120° to 130°) and butter or margarine almost melts; add to flour mixture along with the egg product. Beat with an electric mixer on low speed for 30 seconds, scraping the bowl constantly. Beat on high speed for 3 minutes.

❷ Using a wooden spoon, stir in apricots and remaining flour (batter will be stiff). Spoon the batter into prepared casserole. Cover and let rise in a warm place until nearly double (50 to 60 minutes).

❸ Bake in a 375° oven for 30 minutes. (If necessary, cover the cake loosely with foil the last 10 minutes of baking to prevent overbrowning.) Remove coffee cake from casserole or soufflé dish. Cool slightly on a wire rack. If desired, serve warm cake with apricot spread. Makes 12 servings.

Nutrition facts per serving: 111 calories, **2 g** total fat (**1 g** saturated fat), **5 mg** cholesterol, **77 mg** sodium, **19 g** carbohydrate, **1 g** fiber, **3 g** protein
Daily values: 5% vit. A, **0%** vit. C, **0%** calcium, **8%** iron

tropical COFFEE CAKE

Mango and coconut give this delicious coffee cake an island flair. Yogurt and just a small amount of oil help keep the cake moist. If you can't find mangoes, substitute nectarines or peaches.

Prep: 25 minutes
Bake: 35 minutes

1¼ **cups all-purpose flour**

¼ **cup sugar plus 4 packets heat-stable sugar substitute, or ½ cup sugar**

½ **teaspoon baking powder**

½ **teaspoon baking soda**

¼ **teaspoon salt**

¼ **teaspoon ground nutmeg**

1 **beaten egg**

⅔ **cup plain fat-free yogurt**

2 **tablespoons cooking oil**

½ **teaspoon vanilla**

1 **medium mango, peeled, seeded, and finely chopped (about 1 cup)**

1 **tablespoon all-purpose flour**

2 **tablespoons flaked coconut**

Exchanges: **1½** Starch **½** Fruit **½** Fat

❶ Lightly grease and flour a 9×1½-inch round baking pan; set aside. In a large bowl stir together the 1¼ cups flour, the sugar plus sugar substitute or the sugar, baking powder, baking soda, salt, and nutmeg. Make a well in the center of the flour mixture; set aside.

❷ In a small mixing bowl stir together the egg, yogurt, oil, and vanilla. Add the egg mixture all at once to flour mixture. Stir just until moistened (batter should be slightly lumpy). Toss chopped mango with the 1 tablespoon flour; gently fold into batter. Spread batter into prepared pan.

❸ Sprinkle coconut over batter in pan. Bake in a 350° oven for 35 minutes. Serve warm. Makes 8 servings.

Nutrition facts per serving: 169 calories, **5 g** total fat (**1 g** saturated fat), **27 mg** cholesterol, **194 mg** sodium, **28 g** carbohydrate, **1 g** fiber, **4 g** protein
Daily values: 11% vit. A, **12%** vit. C, **5%** calcium, **7%** iron

Using the ½ cup sugar option: 193 calories and **34 g** carbohydrate

breakfast & brunch

peachy RICE PUDDING

Yogurt makes this rice pudding extra creamy, while fresh peaches add a burst of fruit flavor. This nutritious pudding is suitable for breakfast, snack time, or dessert. Use quick-cooking rice to slash the cooking time.

Start to Finish: 30 minutes

1⅓ cups water

⅔ cup long-grain rice

½ of a 12-ounce can (¾ cup) evaporated fat-free milk

⅓ cup mixed dried fruit bits

2 teaspoons honey

¼ teaspoon pumpkin pie spice or ground cinnamon

⅛ teaspoon salt

1 cup chopped, peeled peaches or frozen sliced peaches, thawed and chopped

¼ cup vanilla fat-free yogurt

Exchanges: 1½ Starch 1 Fruit ½ Milk

1 In a medium saucepan stir together water and uncooked rice. Bring to boiling; reduce heat. Simmer, covered, for 15 to 20 minutes or until rice is tender.

2 Stir evaporated milk, fruit bits, honey, pumpkin pie spice or cinnamon, and salt into cooked rice. Bring just to boiling; reduce heat. Simmer, uncovered, over medium-low heat about 5 minutes or until mixture is thick and creamy, stirring frequently. Serve pudding warm with peaches and yogurt. Makes 4 servings.

Nutrition facts per serving: 213 calories, **0 g** total fat (**0 g** saturated fat), **1 mg** cholesterol, **133 mg** sodium, **46 g** carbohydrate, **1 g** fiber, **7 g** protein
Daily values: 9% vit. A, **5%** vit. C, **12%** calcium, **11%** iron

breakfast & brunch

54

breakfast BREAD PUDDING

Don't think of bread pudding simply as dessert—it's perfect for breakfast or brunch, too. The fruit sauce topping turns an old-fashioned favorite into a nutritious breakfast treat.

Prep: 20 minutes
Bake: 35 minutes
Stand: 15 minutes

6 **slices cinnamon-swirl bread or cinnamon-raisin bread**

Nonstick spray coating

1½ **cups fat-free milk**

¾ **cup refrigerated or frozen egg product, thawed**

3 **tablespoons sugar**

1 **teaspoon vanilla**

¼ **teaspoon ground nutmeg**

1 **5½-ounce can apricot or peach nectar**

2 **teaspoons cornstarch**

Exchanges: 1 Starch **1** Milk

1 To dry bread, place slices in a single layer on a baking sheet. Bake in a 325° oven for 10 minutes, turning once. Cool on a wire rack. Cut into ½-inch cubes (you should have 4 cups).

2 Spray six 6-ounce custard cups with nonstick coating. Divide the bread cubes among the cups. In a medium bowl use a rotary beater or wire whisk to beat together the milk, egg product, sugar, vanilla, and nutmeg. Pour the milk mixture evenly over the bread cubes. Lightly press cubes down with fork or back of a spoon.

3 Place the custard cups in a 13x9x2-inch baking pan. Place pan in oven. Carefully pour hottest tap water available into the baking pan around the custard cups to a depth of 1 inch.

4 Bake in a 325° oven for 35 to 40 minutes or until a knife inserted near center comes out clean. Remove the cups from the baking pan. Let stand for 15 to 20 minutes.

5 Meanwhile, for sauce, in a small saucepan gradually stir nectar into cornstarch. Cook and stir over medium heat until thickened and bubbly. Reduce the heat. Cook and stir for 2 minutes more.

6 To serve, loosen edges of puddings with a knife. Invert into dessert dishes. Serve topped with about 1 tablespoon warm sauce. Makes 6 servings.

Nutrition facts per serving: 164 calories, **2 g** total fat (**1 g** saturated fat), **1 mg** cholesterol, **189 mg** sodium, **28 g** carbohydrate, **0 g** fiber, **8 g** protein
Daily values: 13% vit. A, **15%** vit. C, **9%** calcium, **10%** iron

breakfast & brunch

tex-mex BREAKFAST PIZZA

A Mexican-style omelet meets pizza for a unique breakfast combination. Mildly spiced with jalapeño peppers, the egg mixture is spooned over a bread shell and sliced for out-of-hand eating.

Prep: 25 minutes
Bake: 8 minutes

Nonstick spray coating

1½ **cups frozen loose-pack diced hash brown potatoes, thawed**

2 **green onions, sliced (¼ cup)**

1 **to 2 canned jalapeño peppers or canned whole green chile peppers, drained, seeded, and chopped**

¼ **teaspoon ground cumin**

1 **clove garlic, minced**

1 **cup refrigerated or frozen egg product, thawed**

¼ **cup fat-free milk**

1 **tablespoon snipped fresh cilantro**

1 **16-ounce Italian bread shell (Boboli)**

½ **cup shredded reduced-fat Monterey Jack cheese (2 ounces)**

1 **small tomato, seeded and chopped**

Exchanges: 2 Starch   1 Lean Meat

1 Spray a large skillet with nonstick coating. Preheat over medium heat. Add the potatoes, green onions, peppers, cumin, and garlic. Cook and stir about 3 minutes or until the vegetables are tender.

2 In a small bowl stir together egg product, milk, and cilantro; add to skillet. Cook, without stirring, until mixture begins to set on the bottom and around the edge. Using a spatula, lift and fold the partially cooked mixture so uncooked portion flows underneath. Continue cooking and folding until egg product is cooked through, but is still glossy and moist. Remove from heat.

3 To assemble pizza, place the bread shell on a large baking sheet or a 12-inch pizza pan. Sprinkle half of the cheese over the shell. Top with the egg mixture, tomato, and the remaining cheese.

4 Bake in a 375° oven for 8 to 10 minutes or until cheese is melted. Cut into wedges to serve. Makes 8 servings.

Nutrition facts per serving: 235 calories, **6 g** total fat (**1 g** saturated fat), **8 mg** cholesterol, **424 mg** sodium, **33 g** carbohydrate, **2 g** fiber, **14 g** protein
Daily values: 9% vit. A, **14%** vit. C, **11%** calcium, **15%** iron

banana-STRAWBERRY SHAKE

When time is limited in the mornings, you can prepare this shake in 10 minutes. Store any leftovers in the freezer. Then, thaw and reblend before drinking.

Start to Finish: 10 minutes

1½ **cups vanilla fat-free yogurt with sweetener**

1 **10-ounce package frozen strawberries in light syrup**

1 **medium banana, sliced**

¼ **cup unsweetened pineapple juice or apricot nectar**

3 **tablespoons nonfat dry milk powder**

Exchanges: 1½ Fruit 1 Milk

1 In a blender container combine the yogurt, frozen strawberries, banana, pineapple juice or apricot nectar, and milk powder. Cover and blend until smooth, stopping and scraping down sides of blender container as necessary. Serve immediately. Makes three 1-cup servings.

Nutrition facts per serving: 183 calories, **0 g** total fat (**0 g** saturated fat), **1 mg** cholesterol, **98 mg** sodium, **38 g** carbohydrate, **1 g** fiber, **7 g** protein
Daily values: 4% vit. A, **445%** vit. C, **15%** calcium, **4%** iron

Calcium Kick

A calcium-rich diet is important for keeping bones strong—especially in women. Calcium helps in the prevention of osteoporosis, a degenerative bone disease. Adding nonfat milk powder is one way to boost calcium in your diet. Add a tablespoon or two per serving to foods such as cream soups, creamy casseroles, and milk-based drinks. Each tablespoon contains about 52 mg calcium. Adults 31 to 50 years of age need 1,000 mg per day; adults over 50 need 1,200 mg.

fruity TOFU SHAKE

When you whirl tofu into a fruit smoothie, you're adding more than just a creamy texture. Tofu, made from soybeans, is a great protein source—sans any unhealthy saturated fat.

Start to Finish: 10 minutes

1 10½-ounce package soft tofu (fresh bean curd), drained and cut up

1½ cups unsweetened pineapple juice

1½ cups fruit, such as sliced fresh strawberries; frozen unsweetened whole strawberries; peeled, seeded, and cut-up papaya; or peeled and sliced bananas

2 tablespoons honey

Exchanges: 1 Lean Meat **2** Fruit

❶ In a blender container combine the tofu, pineapple juice, desired fruit, and honey. Cover and blend until nearly smooth. Serve immediately. Makes three 1-cup servings.

Nutrition facts per serving: 189 calories, **3 g** total fat (**0 g** saturated fat), **0 mg** cholesterol, **9 mg** sodium, **37 g** carbohydrate, **2 g** fiber, **6 g** protein
Daily values: 0% vit. A, **92%** vit. C, **5%** calcium, **9%** iron

super SUPPERS

What to have for dinner is an age-old dilemma. These tantalizing entrées, including Chicken with Fruit Salsa, Asian Flank Steak, Spice-Rubbed Pork Chops, or Fish with Cherry Relish, are sure to please you, your family, and dinner guests.

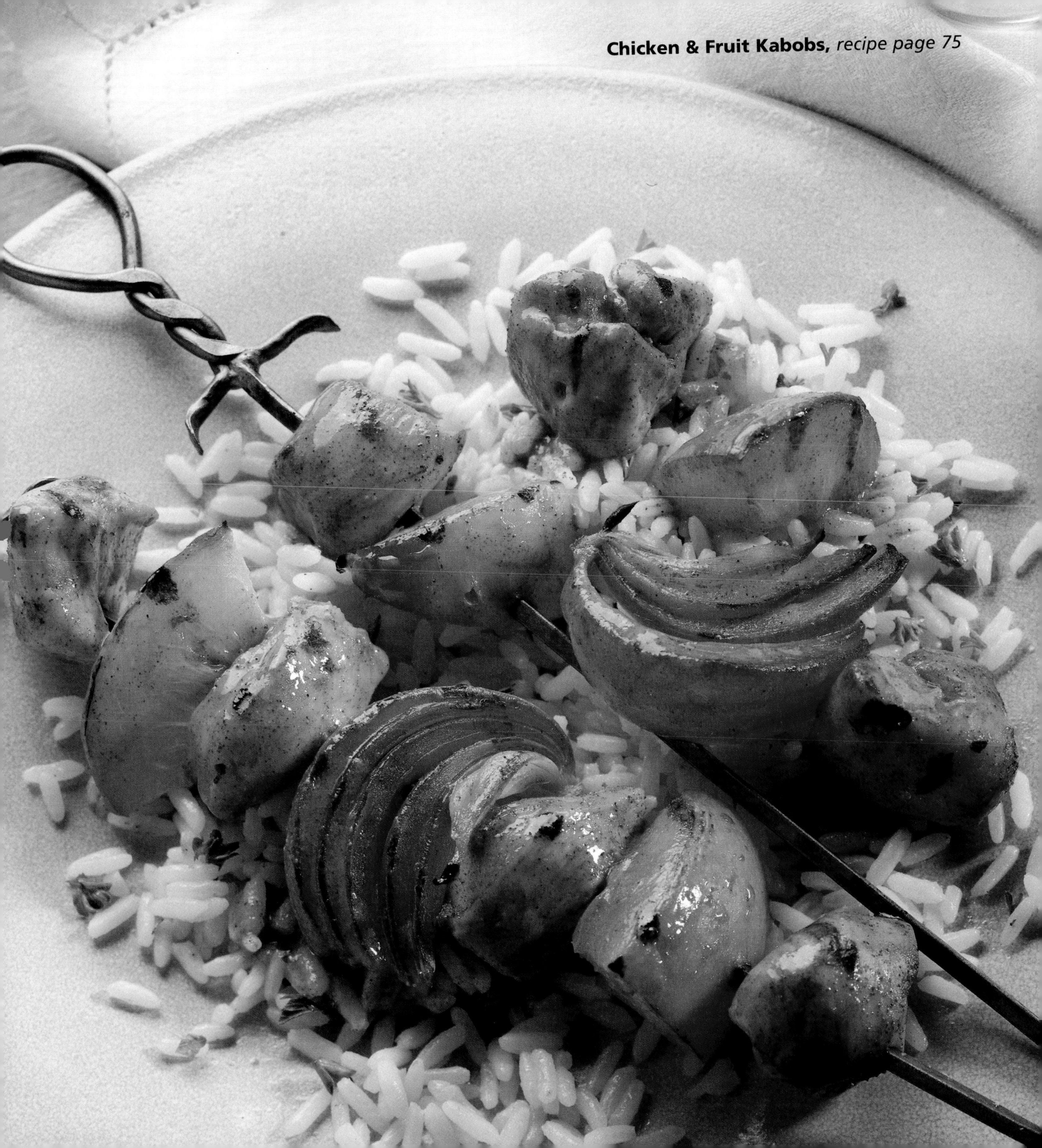

Chicken & Fruit Kabobs, *recipe page 75*

grilled TURKEY MOLE

Mole (MOH-lay), a Mexican specialty, is a rich, reddish-brown sauce that contains an unexpected ingredient—chocolate. Chili powder, garlic, and tomatoes also flavor this sauce, a common accompaniment to poultry.

Prep: 25 minutes
Marinate: 2 to 4 hours
Grill: 8 minutes

- **6 4-ounce turkey breast tenderloin steaks**
- **¼ cup lime juice**
- **1 tablespoon chili powder**
- **2 teaspoons bottled hot pepper sauce**
- **1 tablespoon margarine or butter**
- **½ cup chopped onion**
- **2 teaspoons sugar**
- **1 clove garlic, minced**
- **1 7½-ounce can tomatoes, undrained and cut up**
- **¼ cup canned diced green chile peppers**
- **1½ teaspoons unsweetened cocoa powder**
- **1½ teaspoons chili powder**
- **⅛ teaspoon salt**
- **Fat-free dairy sour cream (optional)**

Exchanges: 2½ Lean Meat 1 Vegetable

1 Rinse turkey; pat dry. Place the turkey in a plastic bag set in a shallow dish. For marinade, in a small bowl stir together the lime juice, the 1 tablespoon chili powder, and the hot pepper sauce. Pour over turkey. Close bag. Marinate in the refrigerator for 2 to 4 hours, turning bag occasionally.

2 Meanwhile, for the mole sauce, in a medium saucepan heat margarine or butter over medium-high heat until melted. Cook and stir the onion, sugar, and garlic in hot margarine or butter about 7 minutes or until onion is tender. Stir in the undrained tomatoes, chile peppers, cocoa powder, the 1½ teaspoons chili powder, and the salt. Bring to boiling; reduce heat. Simmer, covered, for 10 minutes. Remove from heat; set aside.

3 Drain the turkey, discarding the marinade. Grill turkey on the lightly greased rack of an uncovered grill directly over medium coals for 8 to 10 minutes or until turkey is tender and no longer pink, turning once. Serve with mole sauce and, if desired, sour cream. Makes 6 servings.

Nutrition facts per serving: 156 calories, **5 g** total fat (**1 g** saturated fat), **50 mg** cholesterol, **213 mg** sodium, **6 g** carbohydrate, **1 g** fiber, **22 g** protein
Daily values: 9% vit. A, **19%** vit. C, **4%** calcium, **10%** iron

Turkey Talk

Turkey white meat is naturally low in fat. It has a slightly heartier taste than chicken and is versatile enough to be used as a substitute in place of higher fat meats. Like all meats, turkey is a good source of vital iron, zinc, and vitamin B-12. If you only think of turkey at Thanksgiving, think again—whether you broil it, bake it, or grill it, turkey is a versatile meat for any time of year.

super suppers

turkey PAPRIKASH

Paprikash (PAH-pree-kash) is the quintessential comfort food of Hungary. It usually is stewed with bacon drippings. We've updated the traditional method to lower the fat—but kept the rich flavor.

Prep: 25 minutes
Cook: 16 minutes

- 12 **ounces turkey breast tenderloins**
- **Nonstick spray coating**
- 2 **teaspoons cooking oil**
- 2 **cups sliced fresh mushrooms**
- 1 **medium green sweet pepper, cut into thin bite-size strips**
- 1 **medium onion, cut into thin wedges**
- 2 **cloves garlic, minced**
- 2 **tablespoons low-sodium tomato paste**
- 1 **tablespoon paprika**
- ½ **teaspoon dried marjoram, crushed**
- ¼ **teaspoon salt**
- ¼ **teaspoon black pepper**
- 1 **cup reduced-sodium chicken broth**
- 1 **8-ounce carton fat-free dairy sour cream**
- 2 **tablespoons all-purpose flour**
- 2 **cups hot cooked noodles**
- 1 **tablespoon snipped parsley**

Exchanges: 2 Starch **2** Lean Meat **2** Vegetable

1 Rinse turkey; pat dry. Cut the turkey crosswise into ½-inch slices. Spray a large nonstick skillet with the nonstick coating. Preheat skillet over medium-high heat. Brown turkey slices on both sides in skillet. Remove turkey from skillet.

2 Carefully add the oil to hot skillet; add the mushrooms, sweet pepper, onion, and garlic to skillet. Cook and stir the vegetables until crisp-tender. In a bowl combine tomato paste, paprika, marjoram, salt, and black pepper. Gradually stir in about ½ cup of the chicken broth; add mixture to skillet. Add turkey to skillet. Bring to boiling; reduce heat. Simmer, covered, about 15 minutes or until turkey is tender.

3 Meanwhile, stir together sour cream and flour. Stir in remaining chicken broth; add to skillet. Cook and stir until thickened and bubbly. Cook and stir for 1 minute more.

4 To serve, spoon the turkey and sauce mixture over the cooked noodles and sprinkle with parsley. Makes 4 servings.

Nutrition facts per serving: **319** calories, **5 g** total fat (**1 g** saturated fat), **37 mg** cholesterol, **386 mg** sodium, **40 g** carbohydrate, **3 g** fiber, **27 g** protein
Daily values: **20%** vit. A, **37%** vit. C, **9%** calcium, **21%** iron

italian CHICKEN

This dish contains all the best ingredients Italy has to offer—black olives, capers, garlic, basil, wine, olive oil, and tomatoes. Served with a salad and warm crusty bread, it's a memorable taste of Italy from your own kitchen.

Exchanges: **1½** Starch **3** Lean Meat **2** Vegetable

Start to Finish: 40 minutes

- 4 skinless, boneless chicken breast halves (about 1 pound total)
- 2 tablespoons olive oil
- 1 large onion, halved and thinly sliced
- 2 cloves garlic, minced
- 3 large tomatoes, coarsely chopped
- ¼ cup Greek black olives or ripe olives, pitted and sliced
- 1 tablespoon capers, drained
- ¼ teaspoon salt
- ⅛ teaspoon pepper
- ¼ cup dry red wine or reduced-sodium chicken broth
- 2 teaspoons cornstarch
- ¼ cup snipped fresh basil
- 2 cups hot cooked couscous

1 Rinse chicken; pat dry. In a large skillet heat 1 tablespoon of the olive oil over medium-high heat. Add chicken; cook for 4 to 5 minutes on each side or until chicken is tender and no longer pink. Remove from pan and keep warm.

2 For sauce, add the remaining olive oil, onion, and garlic to hot skillet. Cook and stir for 2 minutes. Add the tomatoes, olives, capers, salt, and pepper to skillet. Bring to boiling; reduce heat. Simmer, covered, for 3 minutes. Stir together the wine or broth and cornstarch; add to the skillet. Cook and stir until thickened and bubbly. Cook and stir for 2 minutes more. Stir in basil. Pour sauce over chicken. Serve with couscous. Makes 4 servings.

Nutrition facts per serving: 319 calories, **8 g** total fat (**2 g** saturated fat), **59 mg** cholesterol, **289 mg** sodium, **32 g** carbohydrate, **7 g** fiber, **27 g** protein **Daily values: 8%** vit. A, **42%** vit. C, **3%** calcium, **12%** iron

super suppers

moroccan CHICKEN

The mystique of North Africa is captured in richly flavored recipes such as this one, which are abundant in fruits and aromatic spices. Serve this rich, slow-grilled chicken dish over fluffy couscous or saffron rice.

Prep: 20 minutes
Marinate: 4 to 24 hours
Grill: 50 minutes

- **2 pounds meaty chicken pieces (breasts, thighs, and drumsticks), skinned**
- **2 teaspoons finely shredded orange peel (set aside)**
- **½ cup orange juice**
- **1 tablespoon olive oil**
- **1 tablespoon grated fresh ginger**
- **1 teaspoon paprika**
- **1 teaspoon ground cumin**
- **½ teaspoon ground coriander**
- **¼ teaspoon crushed red pepper**
- **⅛ teaspoon salt**
- **2 tablespoons honey**
- **2 teaspoons orange juice**

Exchanges: 4 Lean Meat **½** Fruit

1 Rinse chicken; pat dry. Place chicken in a plastic bag set in a deep dish. For the marinade, in a small bowl stir together the ½ cup orange juice, the olive oil, ginger, paprika, cumin, coriander, red pepper, and salt. Pour marinade over chicken. Close the bag. Marinate the chicken in the refrigerator for 4 to 24 hours, turning the bag occasionally.

2 Meanwhile, in a small bowl stir together the reserved orange peel, the honey, and the 2 teaspoons orange juice.

3 Drain the chicken, discarding the marinade. In a grill with a cover arrange preheated coals around a drip pan. Test for medium heat above pan. Place chicken, skinned side up, on lightly greased grill rack over drip pan.

4 Cover and grill for 50 to 60 minutes or until the chicken is tender and no longer pink. Occasionally brush chicken with honey mixture during the last 10 minutes of grilling. (Or, to bake, place chicken, skinned side up, in a shallow baking dish. Bake, uncovered, in a 375° oven for 45 to 55 minutes or until chicken is tender and no longer pink. Occasionally brush the chicken with the honey mixture during the last 10 minutes of baking.) Makes 4 servings.

Nutrition facts per serving: 237 calories, **8 g** total fat (**2 g** saturated fat), **92 mg** cholesterol, **98 mg** sodium, **10 g** carbohydrate, **0 g** fiber, **30 g** protein
Daily values: 2% vit. A, **9%** vit. C, **1%** calcium, **9%** iron

feta-stuffed CHICKEN

Feta cheese, popular in eastern Mediterranean countries such as Greece, Israel, and Lebanon, packs a simple chicken breast with tantalizing tang.

Start to Finish: 30 minutes

- ¼ cup crumbled basil-and-tomato feta cheese*
- 2 tablespoons fat-free cream cheese (1 ounce)
- 4 skinless, boneless chicken breast halves (about 1 pound total)
- ¼ to ½ teaspoon pepper
  Dash salt
- 1 teaspoon olive oil or cooking oil
- ¼ cup chicken broth
- 1 10-ounce package prewashed fresh spinach, trimmed (8 cups)
- 2 tablespoons finely chopped toasted walnuts or pecans
- 1 tablespoon lemon juice

Exchanges: **3** Lean Meat **1** Vegetable

1 Combine feta cheese and cream cheese; set aside. Rinse the chicken; pat dry. Cut a horizontal slit through the thickest portion of each chicken breast half to form a pocket. Stuff pockets with the cheese mixture. If necessary, secure openings with wooden picks. Sprinkle chicken with pepper and salt.

2 In a large nonstick skillet heat oil over medium-high heat. Cook chicken, uncovered, in hot oil about 12 minutes or until the chicken is tender and no longer pink, turning once (reduce heat to medium if chicken browns too quickly). Remove the chicken from skillet. Cover to keep chicken warm.

3 Carefully add chicken broth to skillet. Bring to boiling; add half of the spinach. Cover and cook about 3 minutes or until spinach is just wilted. Remove spinach from skillet, reserving liquid in pan. Repeat with remaining spinach. Return all spinach to skillet. Stir in the walnuts or pecans and lemon juice. To serve, divide spinach mixture among 4 plates. Top with chicken breasts. Makes 4 servings.

*Note: If basil-and-tomato feta cheese is not available, add 1 teaspoon each of finely minced fresh basil and snipped oil-packed dried tomatoes, drained, to ¼ cup plain feta cheese.

Nutrition facts per serving: 199 calories, **8 g** total fat (**2 g** saturated fat), **67 mg** cholesterol, **271 mg** sodium, **4 g** carbohydrate, **2 g** fiber, **26 g** protein
Daily values: 51% vit. A, **36%** vit. C, **12%** calcium, **19%** iron

chicken WITH FRUIT SALSA

Juicy chicken breasts go Southwestern with a salsa bursting with flavor. The chipotle chiles—smoked jalapeño peppers—are not for the faint of heart. Use the lower range for a milder salsa.

Prep: 20 minutes
Stand: 30 minutes
Broil: 12 minutes

1½ cups finely chopped
  pineapple

1 to 2 canned chipotle peppers
  in adobo sauce, drained,
  seeded, and finely chopped

2 tablespoons snipped chives

1 tablespoon honey

1 teaspoon finely shredded
  lime peel or lemon peel

2 teaspoons lime juice or lemon
  juice

4 skinless, boneless chicken
  breast halves (about
  1 pound total)

1 teaspoon cooking oil

1 teaspoon dried thyme,
  crushed

¼ teaspoon salt

¼ teaspoon black pepper

Exchanges: 3 Lean Meat **1** Fruit

1 For salsa, in a medium bowl stir together pineapple, chipotle peppers, chives, honey, lime or lemon peel, and lime or lemon juice. Let stand at room temperature for 30 minutes.

2 Meanwhile, rinse chicken; pat dry. Lightly brush chicken with cooking oil. In a small bowl stir together thyme, salt, and black pepper; rub onto both sides of chicken. Place chicken on the unheated rack of broiler pan. Broil 4 to 5 inches from heat for 12 to 15 minutes or until chicken is tender and no longer pink, turning once. (Or, grill chicken on the lightly greased rack of an uncovered grill directly over medium coals for 12 to 15 minutes or until chicken is tender and no longer pink, turning once.) Serve chicken with salsa. Makes 4 servings.

Nutrition facts per serving: 182 calories, **5 g** total fat (**1 g** saturated fat), **59 mg** cholesterol, **227 mg** sodium, **13 g** carbohydrate, **1 g** fiber, **22 g** protein
Daily values: 6% vit. A, **19%** vit. C, **2%** calcium, **8%** iron

soups and stews

chicken WITH POBLANO SALSA

Dark green poblano peppers are very mild, sweet chile peppers with just a whisper of heat. The poblano often is used for classic chiles rellenos. If you can't find poblanos, use Anaheim peppers instead.

Prep: 50 minutes
Bake: 15 minutes

- 1 large fresh poblano pepper
- 1 large clove garlic
  Nonstick spray coating
- ⅓ cup fine dry bread crumbs
- 1 tablespoon chili powder
- 1 teaspoon ground cumin
- 4 skinless, boneless chicken breast halves (about 1 pound total)
- 3 tablespoons refrigerated or frozen egg product, thawed
- ½ cup chopped tomatillo or tomato
- 1 medium tomato, chopped
- ¼ cup finely chopped onion
- 2 tablespoons snipped cilantro

Exchanges: ½ Starch **3** Lean Meat **1** Vegetable

1 To roast poblano pepper and garlic, quarter the pepper, removing seeds and membranes. Place pepper pieces and unpeeled garlic clove on a foil-lined baking sheet. Bake, uncovered, in a 450° oven for 20 to 25 minutes or until the pepper skins are charred. Remove garlic; set aside to cool. Bring up the edges of foil and seal around the pepper pieces. Let pepper stand for 20 minutes to steam. Peel pepper pieces and garlic. Chop pepper; mash garlic.

2 Meanwhile, spray a 2-quart rectangular baking dish with nonstick coating; set aside. In a shallow dish combine the bread crumbs, chili powder, and cumin. Rinse chicken; pat dry. Dip chicken in egg product; coat with bread crumb mixture. Arrange chicken in prepared baking dish. Bake, uncovered, in a 375° oven for 15 to 20 minutes or until chicken is tender and no longer pink.

3 For salsa, in a medium bowl combine the poblano pepper, garlic, tomatillo or tomato, tomato, onion, and cilantro. Serve sauce over chicken. Makes 4 servings.

Nutrition facts per serving: 195 calories, **5 g** total fat (**1 g** saturated fat), **60 mg** cholesterol, **161 mg** sodium, **12 g** carbohydrate, **2 g** fiber, **25 g** protein
Daily values: 13% vit. A, **66%** vit. C, **4%** calcium, **17%** iron

sesame CHICKEN

There's no reason to think of fried chicken as permanently off-limits. For our sesame "fried" chicken recipe, we traded the frying pan for the oven and ended up with a crispy, juicy chicken that only tastes taboo.

Prep: 15 minutes
Bake: 45 minutes

Nonstick spray coating

3 **tablespoons sesame seeds**

3 **tablespoons all-purpose flour**

¼ **teaspoon salt**

¼ **teaspoon ground red pepper**

4 **skinless chicken breast halves (about 2 pounds total)**

3 **tablespoons reduced-sodium teriyaki sauce**

1 **tablespoon margarine or butter, melted**

Exchanges: 5 Lean Meat

❶ Spray a large baking sheet with nonstick coating; set aside. In a large plastic bag combine sesame seeds, flour, salt, and red pepper. Rinse the chicken; pat dry. Dip chicken in teriyaki sauce. Add chicken to the mixture in the plastic bag; close bag. Shake bag to coat chicken.

❷ Place chicken, bone side down, on prepared baking sheet. Drizzle melted margarine or butter over chicken.

❸ Bake in a 400° oven about 45 minutes or until chicken is tender and no longer pink. Makes 4 servings.

Nutrition facts per serving: 275 calories, **11 g** total fat (**2 g** saturated fat), **89 mg** cholesterol, **490 mg** sodium, **7 g** carbohydrate, **1 g** fiber, **35 g** protein
Daily values: 4% vit. A, **0%** vit. C, **2%** calcium, **12%** iron

Butter vs. Margarine

For years, people spread the wrong word about butter—that it's "bad" for you. But when comparing butter and stick margarine, the major difference is taste. Both products have 11 to 12 grams of fat and 100 to 108 calories per tablespoon. Either should be used in small amounts. Many brands of spreads and tub margarine are slightly lower in fat, which makes them lower in calories. These products have been whipped with water to lower the calories and make them easy to spread. Water in the product means water on your toast, causing it to be soggy. Whipped spreads are not recommended for baking. Even stick margarines may not give you the best results, depending on the oil content. Too much oil can wreak havoc with certain baked things, such as pastry or streusel. When in doubt, use butter.

chicken BURRITOS

Say "Con mucho gusto!" to these mango salsa-topped chicken burritos. And, if the heat index starts to climb too high, just dab them with a little palate-soothing light sour cream.

Exchanges: **1** Starch **1** Lean Meat

Start to Finish: 1 hour

½ **cup finely chopped plum tomato**

½ **cup finely chopped, peeled mango**

¼ **cup finely chopped red onion**

4 **tablespoons lime juice**

3 **tablespoons snipped cilantro**

2 **to 3 teaspoons finely chopped, seeded jalapeño pepper**

12 **ounces skinless, boneless chicken breast halves**

½ **cup water**

¼ **teaspoon salt**

⅛ **to ¼ teaspoon ground red pepper**

8 **6-inch corn tortillas**

1½ **cups shredded romaine or leaf lettuce**

¼ **cup light dairy sour cream**

❶ For salsa, in a medium bowl combine the tomato, mango, red onion, 2 tablespoons of the lime juice, the cilantro, and jalapeño pepper. Cover and chill for 30 minutes.

❷ In a large heavy skillet place the chicken and the water. Bring to boiling; reduce heat. Simmer, covered, for 12 to 14 minutes or until chicken is tender and no longer pink. Drain well; let cool until easy to handle. Using two forks, shred the chicken. Toss shredded chicken with the remaining lime juice, the salt, and ground red pepper.

❸ Meanwhile, wrap the tortillas in foil. Bake in a 350° oven for 10 minutes or until warm.

❹ To serve, spoon shredded chicken down centers of warm tortillas. Top each with salsa, romaine or leaf lettuce, and sour cream. Roll up. Makes 8 burritos.

Nutrition facts per burrito: 129 calories, **2 g** total fat (**1 g** saturated fat), **23 mg** cholesterol, **138 mg** sodium, **17 g** carbohydrate, **1 g** fiber, **10 g** protein **Daily values: 9%** vit. A, **22%** vit. C, **5%** calcium, **5%** iron

pesto-stuffed CHICKEN

Fresh sorrel, a sour-tasting herb, looks like thin spinach. Remove any thick stems from the sorrel and spinach before making the homemade pesto. If sorrel isn't available, fill in with extra spinach.

Prep: 30 minutes
Bake: 25 minutes

1 recipe Sorrel Pesto

4 skinless, boneless chicken breast halves (about 1 pound total)

8 teaspoons soft goat cheese (chèvre)

Black pepper

Nonstick spray coating

1 7¼-ounce jar roasted red sweet peppers, drained and chopped (about 1 cup)

½ cup frozen artichoke hearts, thawed and chopped

2 teaspoons snipped fresh oregano or thyme

Exchanges: 3 Lean Meat **1** Vegetable

❶ Prepare Sorrel Pesto. Rinse chicken; pat dry. Place one chicken breast half between 2 pieces of plastic wrap. Pound chicken lightly into a ⅛-inch-thick rectangle. Remove plastic wrap. Spread breast with 1 tablespoon of Sorrel Pesto and 2 teaspoons of goat cheese. Fold in long sides of chicken; roll up from short end. Secure with toothpicks. Season with pepper. Repeat with remaining chicken, pesto, and goat cheese.

❷ Spray a large skillet and a 2-quart square baking dish with nonstick coating; set dish aside. Preheat skillet over medium heat. Place the chicken rolls in hot skillet, turning to brown evenly. Transfer browned chicken rolls to prepared baking dish. Bake in a 375° oven for 25 to 30 minutes or until chicken is tender and no longer pink.

❸ Meanwhile, in a small saucepan combine roasted peppers, artichokes, and oregano or thyme. Cook and stir over medium heat until heated through. Serve over chicken. Makes 4 servings.

Sorrel Pesto: In food processor bowl combine 1 cup firmly packed torn spinach leaves; ½ cup firmly packed torn sorrel leaves; 1 clove garlic, quartered; and ¼ cup finely shredded Asiago cheese. Cover; process with several on-off turns until a paste forms, stopping machine several times to scrape down sides. Combine 1 tablespoon walnut oil or olive oil and 1 tablespoon water. With machine running, gradually add oil mixture; process to consistency of soft butter. Reserve ¼ cup of pesto mixture. Cover and store remaining pesto in refrigerator for later use.

Nutrition facts per serving: 200 calories, **9 g** total fat (**3 g** saturated fat), **70 mg** cholesterol, **164 mg** sodium, **5 g** carbohydrate, **2 g** fiber, **25 g** protein
Daily values: 27% vit. A, **178%** vit. C, **4%** calcium, **12%** iron

fruit & CHICKEN KABOBS

Bring the fresh style and bold flavors of the Caribbean to your backyard grill with these easy fruit-and-chicken kabobs, steeped in a sweet-and-fiery marinade. (See photograph, page 61.)

Prep: 30 minutes
Marinate: 4 hours
Grill: 15 minutes

- 1 **pound skinless, boneless chicken breasts**
- 3 **tablespoons reduced-sodium soy sauce**
- 4 **teaspoons honey**
- 4 **teaspoons red wine vinegar**
- ½ **teaspoon curry powder**
- ½ **teaspoon ground allspice**
- ¼ **teaspoon bottled hot pepper sauce**
- 1 **medium red onion, cut into 1-inch wedges**
- 1 **nectarine, seeded and cut into 1-inch pieces, or 1 papaya, peeled, seeded, and cut into 1-inch pieces**
- 2 **cups hot cooked couscous or rice**

Exchanges: 2 Starch **3** Lean Meat **1** Fruit

1 Rinse chicken; pat dry. Cut chicken into 1-inch pieces. Place chicken in a plastic bag set in a shallow dish. For marinade, in a small bowl stir together soy sauce, honey, vinegar, curry powder, allspice, and hot pepper sauce. Pour over chicken. Close the bag. Marinate chicken in the refrigerator for 4 hours, turning bag occasionally. Remove chicken from marinade, reserving the marinade.

2 In a saucepan cook the onion in a small amount of boiling water for 3 minutes; drain. Thread the chicken, nectarine or papaya pieces, and partially cooked onion alternately onto eight 6-inch metal skewers.

3 Grill the kabobs on the rack of an uncovered grill directly over medium-hot coals about 15 minutes or until chicken is tender and no longer pink, turning skewers occasionally. Place reserved marinade in a small saucepan. Bring to boiling. Cook, uncovered, for 1 minute. Pour marinade through a strainer, reserving liquid.

4 Before serving, brush kabobs with the strained marinade. Serve kabobs with hot cooked couscous or rice. Pass any remaining marinade. Makes 4 servings.

Nutrition facts per serving: 374 calories, **4 g** total fat (**1 g** saturated fat), **59 mg** cholesterol, **462 mg** sodium, **54 g** carbohydrate, **9 g** fiber, **30 g** protein
Daily values: 7% vit. A, **37%** vit. C, **3%** calcium, **12%** iron

ginger beef STIR-FRY

When you crave steak, but don't crave high fat and calories, try this stir-fry. Lean beef and crispy spring vegetables stir-fry together for a full-flavored dinner you can toss together in 30 minutes.

Start to Finish: 30 minutes

- **8** ounces beef top round steak
- **½** cup beef broth
- **3** tablespoons reduced-sodium soy sauce
- **2½** teaspoons cornstarch
- **1** teaspoon sugar
- **½** teaspoon grated fresh ginger
- Nonstick spray coating
- **12** ounces asparagus spears, trimmed and cut into 1-inch-long pieces (2 cups)
- **1½** cups sliced fresh mushrooms
- **1** cup small broccoli flowerets
- **4** green onions, bias-sliced into 1-inch lengths (½ cup)
- **1** tablespoon cooking oil
- **2** cups hot cooked rice

Exchanges: 1 Starch **2** Lean Meat **3** Vegetable

1 Trim fat from beef. Partially freeze beef; thinly slice across the grain into bite-size strips. Set aside. For the sauce, in a small bowl stir together the beef broth, soy sauce, cornstarch, sugar, and ginger; set aside.

2 Spray a cold wok or large skillet with nonstick coating. Preheat over medium-high heat. Add asparagus, mushrooms, broccoli, and green onions. Stir-fry for 3 to 4 minutes or until vegetables are crisp-tender. Remove from wok or skillet.

3 Carefully add the oil to wok or skillet. Add beef; stir-fry for 2 to 3 minutes or until desired doneness. Push the beef from center of wok or skillet. Stir sauce; add to the wok or skillet. Cook and stir until thickened and bubbly.

4 Return vegetables to wok or skillet. Stir all ingredients together to coat with sauce; heat through. Serve immediately with hot cooked rice. Makes 4 servings.

Nutrition facts per serving: 270 calories, **7 g** total fat (**2 g** saturated fat), **36 mg** cholesterol, **541 mg** sodium, **32 g** carbohydrate, **4 g** fiber, **21 g** protein
Daily values: 15% vit. A, **107%** vit. C, **4%** calcium, **25%** iron

super suppers

77

spiced beef STIR-FRY

This is no ordinary stir-fry! The aromatic blend of five spices infuses bold flavors into this dish. Fresh mint and cilantro add further intrigue to the mix.

Start to Finish: 40 minutes

- 1 teaspoon ground cumin
- ½ teaspoon garlic powder
- ½ teaspoon ground ginger
- ½ teaspoon ground allspice
- ½ teaspoon paprika
- ¼ teaspoon salt
- ¼ teaspoon pepper
- 1 pound boneless beef sirloin steak, cut into ¾-inch cubes
- 1 14½-ounce can reduced-sodium chicken broth
- 1¼ cups couscous
- 3 plum tomatoes, chopped
- ½ of a medium cucumber, halved lengthwise and sliced
- 2 tablespoons snipped cilantro or parsley
- 1 tablespoon snipped mint
  Nonstick spray coating
- 8 green onions, bias-sliced into 1-inch lengths (1 cup)
- 2 teaspoons cooking oil

Exchanges: 2 Starch **3** Lean Meat **2** Vegetable

1 In a plastic bag combine cumin, garlic powder, ginger, allspice, paprika, salt, and pepper. Add beef. Close bag. Toss to coat beef with spice mixture; set aside.

2 In a medium saucepan bring the chicken broth to boiling. Stir in the couscous. Remove from heat. Cover; let stand for 5 minutes. Stir in tomato, cucumber, cilantro or parsley, and mint. Cover to keep warm.

3 Spray a large nonstick skillet with nonstick coating. Preheat over medium-high heat. Add green onions. Stir-fry for 2 to 3 minutes or until crisp-tender. Remove green onions from skillet.

4 Carefully add 1 teaspoon of the oil to the skillet. Add half of the beef. Stir-fry for 2 to 3 minutes or to desired doneness. Remove from the skillet. Repeat with the remaining oil and beef. Return all beef to skillet; heat through.

5 To serve, divide couscous mixture among 5 plates. Top each with some of the beef and green onions. Makes 5 servings.

Nutrition facts per serving: 378 calories, **11 g** total fat (**4 g** saturated fat), **60 mg** cholesterol, **394 mg** sodium, **40 g** carbohydrate, **8 g** fiber, **28 g** protein
Daily values: **9%** vit. A, **23%** vit. C, **3%** calcium, **26%** iron

asian FLANK STEAK

Sweet and spicy Szechwan-style cooking promises palate-pleasing diversity for your taste buds. Preparing and marinating the steak the day before allows you to pop it under the broiler and have it on the table in short order.

Prep: 15 minutes
Marinate: 4 to 24 hours
Broil: 12 minutes

1   1¼-pounds beef flank steak
½   cup beef broth
⅓   cup hoisin sauce
¼   cup reduced-sodium soy
     sauce
¼   cup sliced green onions
3   tablespoons dry sherry or
     apple, orange, or pineapple
     juice
1   tablespoon sugar
1   teaspoon grated fresh ginger
4   cloves garlic, minced
     Nonstick spray coating

Exchanges: 2½ Lean Meat

❶ Trim fat from beef. Place beef in a plastic bag set in a shallow dish. For marinade, in a small bowl stir together beef broth, hoisin sauce, soy sauce, green onions, sherry or juice, sugar, ginger, and garlic. Pour over beef. Close bag. Marinate in refrigerator for 4 to 24 hours, turning bag occasionally.

❷ Drain beef, discarding the marinade. Spray the unheated rack of a broiler pan with nonstick coating. Place beef on the prepared rack. Broil 4 to 5 inches from the heat to desired doneness, turning once. Allow 12 to 14 minutes for medium. (Or, grill the beef on the rack of an uncovered grill directly over medium coals to desired doneness, turning once. Allow 12 to 14 minutes for medium.) To serve, thinly slice beef across the grain. Makes 6 servings.

Nutrition facts per serving: 144 calories, **7 g** total fat (**3 g** saturated fat), **44 mg** cholesterol, **113 mg** sodium, **1 g** carbohydrate, **0 g** fiber, **18 g** protein
Daily values: 0% vit. A, **0%** vit. C, **0%** calcium, **11%** iron

No Beef With Beef

Protein is a vital nutrient that our bodies need for a variety of functions, such as building tissue and keeping the immune system strong. Many people enjoy meat as their primary source of protein in the diet. Red meat is one of the best sources of iron and zinc—two minerals in short dietary supply for many people. Today's beef comes from cattle that are raised to be leaner, with some cuts—such as flank and tenderloin steak—having less fat than dark meat poultry. Beef also is closely trimmed of fat by butchers. All of this makes beef a viable participant in a healthful diet.

horseradish FLANK STEAK

A classic at British clubs, this supper works well as a salad, too. Serve thin strips of this grilled flank steak cold on a bed of mixed greens. Top with the mustard sauce or dress with bottled fat-free Italian dressing.

Prep: 20 minutes
Marinate: 6 to 24 hours
Grill: 12 minutes

1 **1-pound beef flank steak**

3 **tablespoons Dijon-style mustard**

3 **tablespoons lemon juice**

4½ **teaspoons reduced-sodium Worcestershire sauce**

⅓ **cup fat-free dairy sour cream or fat-free mayonnaise or salad dressing**

1 **green onion, finely chopped (2 tablespoons)**

1 **to 2 teaspoons prepared horseradish**

Exchanges: ½ Starch 3 Lean Meat

1 Trim fat from beef. Use a sharp knife to score beef by making shallow diagonal cuts at 1-inch intervals in a diamond pattern. Repeat on other side. Place beef in a plastic bag set in a shallow dish.

2 For marinade, in a small bowl combine 2 tablespoons of the Dijon-style mustard, the lemon juice, and Worcestershire sauce. Pour over beef. Close the bag. Marinate beef in the refrigerator for 6 to 24 hours, turning the bag occasionally.

3 In a small bowl combine the remaining Dijon-style mustard; the sour cream, mayonnaise, or salad dressing; green onion; and horseradish. Cover and refrigerate. Remove from refrigerator 30 minutes before serving time.

4 Drain the beef, discarding the marinade. Grill on the rack of an uncovered grill directly over medium coals to desired doneness, turning once. Allow 12 to 14 minutes for medium.

5 To serve, thinly slice beef across the grain. Serve with sour cream mixture. Makes 4 servings.

Nutrition facts per serving: 208 calories, **9 g** total fat (**3 g** saturated fat), **53 mg** cholesterol, **398 mg** sodium, **6 g** carbohydrate, **0 g** fiber, **24 g** protein
Daily values: 3% vit. A, 26% vit. C, 3% calcium, 16% iron

deviled ROAST BEEF

For the mustard lover in your midst, here's a "deviled" beef dish that is sinfully delicious. One taste and you may be willing to barter anything for another helping.

Prep: 25 minutes
Roast: 1½ hours
Stand: 15 minutes

1 **2- to 2½-pounds beef eye of round roast**

¼ **cup Dijon-style mustard**

¼ **teaspoon coarsely ground pepper**

2 **cups sliced fresh mushrooms**

1 **cup beef broth**

1 **small onion, cut into thin wedges**

¼ **cup water**

2 **cloves garlic, minced**

1 **teaspoon Worcestershire sauce**

¼ **teaspoon dried thyme, crushed**

½ **cup fat-free milk**

3 **tablespoons all-purpose flour**

Exchanges: 3 Lean Meat **1** Vegetable

1 Trim fat from beef. In a small bowl stir together 2 tablespoons of the Dijon-style mustard and the pepper; rub onto the beef. Place the beef on a rack in a shallow roasting pan. Insert a meat thermometer. Roast beef in a 325° oven until thermometer registers 140° for medium-rare (1½ to 2 hours) or 155° for medium (1¾ to 2¼ hours). Cover with foil; let stand for 15 minutes before carving. (The temperature of the meat will rise 5° during standing.)

2 Meanwhile, for sauce, in a medium saucepan combine the mushrooms, beef broth, onion, water, garlic, Worcestershire sauce, and thyme. Bring to boiling; reduce heat. Simmer, covered, about 5 minutes or until vegetables are tender. In a small bowl stir together milk and remaining Dijon-style mustard; gradually stir into flour. Add to mushroom mixture in saucepan. Cook and stir over medium heat until thickened and bubbly. Cook and stir for 1 minute more.

3 To serve, thinly slice beef across the grain. Arrange on a serving platter. Spoon some of the sauce over beef. Pass remaining sauce. Makes 8 to 10 servings.

Nutrition facts per serving: 217 calories, **9 g** total fat (**3 g** saturated fat), **78 mg** cholesterol, **342 mg** sodium, **5 g** carbohydrate, **0 g** fiber, **28 g** protein
Daily values: 0% vit. A, **4%** vit. C, **2%** calcium, **22%** iron

super suppers

cranberry PORK CHOPS

For a holiday or everyday dinner, the combination of tart cranberries and succulent pork chops is a winner worth celebrating. Complement this festive main dish with steamed Brussels sprouts and a wild rice mix.

Start to Finish: 30 minutes

½ teaspoon pepper

¼ teaspoon celery salt

4 pork loin chops (about 12 ounces total)

2 teaspoons cooking oil

1 large onion, thinly sliced and separated into rings

2 tablespoons water

¾ cup cranberries

¼ cup sugar

3 tablespoons water

2 tablespoons frozen orange juice concentrate, thawed

1 teaspoon finely shredded orange peel

½ teaspoon ground sage

¼ teaspoon salt

Exchanges: 2 Lean Meat **1½** Fruit

1 In a small bowl stir together pepper and celery salt; rub onto both sides of chops. In a medium skillet heat oil over medium-high heat. Cook chops and onion rings in hot oil until chops are browned, turning once. Carefully add the 2 tablespoons water to skillet. Cover and cook over medium heat for 15 to 20 minutes more or until no pink remains and juices run clear. Transfer chops to serving plates; keep warm. Remove onions from juices with a slotted spoon; set aside.

2 Meanwhile, for the sauce, in a medium saucepan combine the cranberries, sugar, the 3 tablespoons water, the orange juice concentrate, orange peel, sage, and salt. Cook and stir over medium heat about 10 minutes or until the cranberry skins pop and mixture thickens. Stir in the onions; heat through. Remove from heat.

3 To serve, spoon about ¼ cup sauce over each pork chop. Makes 4 servings.

Nutrition facts per serving: 209 calories, **8 g** total fat (**2 g** saturated fat), **38 mg** cholesterol, **264 mg** sodium, **22 g** carbohydrate, **2 g** fiber, **13 g** protein
Daily values: 0% vit. A, **31%** vit. C, **1%** calcium, **5%** iron

super suppers

blue cheese 'N' CHOPS

Looking for something impressive to serve guests? Try these herb-rubbed pork chops. Pan-sizzled in their own juices, the chops are then baked along with rice. Fresh pear and blue cheese are the final touch.

Prep: 15 minutes
Bake: 30 minutes

Nonstick spray coating

2½ cups cooked brown rice

4 green onions, sliced (½ cup)

⅓ cup apple juice

¼ cup chopped toasted walnuts (optional)

¼ teaspoon salt

⅛ teaspoon pepper

1 teaspoon dried thyme, crushed

¼ teaspoon salt

¼ to ½ teaspoon pepper

4 boneless pork loin chops, cut ½ to ¾ inch thick (about 12 ounces total)

1 red pear, cored and chopped

¼ cup crumbled blue cheese

Exchanges: 2 Starch **2** Lean Meat **½** Fruit

❶ Spray a 2-quart square baking dish and a large skillet with nonstick coating; set aside. In a large bowl combine the cooked rice, green onions, 2 tablespoons of the apple juice, the walnuts (if desired), ¼ teaspoon salt, and the ⅛ teaspoon pepper. Spoon rice mixture into prepared baking dish.

❷ In a small bowl stir together the thyme, ¼ teaspoon salt, and the ¼ to ½ teaspoon pepper. Rub onto both sides of chops. Cook chops in skillet over medium-high heat until browned, turning once. Arrange browned chops on top of rice mixture. Pour remaining apple juice over chops.

❸ Bake, covered, in a 350° oven about 30 minutes or until no pink remains in chops and juices run clear. Transfer chops to serving plates. Stir chopped pear and blue cheese into hot rice mixture; serve with chops. Makes 4 servings.

Nutrition facts per serving: **305** calories, **9 g** total fat (**5 g** saturated fat), **45 mg** cholesterol, **416 mg** sodium, **38 g** carbohydrate, **3 g** fiber, **17 g** protein
Daily values: **2%** vit. A, **7%** vit. C, **3%** calcium, **11%** iron

super suppers

onion-glazed PORK

Glazing the onions allows their natural sweetness to come through, forming a perfect partnership with the juicy pork tenderloin medallions. For extra flavor, use a variety of sweet onions such as Maui, Walla Walla, or Vidalia.

Start to Finish: 35 minutes

- 1 **12-ounce pork tenderloin**
  Nonstick spray coating
- 1 **tablespoon olive oil**
- 2 **medium onions, sliced and separated into rings**
- 1 **tablespoon brown sugar**
- ⅓ **cup water**
- 3 **tablespoons balsamic vinegar or white wine vinegar**
- 2 **teaspoons cornstarch**
- ¼ **teaspoon salt**
- ¼ **teaspoon pepper**
- 2 **tablespoons snipped parsley**

Exchanges: 2 Lean Meat **2** Vegetable

① Trim any fat from pork. Cut pork crosswise into ½-inch-thick slices. Spray a large nonstick skillet with nonstick coating. Preheat skillet over medium-high heat. Cook half of the pork in the hot skillet for 3½ to 4 minutes or until pork is slightly pink in the center and the juices run clear, turning once. Remove pork from skillet; keep warm. Repeat with remaining pork.

② Carefully add oil to skillet; add the onions. Cook, covered, over medium-low heat for 13 to 15 minutes or until onions are tender. Uncover; stir in the brown sugar. Cook and stir over medium-high heat for 4 to 5 minutes or until onions are golden.

③ Meanwhile, in a small bowl stir together water, vinegar, cornstarch, salt, and pepper; carefully stir into onion mixture in skillet. Cook and stir until thickened and bubbly. Cook and stir for 2 minutes more. Return pork to skillet; heat through.

④ To serve, transfer the pork and onion mixture to a serving platter. Sprinkle with parsley. Makes 4 servings.

Nutrition facts per serving: 179 calories, **7 g** total fat (**2 g** saturated fat), **60 mg** cholesterol, **182 mg** sodium, **10 g** carbohydrate, **1 g** fiber, **19 g** protein
Daily values: 1% vit. A, **10%** vit. C, **1%** calcium, **11%** iron

Flavor Boosters

Many dishes rely on fat and sodium for flavoring, but there are other ways to get great taste without compromising a well-managed diet. Acidic flavors from citrus and vinegars stimulate the taste buds while adding few, if any, calories and no fat. Herbs pack a lot of concentrated punch into a recipe without adding fat and very few calories. When using fresh herbs, snip or mince them and toss them into the final dish just before serving.

peachy PORK TENDERLOIN

Fruit and pork have been a dynamic duet for centuries because of the way the fruit enhances the taste of the pork. This simple, five-ingredient recipe showcases the harmony of these two flavor notes.

Prep: 10 minutes
Marinate: 4 to 24 hours
Grill: 30 minutes

- 1 **12-ounce pork tenderloin**
- ⅓ **cup peach nectar**
- 3 **tablespoons light teriyaki sauce**
- 2 **tablespoons snipped fresh rosemary or 2 teaspoons dried rosemary, crushed**
- 1 **tablespoon olive oil**

Exchanges: 2½ Lean Meat ½ Fruit

1 Trim any fat from pork. Place the pork in a plastic bag set in a shallow dish. For the marinade, in a small bowl combine peach nectar, teriyaki sauce, rosemary, and olive oil. Pour over pork. Close bag. Marinate in refrigerator for 4 to 24 hours, turning bag occasionally. Drain the pork, discarding marinade.

2 In a grill with a cover arrange preheated coals around a drip pan. Test for medium heat above the pan. Place pork on grill rack directly over the drip pan. Cover and grill about 30 minutes or until no pink remains and the juices run clear. Makes 4 servings.

Nutrition facts per serving: 162 calories, **7 g** total fat (**2 g** saturated fat), **60 mg** cholesterol, **285 mg** sodium, **6 g** carbohydrate, **0 g** fiber, **19 g** protein
Daily values: 0% vit. A, **2%** vit. C, **1%** calcium, **8%** iron

Lean on Pork

Q: Can pork find a place in a healthful diet?
A: Definitely! Today's pork comes from hogs that are bred to be lean. Also, the visible fat is trimmed more closely from the meat than in the past. In fact, pork compares favorably to the white meat of chicken. A 3-ounce portion of roasted pork tenderloin, for example, has 139 calories and 4 grams of fat. The same portion of roasted chicken (breast meat with no skin) has 142 calories and 3 grams of fat.

spice-rubbed PORK CHOPS

Big, meaty pork chops pair well with full-flavored ingredients. This lime and chili powder marinade is just the ticket. Add more or less of the hot pepper sauce to suit your taste.

Prep: 15 minutes
Marinate: 4 to 24 hours
Broil: 6 minutes

- **4 boneless pork loin chops, cut ½ inch thick (about 1 pound total)**
- **¼ cup lime juice**
- **2 tablespoons chili powder**
- **1 tablespoon olive oil**
- **1 clove garlic, minced**
- **1½ teaspoons ground cumin**
- **1½ teaspoons ground cinnamon**
- **½ teaspoon bottled hot pepper sauce**
- **¼ teaspoon salt**

Exchanges: 2 Lean Meat 1 Fat

1 Place chops in a plastic bag set in a shallow dish. For the marinade, in a small bowl stir together the lime juice, chili powder, olive oil, garlic, cumin, cinnamon, hot pepper sauce, and salt. Pour over chops. Close bag. Marinate in refrigerator for 4 to 24 hours, turning the bag occasionally. Drain chops, discarding marinade.

2 Place chops on the unheated rack of a broiler pan. Broil 3 to 4 inches from the heat for 6 to 8 minutes or until no pink remains and juices run clear, turning once. Makes 4 servings.

Nutrition facts per serving: **163** calories, **10 g** total fat (**3 g** saturated fat), **51 mg** cholesterol, **128 mg** sodium, **3 g** carbohydrate, **1 g** fiber, **17 g** protein
Daily values: **7%** vit. A, **7%** vit. C, **1%** calcium, **10%** iron

super suppers

fish WITH CHERRY RELISH

By making the relish a day ahead, you save time and allow the flavors to blend. If swordfish is unavailable, or if you prefer a different fish, try halibut, tuna, or any other firm-fleshed fish.

Prep: 20 minutes
Grill: 6 minutes

4 fresh or frozen swordfish steaks, ¾ inch thick (about 1¼ pounds total)

½ cup dried tart cherries, snipped

2 tablespoons raspberry vinegar, balsamic vinegar, or white wine vinegar

1 tablespoon water

⅓ cup chopped red onion

1 teaspoon olive oil

1½ teaspoons sugar

Dash bottled hot pepper sauce

½ teaspoon dried thyme, crushed

¼ teaspoon paprika

¼ teaspoon black pepper

⅛ teaspoon onion powder

⅛ teaspoon ground red pepper

1 teaspoon olive oil

1 teaspoon raspberry vinegar, balsamic vinegar, or white wine vinegar

Nonstick spray coating

Exchanges: **4** Lean Meat **1** Fruit

1 Thaw swordfish, if frozen. Rinse swordfish; pat dry. Set aside.

2 For the relish, in a small bowl stir together the cherries, the 2 tablespoons vinegar, and water; set aside. In a small saucepan cook the onion in 1 teaspoon olive oil until tender. Stir in cherry mixture, sugar, and hot pepper sauce. Keep warm over low heat until serving time, stirring occasionally.

3 In a small bowl stir together thyme, paprika, black pepper, onion powder, and ground red pepper. Combine 1 teaspoon olive oil and the 1 teaspoon vinegar. Lightly brush both sides of swordfish with the oil mixture. Rub the herb mixture onto both sides of the swordfish.

4 Spray a cold grill rack with nonstick coating. Grill swordfish on the sprayed rack of an uncovered grill directly over medium coals for 6 to 9 minutes or until swordfish flakes easily when tested with a fork, turning once. (Or, spray the unheated rack of a broiler pan with nonstick spray coating. Place the swordfish on the rack. Broil 4 inches from the heat for 6 to 9 minutes or until swordfish flakes easily when tested with a fork). Serve with relish. Makes 4 servings.

Nutrition facts per serving with about 2 tablespoons relish: 254 calories, **8 g** total fat (**2 g** saturated fat), **56 mg** cholesterol, **128 mg** sodium, **16 g** carbohydrate, **1 g** fiber, **29 g** protein **Daily values: 14%** vit. A, **3%** vit. C, **1%** calcium, **9%** iron

super suppers

89

rosemary tuna KABOBS

Seafood has a reputation for being delicate. Not so with swordfish and tuna. These varieties are sturdy enough to marinate, skewer, and grill. Don't marinate for longer than 2 hours or the fish will toughen.

Prep: 25 minutes
Marinate: 2 hours
Broil: 8 minutes

¾ **pound fresh or frozen tuna steaks, 1 inch thick**

1 **teaspoon finely shredded lemon peel**

¼ **cup lemon juice**

1 **tablespoon cooking oil**

1 **tablespoon snipped fresh rosemary or 1 teaspoon dried rosemary, crushed**

2 **cloves garlic, minced**

¼ **teaspoon salt**

⅛ **teaspoon pepper**

8 **to 10 whole tiny new potatoes (about ¾ pound)**

4 **baby pattypan squash, halved lengthwise, or 1 medium zucchini, halved lengthwise and cut into 1-inch pieces**

Nonstick spray coating

4 **cherry tomatoes**

Hot cooked rice (optional)

Exchanges: 1 Starch 2 Lean Meat 1 Vegetable

❶ Thaw tuna, if frozen. Rinse tuna; pat dry. Cut into 1-inch pieces. Place tuna in a plastic bag set in a shallow dish. For the marinade, in a small bowl stir together the lemon peel, lemon juice, cooking oil, rosemary, garlic, salt, and pepper. Pour over tuna. Close bag. Marinate in refrigerator for 2 hours, turning bag occasionally.

❷ Meanwhile, scrub potatoes; cut any large potatoes in half. In a medium saucepan cook potatoes in a small amount of boiling water for 15 to 20 minutes or just until tender; drain. Rinse with cold water. Set aside.

❸ Drain tuna, reserving marinade. On 4 long metal skewers, alternately thread the tuna, potatoes, and squash or zucchini, leaving about ¼-inch space between pieces. Spray the unheated rack of a broiler pan with nonstick coating. Place kabobs on rack. Brush with marinade. Broil 4 inches from heat for 5 minutes. Turn kabobs; brush with some of the marinade. Discard remaining marinade. Broil kabobs for 3 to 4 minutes more or until tuna flakes easily when tested with a fork and squash is tender. To serve, place a tomato on the end of each kabob. If desired, serve with rice. Makes 4 servings.

Nutrition facts per serving: 235 calories, **7 g** total fat (**1 g** saturated fat), **34 mg** cholesterol, **220 mg** sodium, **23 g** carbohydrate, **2 g** fiber, **19 g** protein
Daily values: 5% vit. A, **45%** vit. C, **2%** calcium, **16%** iron

super suppers

apricot-sauced SALMON

Salmon is one of the richest sources for the omega-3 fatty acids that help protect against heart disease. Apricots are rich in cancer-fighting antioxidants. Teamed together, the result is a delicious and dynamite health duo.

Prep: 20 minutes
Broil: 8 minutes

4 **fresh or frozen salmon steaks, ¾ inch thick (about 1¼ pounds total)**

Nonstick spray coating

2 **teaspoons cornstarch**

¼ **teaspoon salt**

Dash ground red pepper

1 **5½-ounce can apricot nectar**

1 **tablespoon honey**

1 **tablespoon white wine vinegar**

2 **cups watercress leaves or shredded spinach or romaine**

½ **of a medium cucumber, thinly sliced**

1 **tablespoon white wine vinegar**

2 **green onions, sliced (¼ cup)**

Exchanges: 3 Lean Meat **½** Fruit

1 Thaw the salmon, if frozen. Rinse salmon; pat dry. Spray the unheated rack of a broiler pan with nonstick coating. Place salmon on rack. Broil 4 to 5 inches from heat for 8 to 12 minutes or until the salmon flakes easily when tested with a fork. (Or, spray a grill basket with nonstick coating. Place salmon in basket. Grill salmon on the grill rack of an uncovered grill directly over medium coals for 8 to 12 minutes or until salmon flakes easily with a fork, turning once.)

2 Meanwhile, for sauce, in a small saucepan combine the cornstarch, salt, and ground red pepper. Gradually stir in the nectar; add honey and 1 tablespoon vinegar. Cook and stir over medium heat until thickened and bubbly. Cook and stir for 2 minutes more. Remove from heat. Cover; keep warm.

3 In a large bowl toss together the watercress, spinach, or romaine; cucumber; and 1 tablespoon vinegar. Divide among 4 serving plates. To serve, place salmon on watercress mixture and spoon sauce over each serving. Sprinkle with green onions. Makes 4 servings.

Nutrition facts per serving: 181 calories, **5 g** total fat (**1 g** saturated fat), **25 mg** cholesterol, **228 mg** sodium, **13 g** carbohydrate, **1 g** fiber, **21 g** protein
Daily values: 18% vit. A, **39%** vit. C, **3%** calcium, **8%** iron

super suppers

91

vegetable STRUDEL

Calzone lovers will appreciate this flaky phyllo dough strudel studded with vegetables, tomatoes, and cheese. Remember to place the frozen phyllo in the fridge the day before using to allow for thawing.

Prep: 40 minutes
Bake: 25 minutes
Stand: 10 minutes

5 **cups fresh spinach leaves**

2 **medium red sweet peppers, cut into 1-inch strips**

1 **medium yellow summer squash, cut into 1-inch strips**

2 **carrots, shredded**

½ **cup sliced fresh mushrooms**

4 **green onions, sliced (½ cup)**

¼ **cup oil-packed dried tomatoes, drained and chopped**

3 **tablespoons grated Parmesan cheese**

1 **tablespoon snipped fresh oregano or ½ teaspoon dried oregano, crushed**

⅛ **teaspoon salt**

⅛ **teaspoon black pepper**

Dash ground red pepper

Butter-flavor nonstick spray coating

6 **sheets frozen phyllo dough, thawed**

2 **tablespoons fine dry bread crumbs**

Exchanges: 1 Starch 3 Vegetable

❶ For filling, place the spinach in large colander; set aside. In a large saucepan cook sweet peppers, summer squash, carrots, mushrooms, and green onions in 4 cups boiling water for 2 to 3 minutes. Pour over spinach to drain; rinse immediately with cold water. Drain well, pressing out excess moisture. Transfer vegetables to a large bowl. Stir in the dried tomatoes, 2 tablespoons of the Parmesan cheese, the oregano, salt, black pepper, and ground red pepper. Set filling aside.

❷ Spray a large baking sheet with nonstick coating. Place 1 sheet of phyllo on a dry kitchen towel. (Keep remaining sheets covered with plastic wrap to prevent drying out.) Spray with nonstick coating. Place another sheet on top; spray with nonstick coating. Sprinkle with half of the bread crumbs. Place 2 more sheets of phyllo on top, spraying each with nonstick coating. Sprinkle with remaining crumbs. Add remaining 2 sheets of phyllo, spraying each with nonstick coating.

❸ Spoon filling along 1 long side of phyllo stack about 1½ inches from edges. Fold in the short sides over the filling. Starting from the long side with filling, roll up jelly-roll style.

❹ Place strudel, seam side down, on the prepared baking sheet. Spray top with nonstick coating. Using a sharp knife, score into 8 slices, cutting through the top layer only. Sprinkle with remaining Parmesan cheese.

❺ Bake in a 375° oven for 25 to 30 minutes or until the strudel is golden. Let stand for 10 minutes before serving. To serve, cut along scored lines into slices. Makes 4 servings.

Nutrition facts per serving: 182 calories, **5 g** total fat (**1 g** saturated fat), **4 mg** cholesterol, **466 mg** sodium, **29 g** carbohydrate, **4 g** fiber, **8 g** protein
Daily values: 156% vit. A, **158%** vit. C, **14%** calcium, **24%** iron

super suppers

soups
& STEWS

A hearty soup paired with salad or bread is a satisfying meal. Generally, soups are chock-full of vegetables, making them a nutritious choice. From hot to cold to meatless to meat-brimmed, this chapter includes a variety of soups and stews to enjoy for lunch or dinner.

Shrimp Gazpacho, *recipe page 116*

mulligatawny SOUP

Nourishing and delicious are the best words to describe this hearty chicken soup. To reap all the rewards of this Indian-inspired dish, sop up the rich, curried broth with chunks of warm bread.

soups & stews

Prep: 25 minutes
Cook: 35 minutes

- 1 **tablespoon cooking oil**
- 1 **cup chopped onion**
- 1 **cup coarsely chopped carrots**
- 1 **cup sliced celery**
- 1⅓ **cups chopped, peeled, tart apples**
- 2 **to 3 teaspoons curry powder**
- ¼ **teaspoon salt**
- 3 **cups reduced-sodium chicken broth**
- 3 **cups water**
- 1 **14½-ounce can low-sodium stewed tomatoes**
- 2 **cups chopped cooked chicken or turkey**

Exchanges: 2 Lean Meat **1** Vegetable **1** Fruit ½ Fat

❶ In a Dutch oven heat cooking oil over medium heat. Cook and stir onion, carrots, and celery in hot oil about 10 minutes or until crisp-tender. Reduce heat to medium-low; add apples, curry powder, and salt. Cook, covered, for 5 minutes. Stir in the chicken broth, water, and undrained tomatoes. Bring to boiling; reduce heat. Simmer, covered, for 10 minutes. Stir in the chicken or turkey; simmer for 10 minutes more. Makes six 1⅔-cup servings.

Nutrition facts per serving: 197 calories, **7 g** total fat (**1 g** saturated fat), **45 mg** cholesterol, **517 mg** sodium, **17 g** carbohydrate, **4 g** fiber, **17 g** protein
Daily values: 62% vit. A, **16%** vit. C, **3%** calcium, **8%** iron

chicken chili MONTEREY

This "white" chili packs all the punch of the traditional "bowl of red," and then some. For a distinctive look, use blue corn tortillas instead of the more traditional yellow ones.

soups & stews

Prep: 20 minutes
Cook: 10 minutes

1   **tablespoon cooking oil**

½   **cup chopped onion**

2   **cloves garlic, minced**

2   **to 3 teaspoons chili powder**

½   **teaspoon ground cumin**

1   **15-ounce can reduced-sodium navy beans, great Northern beans, or white kidney beans, rinsed and drained**

1   **14½-ounce can reduced-sodium chicken broth**

1¾ **cups water**

½   **of a 4½-ounce can (about ¼ cup) diced green chile peppers**

1½ **cups chopped cooked chicken**

1   **to 2 tablespoons snipped fresh cilantro or parsley**

2   **6-inch corn tortillas, cut into thin, bite-size strips**

¼   **cup shredded reduced-fat Monterey Jack cheese**

Exchanges: 1½ Starch **3** Lean Meat

1 In a large saucepan heat oil over medium heat. Cook and stir the onion and garlic in hot oil about 4 minutes or until onion is tender; stir in the chili powder and cumin. Cook and stir for 1 minute more. Stir in beans, chicken broth, water, and chile peppers. Bring to boiling; reduce heat. Simmer, covered, for 10 minutes, stirring occasionally. Stir in the chicken and cilantro or parsley. Heat through. Top each serving with tortilla strips and cheese. Makes four 1½-cup servings.

Nutrition facts per serving: 301 calories, **11 g** total fat (**2 g** saturated fat), **56 mg** cholesterol, **472 mg** sodium, **26 g** carbohydrate, **6 g** fiber, **27 g** protein
Daily values: 6% vit. A, **11%** vit. C, **13%** calcium, **22%** iron

5-spice CHICKEN NOODLE SOUP

Asian dishes abound with flavor-packed ingredients. This soup is no exception, with its highlights of soy, five-spice powder, and ginger. All add a flavor punch without adding lots of calories or fat.

Start to Finish: 20 minutes

2½ cups water

1¼ cups reduced-sodium chicken broth

2 green onions, thinly bias-sliced

2 teaspoons reduced-sodium soy sauce

2 cloves garlic, minced

¼ teaspoon five-spice powder

⅛ teaspoon ground ginger

2 cups chopped bok choy

1 medium red sweet pepper, thinly sliced into strips

2 ounces dried somen noodles, broken into 2-inch lengths, or 2 ounces dried fine noodles

1½ cups chopped cooked chicken

Exchanges: ½ Starch **2** Lean Meat **1** Vegetable

1 In a large saucepan combine water, chicken broth, green onions, soy sauce, garlic, five-spice powder, and ginger. Bring to boiling. Stir in bok choy, sweet pepper strips, and noodles. Return to boiling; reduce heat. Boil gently, uncovered, for 3 to 5 minutes or until noodles are just tender. Stir in the cooked chicken. Heat through. Makes four 1½-cup servings.

Nutrition facts per serving: 181 calories, **4 g** total fat (**1 g** saturated fat), **51 mg** cholesterol, **556 mg** sodium, **14 g** carbohydrate, **1 g** fiber, **20 g** protein
Daily values: 27% vit. A, **83%** vit. C, **4%** calcium, **8%** iron

soups & stews

wild rice CHICKEN SOUP

The flavors of Mediterranean cuisine shine through in this recipe with zucchini, garlic, fresh herbs, and Madeira. It's a sunny twist on old-fashioned chicken and rice soup.

soups & stews

Start to Finish: 25 minutes

- 1 6.2-ounce package quick-cooking long-grain and wild rice mix
- 2 14½-ounce cans reduced-sodium chicken broth
- 4 cloves garlic, minced
- 1 tablespoon snipped fresh thyme or 1 teaspoon dried thyme, crushed
- 4 cups chopped tomatoes
- 1 9-ounce package frozen chopped cooked chicken
- 1 cup finely chopped zucchini
- ¼ teaspoon freshly ground pepper
- 1 tablespoon Madeira or dry sherry (optional)

Exchanges: **2** Starch **1** Lean Meat **1** Vegetable

1 Prepare rice mix according to package directions, except omit the seasoning packet and the margarine.

2 Meanwhile, in a Dutch oven combine chicken broth, garlic, and dried thyme (if using); bring to boiling. Stir in the tomatoes, chicken, zucchini, fresh thyme (if using), and pepper. Return to boiling; reduce heat. Simmer, covered, for 5 minutes. Stir in cooked rice and, if desired, Madeira or dry sherry. Heat through. Makes six 1⅔-cup servings.

Nutrition facts per serving: 236 calories, **5 g** total fat (**1 g** saturated fat), **38 mg** cholesterol, **440 mg** sodium, **31 g** carbohydrate, **2 g** fiber, **18 g** protein
Daily values: 10% vit. A, **48%** vit. C, **2%** calcium, **16%** iron

Living Wild

Wild rice is known for its chewy texture and nutlike flavor. But its name is a misnomer—it isn't rice at all. It's a long-grain marsh grass. Wild rice takes longer to cook than other rices (up to an hour) and costs more, too. Fortunately, wild rice is available in timesaving rice mixes (such as the one called for above) that allow you to enjoy it more conveniently and less expensively.

moroccan CHICKEN SOUP

Spices were a big commodity along the ancient trade routes that ran through the North African countries between Asia and Europe. That legacy is still apparent in modern Moroccan cuisine.

Prep: 30 minutes
Cook: 12 minutes

1 teaspoon paprika

1 teaspoon ground cumin

¼ teaspoon ground coriander

¼ teaspoon ground turmeric
   Dash ground red pepper

12 ounces skinless, boneless chicken breast halves

2 teaspoons olive oil

¾ cup chopped onion

2 cloves garlic, minced

1 14½-ounce can reduced-sodium chicken broth

1¾ cups water

1 cup cubed, peeled acorn squash or butternut squash

1 cup cubed, peeled turnip

½ cup bias-sliced carrot

⅛ teaspoon salt

1 tablespoon lemon juice

Exchanges: ½ Starch **2** Lean Meat **1** Vegetable

❶ In a small bowl stir together paprika, cumin, coriander, turmeric, and red pepper; set aside. Rinse chicken; pat dry. Cut chicken into bite-size strips. Toss chicken with 2 teaspoons of the spice mixture, reserving remaining spice mixture.

❷ In a large saucepan heat olive oil over medium-high heat. Cook and stir chicken in hot oil for 3 to 4 minutes or until chicken is no longer pink. Use a slotted spoon to remove chicken from pan; keep warm.

❸ Add onion and garlic to drippings in pan. (If necessary, add an additional 1 teaspoon olive oil to pan.) Cook and stir until onion is tender. Stir in chicken broth, water, squash, turnip, carrot, salt, and reserved spice mixture. Bring to boiling; reduce heat. Simmer, covered, for 12 to 15 minutes or until vegetables are tender. Stir in chicken and lemon juice. Heat through. Makes six 1½-cup servings.

Nutrition facts per serving: 166 calories, **6 g** total fat (**1 g** saturated fat), **45 mg** cholesterol, **431 mg** sodium, **11 g** carbohydrate, **3 g** fiber, **19 g** protein
Daily values: **64%** vit. A, **21%** vit. C, **4%** calcium, **12%** iron

chicken TORTELLINI SOUP

This soup is no ordinary chicken soup. Chunks of chicken and vegetables share the bowl with lightly cooked, iron-rich leafy greens and plump, cheesy tortellini.

Start to Finish: 40 minutes

12 ounces skinless, boneless chicken breast halves

2 teaspoons olive oil

3 cloves garlic, minced

2 14½-ounce cans reduced-sodium chicken broth

3 cups sliced fresh mushrooms

1¾ cups water

2 medium carrots, cut into matchstick strips (1 cup)

2 cups packed torn fresh purple kale or spinach

1 teaspoon dried tarragon, crushed

1 9-ounce package refrigerated cheese-filled tortellini

Exchanges: 1 Starch **2** Lean Meat **2** Vegetable

1 Rinse chicken; pat dry. Cut the chicken into ¾-inch pieces. In a Dutch oven heat olive oil over medium-high heat. Cook and stir chicken and garlic in hot oil for 5 to 6 minutes or until chicken is no longer pink. Stir in chicken broth, mushrooms, water, carrots, kale (if using), and tarragon.

2 Bring mixture to boiling; reduce heat. Simmer, covered, for 2 minutes. Add tortellini. Simmer, covered, for 5 to 6 minutes more or until tortellini is tender. Stir in the spinach (if using). Makes six 1⅓-cup servings.

Nutrition facts per serving: 254 calories, **7 g** total fat (**2 g** saturated fat), **50 mg** cholesterol, **596 mg** sodium, **27 g** carbohydrate, **3 g** fiber, **21 g** protein
Daily values: 90% vit. A, **33%** vit. C, **10%** calcium, **16%** iron

turkey NOODLE SOUP

The tangy flavor of lemon lends a delightfully brisk lift to a classic turkey noodle soup. The tangy addition is a refreshing variation on a timeless favorite.

soups & stews

Prep: 20 minutes
Cook: 26 minutes

3 cups reduced-sodium chicken
broth

2¼ cups water

1½ cups chopped cooked turkey
or chicken

1 cup thinly sliced carrots

1 medium onion, cut into thin
wedges

½ cup thinly sliced celery

2 teaspoons snipped fresh
thyme or 1 teaspoon dried
thyme, crushed

2 cups dried wide noodles

1 medium yellow summer
squash, quartered
lengthwise and sliced
(1⅓ cups)

2 tablespoons lemon juice

Exchanges: 1 Starch **2** Lean Meat **1** Vegetable

1 In a large saucepan combine the chicken broth, water, turkey or chicken, carrots, onion, celery, and dried thyme (if using). Bring mixture to boiling; reduce heat. Simmer, covered, for 15 minutes.

2 Stir in the noodles and squash. Cook, uncovered, for 10 to 12 minutes more or until the noodles are tender. Stir in the lemon juice and fresh thyme (if using). Cook, uncovered, for 1 minute more. Makes five 1½-cup servings.

Nutrition facts per serving: 192 calories, **4 g** total fat (**1 g** saturated fat), **41 mg** cholesterol, **459 mg** sodium, **20 g** carbohydrate, **3 g** fiber, **18 g** protein
Daily values: 66% vit. A, **10%** vit. C, **2%** calcium, **9%** iron

cajun BEAN SOUP

True Cajun cooks will tell you that it isn't the spices that make a dish authentic, it's the trio of onion, sweet peppers, and celery. The hot sauce in this recipe is optional, but it adds a spirited touch.

Start to Finish: 35 minutes

2 teaspoons cooking oil

1¼ cups chopped onion

1¼ cups chopped green sweet pepper

¾ cup finely chopped celery

3 cloves garlic, minced

2½ cups reduced-sodium chicken broth

2½ cups water

1 14½-ounce can low-sodium stewed tomatoes

2 cups sliced fresh or frozen okra

1 15-ounce can reduced-sodium navy beans, rinsed and drained

1 15-ounce can reduced-sodium red kidney beans, rinsed and drained

4 ounces cooked smoked turkey sausage, halved lengthwise and sliced

1 bay leaf

1 teaspoon dried thyme, crushed

¼ teaspoon black pepper

⅛ teaspoon salt

Bottled hot pepper sauce (optional)

4 cups hot cooked rice

Exchanges: 2½ Starch 2 Vegetable

① In a Dutch oven heat oil over medium-high heat. Cook and stir the onion, sweet pepper, celery, and garlic in the hot oil for 8 to 10 minutes or until vegetables are tender, stirring occasionally.

② Stir in the broth, water, undrained tomatoes, okra, beans, sausage, bay leaf, thyme, black pepper, salt, and, if desired, hot pepper sauce. Bring to boiling; reduce heat. Simmer, covered, about 10 minutes or until okra is tender. Discard the bay leaf. Serve over hot rice. Makes eight 1½-cup servings.

Nutrition facts per serving: 274 calories, **4 g** total fat (**0 g** saturated fat), **7 mg** cholesterol, **430 mg** sodium, **50 g** carbohydrate, **7 g** fiber, **13 g** protein **Daily values: 6%** vit. A, **44%** vit. C, **8%** calcium, **21%** iron

sausage & PEPPERS SOUP

Serve this soup on a cold and wintry day. It's hearty, it's healthy, it's spicy—and best of all, it's Italian. Did we mention that it can be made in under 30 minutes?

Prep: 10 minutes
Cook: 15 minutes

¼ **pound bulk hot Italian turkey sausage**

1 **small green sweet pepper, thinly sliced**

1 **small yellow sweet pepper, thinly sliced**

1 **medium onion, cut into thin wedges**

2 **cloves garlic, minced**

1 **14½-ounce can reduced-sodium chicken broth**

1¾ **cups water**

1 **14½-ounce can low-sodium tomatoes, undrained and cut up**

1½ **cups cubed potatoes**

1 **tablespoon snipped fresh basil or 1 teaspoon dried basil, crushed**

¼ **teaspoon crushed red pepper (optional)**

Exchanges: 1 Starch **1** Lean Meat **1** Vegetable

1 In a large saucepan cook and stir sausage, sweet peppers, onion, and garlic over medium heat about 5 minutes or until sausage is browned. Drain off fat.

2 Stir in broth, water, undrained tomatoes, potatoes, and dried basil (if using). Bring to boiling; reduce heat. Simmer, covered, for 10 to 15 minutes or until potatoes are just tender. Stir in the fresh basil (if using), and, if desired, the crushed red pepper. Makes four 1½-cup servings.

Nutrition facts per serving: 146 calories, **4 g** total fat (**1 g** saturated fat), **21 mg** cholesterol, **472 mg** sodium, **21 g** carbohydrate, **2 g** fiber, **8 g** protein
Daily values: 21% vit. A, **94%** vit. C, **4%** calcium, **13%** iron

Broth Basics

Although there is no Recommended Daily Allowance set for sodium, a daily limit of 2,400 mg of sodium is commonly suggested. A comparison of three chicken broth products illustrates the difference in the sodium content of each (note: brands will vary). All are based on 1 cup chicken broth:

Low sodium: 54 mg	
Reduced sodium: 620 mg*	
Regular: 985 mg	
1 bouillon cube: 900 to 1,000 mg	

*Due to better flavor, reduced-sodium broth rather than low-sodium broth is generally used in recipes in this book.

vegetable BEEF SOUP

Here's a home and hearth recipe that's great for cold evenings. Huge chunks of beef, a lot of fall vegetables, and hearty noodles turn a brimming bowl of soup into a bona fide, stick-to-your ribs meal.

Prep: 25 minutes
Cook: 65 minutes

- 1 **pound boneless beef top round steak**
- 2 **teaspoons olive oil**
- 1½ **cups chopped onion**
- 2½ **cups water**
- 1 **14½-ounce can beef broth**
- 1 **14½-ounce can low-sodium stewed tomatoes**
- 2 **teaspoons Italian seasoning, crushed**
- ½ **teaspoon pepper**
- 1 **bay leaf**
- 3 **medium turnips, peeled and cut into ½-inch pieces (3 cups)**
- 1½ **cups cubed red potatoes**
- 1 **cup sliced carrots**
- 1½ **cups dried wide noodles**
- 2 **tablespoons snipped fresh oregano or thyme (optional)**

Exchanges: 1½ Starch 2 Lean Meat 2 Vegetable

1 Trim fat from beef. Cut beef into 1-inch cubes. In a Dutch oven heat olive oil over medium-high heat. Cook and stir beef and onion in hot oil until beef is browned. Stir in the water, beef broth, undrained tomatoes, Italian seasoning, pepper, and bay leaf. Bring to boiling; reduce heat. Simmer, covered, for 40 minutes.

2 Stir in the turnips, potatoes, and carrots. Simmer, covered, for 15 minutes. Stir in the noodles. Simmer, uncovered, about 10 minutes more or until noodles and vegetables are tender. Remove bay leaf. If desired, stir in oregano or thyme. Makes six 1½-cup servings.

Nutrition facts per serving: 272 calories, **6 g** total fat (**2 g** saturated fat), **60 mg** cholesterol, **345 mg** sodium, **32 g** carbohydrate, **6 g** fiber, **23 g** protein
Daily values: **62%** vit. A, **34%** vit. C, **5%** calcium, **25%** iron

teriyaki beef SOUP

For an even faster stove top-to-table time, cut up the beef and vegetables for this "on-the-fly" soup the evening before. The next day, you'll be able to toss the whole meal together in the time it takes to cook the rice.

soups & stews

Prep: 20 minutes
Cook: 18 minutes

8 ounces boneless beef sirloin steak

2 teaspoons olive oil

1 large shallot, cut into thin rings

4 cups water

1 cup unsweetened apple juice

2 carrots, cut into matchstick strips (1 cup)

⅓ cup long-grain rice

1 tablespoon grated fresh ginger

1 teaspoon instant beef bouillon granules

3 cloves garlic, minced

2 cups coarsely chopped broccoli

1 to 2 tablespoons reduced-sodium teriyaki sauce

1 tablespoon dry sherry (optional)

Exchanges: ½ Starch **1** Lean Meat **2** Vegetable ½ Fruit ½ Fat

1 Trim fat from beef. Cut beef into bite-size strips. In a large saucepan heat olive oil over medium-high heat. Cook and stir beef and shallot in hot oil for 2 to 3 minutes or until beef is brown. Remove beef mixture with a slotted spoon; set aside.

2 In the same saucepan combine water, apple juice, carrots, uncooked rice, ginger, bouillon granules, and garlic. Bring to boiling; reduce heat. Simmer, covered, about 15 minutes or until the carrots are tender.

3 Stir in the broccoli and beef mixture. Simmer, covered, for 3 minutes. Stir in the teriyaki sauce and, if desired, the dry sherry. Makes five 1½-cup servings.

Nutrition facts per serving: 197 calories, **6 g** total fat (**2 g** saturated fat), **30 mg** cholesterol, **382 mg** sodium, **22 g** carbohydrate, **2 g** fiber, **13 g** protein
Daily values: 76% vit. A, **58%** vit. C, **3%** calcium, **16%** iron

chipotle BEEF CHILI

Smoked jalapeños are called "chipotles." They have all the heat of jalapeño peppers, plus a mellow smoky flavor. Look for chipotles en adobo in Mexican or Latin American groceries or large supermarkets.

soups & stews

Prep: 15 minutes
Cook: 20 minutes

8 ounces beef top sirloin steak
Nonstick spray coating
1 teaspoon olive oil
1 cup chopped onion
2 cloves garlic, minced
1 14½-ounce can low-sodium tomatoes, undrained and cut up
1 8-ounce can low-sodium tomato sauce
1 cup water
2 to 3 teaspoons chopped, canned chipotle peppers in adobo sauce
1 teaspoon dried basil, crushed
1 teaspoon dried oregano, crushed
1 teaspoon chili powder
¼ teaspoon salt (optional)
¼ teaspoon ground cumin
1½ cups frozen whole kernel corn

Exchanges: **1½** Starch **2** Lean Meat **3** Vegetable **1** Fat

❶ Trim fat from beef. Cut beef into bite-size strips. Spray a large saucepan with nonstick coating. Preheat on medium-high heat. Cook and stir beef in saucepan over medium-high heat for 2 to 3 minutes or until beef is browned. Remove beef from saucepan; set aside.

❷ Carefully add oil to hot saucepan. Cook onion and garlic in hot oil until tender. Stir in undrained tomatoes, tomato sauce, water, chipotle peppers, basil, oregano, chili powder, salt (if desired), and cumin. Bring to boiling; reduce heat. Simmer, covered, for 15 minutes, stirring occasionally.

❸ Add the frozen corn. Return to simmering. Simmer, covered, for 5 minutes more, stirring occasionally. Return beef to saucepan. Heat through. Makes three 1½-cup servings.

Nutrition facts per serving: 355 calories, **12 g** total fat (**3 g** saturated fat), **50 mg** cholesterol, **598 mg** sodium, **43 g** carbohydrate, **4 g** fiber, **23 g** protein
Daily values: **84%** vit. A, **65%** vit. C, **9%** calcium, **33%** iron

beef goulash SOUP

A single teaspoon of unsweetened cocoa powder contributes a hint of New World uniqueness to an Old World Hungarian goulash. Don't be surprised if your family asks for this soup time and time again.

Prep: 25 minutes
Cook: 30 minutes

- 6 ounces boneless beef sirloin steak
- 1 teaspoon olive oil
- 1 medium onion, cut into thin wedges
- 2 cups water
- 1 14½-ounce can beef broth
- 1 14½-ounce can low-sodium tomatoes, undrained and cut up
- ½ cup thinly sliced carrot
- 1 teaspoon unsweetened cocoa powder
- 1 clove garlic, minced
- 1 cup thinly sliced cabbage
- 1 ounce dried wide noodles (about ¾ cup)
- 2 teaspoons paprika
- ¼ cup fat-free dairy sour cream

Exchanges: ½ Starch **1** Medium-Fat Meat **2** Vegetable

1 Trim fat from beef. Cut beef into ½-inch cubes. In a large saucepan heat olive oil over medium-high heat. Cook and stir beef in hot oil over medium-high heat about 6 minutes or until beef is browned. Add onion wedges; cook and stir about 3 minutes or until tender.

2 Stir in the water, beef broth, undrained tomatoes, carrot, cocoa powder, and garlic. Bring to boiling; reduce heat. Simmer about 15 minutes or until beef is tender. Stir in the cabbage, noodles, and paprika. Simmer for 5 to 7 minutes more or until noodles are tender but firm. Remove from heat; stir in sour cream until combined. Makes four 1½-cup servings.

Nutrition facts per serving: 178 calories, **6 g** total fat (**2 g** saturated fat), **34 mg** cholesterol, **400 mg** sodium, **17 g** carbohydrate, **2 g** fiber, **15 g** protein
Daily values: 55% vit. A, **47%** vit. C, **7%** calcium, **18%** iron

Red Meat Facts

Including beef in a healthful diet is fine—just choose lean cuts most often. Also, remove all visible fat. Select the following for the leanest cuts: arm pot roast, bottom round roast, eye round roast, round tip roast, top round roast or steak, sirloin steak, T-bone steak, or top loin steak.

oven-baked CASSOULET

A French cassoulet traditionally is simmered for hours. Baking this version in the oven slashes the cooking time to about 40 minutes. For a touch of freshness, top with snipped parsley just before serving.

soups & stews

Prep: 20 minutes
Bake: 40 minutes

Nonstick spray coating

12 ounces lean boneless pork, cut into ½-inch cubes

1 teaspoon cooking oil

1 cup chopped onion

1 cup chopped carrots

3 cloves garlic, minced

2 15-ounce cans white kidney beans, rinsed and drained

4 plum tomatoes, chopped

⅔ cup reduced-sodium chicken broth

⅔ cup water

2 ounces cooked turkey kielbasa, halved lengthwise and cut into ¼-inch-thick slices

1 teaspoon dried thyme, crushed

¼ teaspoon dried rosemary, crushed

¼ teaspoon pepper

2 tablespoons snipped fresh parsley

Exchanges: 1 Starch **2** Lean Meat **2** Vegetable

1 Spray a Dutch oven with nonstick coating. Preheat over medium-high heat. Cook and stir pork in Dutch oven until pork is browned. Remove pork from pan. Reduce heat. Carefully add cooking oil to hot Dutch oven. Cook the onion, carrots, and garlic in hot oil until onion is tender.

2 Stir pork, beans, tomatoes, chicken broth, water, kielbasa, thyme, rosemary, and pepper into Dutch oven. Bake, covered, in a 325° oven for 40 to 45 minutes or until pork and carrots are tender. To serve, sprinkle each serving with parsley. Makes five 1⅓-cup servings.

Range-top method: Prepare as directed above, except instead of baking, cover and simmer about 15 minutes or until the pork and carrots are tender.

Nutrition facts per serving: 243 calories, **7 g** total fat (**2 g** saturated fat), **38 mg** cholesterol, **497 mg** sodium, **32 g** carbohydrate, **10 g** fiber, **23 g** protein
Daily values: 68% vit. A, **26%** vit. C, **5%** calcium, **21%** iron

pork & CABBAGE SOUP

Good old-fashioned pork and beans are treated to a new-fashioned, upscale makeover. For convenience, use coleslaw mix, found in the produce section, in place of the chopped cabbage.

Start to Finish: 35 minutes

- 2 **teaspoons olive oil**
- 12 **ounces pork tenderloin, cut into ¾-inch cubes**
- 1 **cup chopped onion**
- 3 **cloves garlic, minced**
- 2 **14½-ounce cans reduced-sodium chicken broth**
- 3 **cups chopped cabbage**
- 1 **14½-ounce can low-sodium stewed tomatoes**
- 1 **teaspoon dried sage, crushed**
- ½ **teaspoon dried rosemary, crushed**
- ¼ **teaspoon ground nutmeg**
- ⅛ **teaspoon ground red pepper**
- 2 **15-ounce cans reduced-sodium navy beans or great Northern beans, rinsed and drained**
- ½ **cup finely shredded Parmesan cheese (optional)**

Exchanges: 1 Starch **2** Lean Meat **3** Vegetable

1 In a Dutch oven heat olive oil over medium-high heat. Cook and stir the pork, onion, and garlic in hot oil until pork is no longer pink. Stir in chicken broth, cabbage, undrained tomatoes, sage, rosemary, nutmeg, and red pepper.

2 Bring mixture to boiling; reduce heat. Simmer, covered, about 10 minutes or until cabbage is tender. Stir in beans. Heat through. If desired, sprinkle each serving with Parmesan cheese. Makes about six 1½-cup servings.

Nutrition facts per serving: 260 calories, **5 g** total fat (**1 g** saturated fat), **40 mg** cholesterol, **466 mg** sodium, **32 g** carbohydrate, **10 g** fiber, **23 g** protein
Daily values: 6% vit. A, **49%** vit. C, **9%** calcium, **24%** iron

salmon CHOWDER

Rosy-pink salmon is a popular fish because of its great taste. But it also is a rich source of omega-3 oils that help protect the cardiovascular system.

Start to Finish: 45 minutes

Exchanges: 1 Starch **1** Lean Meat **2** Vegetable **½** Fat

1 **pound fresh skinless salmon fillets or one 15-ounce can salmon, rinsed, drained, flaked, and skin and bones removed**

1 **tablespoon cooking oil**

2 **cups shredded carrots**

1 **cup finely chopped onion**

½ **cup thinly sliced celery**

1½ **cups water**

4 **cups reduced-sodium chicken broth**

2½ **cups cubed red-skinned potatoes (3 medium)**

1 **10-ounce package frozen whole kernel corn**

1 **teaspoon snipped fresh dill or ½ teaspoon dried dillweed**

¼ **teaspoon salt**

2 **cups fat-free milk**

2 **tablespoons cornstarch**

1 Rinse fresh salmon; pat dry. Set aside. In a large saucepan heat oil over medium-high heat. Cook and stir carrots, onion, and celery in hot oil about 10 minutes or until the vegetables are tender, stirring occasionally.

2 Meanwhile, to poach fresh salmon, in a large skillet bring water to boiling. Add salmon. Return to boiling; reduce heat. Simmer, covered, for 6 to 8 minutes or until the salmon flakes easily with a fork. Remove salmon from skillet, discarding poaching liquid. Flake salmon into ½-inch pieces; set aside.

3 Stir the broth, potatoes, corn, dill, and salt into vegetables in saucepan. Bring to boiling; reduce heat. Cook, covered, over medium-low heat about 15 minutes or until the potatoes are tender, stirring occasionally.

4 Stir together ½ cup of the milk and cornstarch. Add milk mixture to saucepan. Stir in remaining milk. Cook and stir over medium heat until thickened and bubbly. Cook and stir for 2 minutes more. Gently stir in poached salmon or canned salmon. Heat through. Makes eight 1¼-cup servings.

Nutrition facts per serving: 211 calories, **5 g** total fat (**1 g** saturated fat), **11 mg** cholesterol, **487 mg** sodium, **30 g** carbohydrate, **3 g** fiber, **14 g** protein
Daily values: 91% vit. A, **14%** vit. C, **8%** calcium, **7%** iron

shrimp GAZPACHO

Gazpacho—a Spanish soup with tomatoes and onions—traditionally is served cold. We've made this gazpacho into a complete meal by adding succulent shrimp for a zingy thrill of a chill. (See photograph, page 95.)

(See photograph, page 95.)

Prep: 35 minutes
Chill: 4 to 24 hours

- 8 **medium ripe tomatoes, peeled, if desired, and chopped (2½ pounds)**
- 1 **medium cucumber, chopped**
- 1 **medium green or red sweet pepper, seeded and chopped**
- ¾ **cup low-sodium vegetable juice or low-sodium tomato juice**
- ½ **cup clam juice**
- ¼ **cup chopped onion**
- 3 **tablespoons red wine vinegar**
- 2 **tablespoons snipped fresh cilantro**
- 2 **tablespoons olive oil**
- 1 **clove garlic, minced**
- ¼ **teaspoon ground cumin**
- 1 **8-ounce package frozen, peeled, cooked small shrimp, thawed**

  Fat-free dairy sour cream (optional)

Exchanges: 1 Lean Meat **3** Vegetable

1 In a large mixing bowl combine tomatoes, cucumber, sweet pepper, vegetable juice or tomato juice, clam juice, onion, vinegar, cilantro, olive oil, garlic, and cumin. Gently fold the shrimp into the tomato mixture.

2 Cover and chill 4 to 24 hours to allow flavors to blend. To serve, ladle into serving bowls. If desired, top each with a spoonful of sour cream. Makes six 1½-cup servings.

Nutrition facts per serving: 141 calories, **6 g** total fat (**1 g** saturated fat), **74 mg** cholesterol, **154 mg** sodium, **15 g** carbohydrate, **4 g** fiber, **11 g** protein
Daily values: 22% vit. A, **121%** vit. C, **3%** calcium, **37%** iron

Shellfish Facts

Cholesterol is something shrimp have a lot of. These denizens of the deep contain 166 mg cholesterol per 3-ounce serving, about half of the recommended daily limit (300 mg). But that doesn't mean you need to go fishing for something else when you have a hankering for shrimp. Shrimp have some great attributes—they are low in fat, saturated fat, and calories. So, go ahead and satisfy your craving—just watch your total cholesterol intake from all foods.

crab & corn CHOWDER

So rich and creamy, you'll be tempted to feel guilty. There's no need! This chowder has only 1 gram of fat. If you like, substitute one 6-ounce package of chunk-style imitation crab meat for the cooked crab.

Exchanges: 1½ Starch 1 Lean Meat 1 Vegetable ½ Milk

Start to Finish: 30 minutes

1½ cups reduced-sodium chicken broth

1⅓ cups water

1 10-ounce package frozen whole kernel corn

⅔ cup cubed, peeled potato

⅓ cup finely chopped carrot

2 teaspoons snipped fresh thyme or ½ teaspoon dried thyme, crushed

2 cloves garlic, minced

¼ teaspoon salt

¼ teaspoon pepper

1 cup evaporated fat-free milk

2 tablespoons cornstarch

6 ounces cooked crabmeat, cut into bite-size pieces (about 1 cup)

¼ cup sliced green onions

1 In a medium saucepan combine the broth, water, corn, potato, carrot, dried thyme (if using), garlic, salt, and pepper. Bring to boiling; reduce heat. Simmer, covered, for 15 to 20 minutes or until potato is tender.

2 Gradually stir the evaporated milk into the cornstarch; stir into the corn mixture. Cook and stir over medium heat until thickened and bubbly. Cook and stir for 2 minutes more. Gently stir in the fresh thyme (if using), crabmeat, and green onions. Heat through. Makes four 1½-cup servings.

Nutrition facts per serving: **212** calories, **1 g** total fat (**0 g** saturated fat), **45 mg** cholesterol, **520 mg** sodium, **34 g** carbohydrate, **1 g** fiber, **17 g** protein
Daily values: **37%** vit. A, **20%** vit. C, **20%** calcium, **8%** iron

spicy SEAFOOD STEW

Health experts recommend eating at least one meal per week that includes fish—let it be this one. Boneless fish fillets and whole shrimp simmer with garlic, herbs, and cajun spices in a bayou blockbuster of a stew.

Prep: 15 minutes
Cook: 25 minutes

8   ounces fresh or frozen skinless fish fillets (halibut, orange roughy, or sea bass)

6   ounces fresh or frozen peeled and deveined shrimp

2   teaspoons olive oil

⅔   cup chopped onion

½   cup finely chopped carrot

½   cup chopped red or green sweet pepper

2   cloves garlic, minced

1   14½-ounce can low-sodium tomatoes, undrained and cut up

1   8-ounce can low-sodium tomato sauce

1   cup reduced-sodium chicken broth

¼   cup dry red wine or reduced-sodium chicken broth

2   bay leaves

1   tablespoon snipped fresh thyme or 1 teaspoon dried thyme, crushed

½   teaspoon Cajun seasoning

¼   teaspoon ground cumin

¼   teaspoon crushed red pepper (optional)

Exchanges: 2 Lean Meat   3 Vegetable

① Thaw fish and shrimp, if frozen. Rinse fish and shrimp; pat dry. Cut the fish into 1-inch pieces. Cover and chill fish pieces and shrimp until needed.

② In a large saucepan heat olive oil over medium-high heat. Cook and stir onion, carrot, sweet pepper, and garlic in hot oil until tender. Stir in the undrained tomatoes, tomato sauce, chicken broth, wine or chicken broth, bay leaves, dried thyme (if using), Cajun seasoning, cumin, and, if desired, crushed red pepper. Bring the mixture to boiling; reduce heat. Simmer, covered, for 20 minutes.

③ Gently stir in the fish pieces, shrimp, and fresh thyme (if using). Cover and simmer about 5 minutes more or until the fish flakes easily when tested with a fork and shrimp are opaque. Remove the bay leaves before serving. Makes four 1⅓-cup servings.

Nutrition facts per serving: 199 calories, **5 g** total fat (**1 g** saturated fat), **84 mg** cholesterol, **341 mg** sodium, **15 g** carbohydrate, **3 g** fiber, **22 g** protein
Daily values: 69% vit. A, **82%** vit. C, **8%** calcium, **23%** iron

black bean CHILLED SOUP

The Spaniards may have conquered the Southwest, but the Southwest has conquered classical Spanish gazpacho with this recipe. Traditionally served chilled, you can defy tradition and serve it warm.

soups & stews

Prep: 20 minutes
Chill: 4 to 24 hours

- 4 **cups seeded and quartered tomatoes**
- 1½ **cups hot-style vegetable juice**
- 1 **15-ounce can reduced-sodium black beans, rinsed and drained**
- 1 **cup finely chopped, seeded cucumber**
- 1 **cup finely chopped red or yellow sweet pepper**
- ½ **cup finely chopped red onion**
- 2 **tablespoons balsamic vinegar**
- ¾ **cup plain fat-free yogurt or dairy sour cream**

Exchanges: 1 Starch 2 Vegetable

❶ In a food processor bowl or blender container combine half of the tomatoes and ¼ cup of the vegetable juice. Cover and process or blend until tomatoes are coarsely chopped. Pour into a large bowl. Repeat with the remaining tomatoes and ¼ cup more vegetable juice.

❷ Stir in the remaining vegetable juice, the beans, cucumber, sweet pepper, onion, and vinegar. Cover and refrigerate for 4 to 24 hours. To serve, ladle soup into bowls. Top each serving with 2 tablespoons of the yogurt or sour cream. Makes six 1-cup servings.

Nutrition facts per serving: 122 calories, **1 g** total fat (**0 g** saturated fat), **2 mg** cholesterol, **430 mg** sodium, **23 g** carbohydrate, **5 g** fiber, **7 g** protein
Daily values: 31% vit. A, **107%** vit. C, **7%** calcium, **14%** iron

Bean There, Done That

Canned beans are so convenient—after all, you don't always have the time to cook them from the dried stage. But what about the sodium? Don't worry! Many brands of canned beans now come in low-sodium versions. And canned beans are as nutritionally beneficial as those cooked from dried—with protein, minerals, and lots of fiber.

vegetable BARLEY SOUP

Barley has been nourishing folks for thousands of years. This pearl of a grain is so packed with protein that it makes this meatless soup hearty enough to serve as a main dish.

Prep: 15 minutes
Cook: 25 minutes

- 1 14½-ounce can reduced-sodium chicken broth
- 1 14½-ounce can low-sodium tomatoes, undrained and cut up
- 1 cup chopped onion
- ¾ cup vegetable juice
- ½ cup quick-cooking barley
- ½ cup sliced celery
- ½ cup sliced carrot
- 1 tablespoon snipped fresh basil or 1 teaspoon dried basil, crushed
- 1½ teaspoons snipped fresh marjoram or ½ teaspoon dried marjoram, crushed
- 2 cloves garlic, minced
- ¼ teaspoon pepper
- 1 medium yellow summer squash, cut into ¼-inch slices
- 1 9-ounce package frozen cut green beans

Exchanges: 1 Starch **3** Vegetable

1 In a large saucepan stir together the chicken broth, undrained tomatoes, onion, vegetable juice, barley, celery, carrot, dried basil (if using), dried marjoram (if using), garlic, and pepper. Bring to boiling; reduce heat. Simmer, covered, for 20 minutes.

2 Stir in the squash, green beans, fresh basil (if using), and fresh marjoram (if using). Return mixture to boiling. Simmer, covered, 5 to 10 minutes more or until vegetables are tender. Makes five 1¾-cup servings.

Nutrition facts per serving: 173 calories, **2 g** total fat (**0 g** saturated fat), **0 mg** cholesterol, **480 mg** sodium, **36 g** carbohydrate, **5 g** fiber, **7 g** protein
Daily values: 56% vit. A, **55%** vit. C, **7%** calcium, **13%** iron

121

CHUNKY minestrone

Minestrone is Italian for "big soup," and this one is big indeed—full of zucchini, onion, and carrot. For a vegetarian version, substitute vegetable broth for the chicken broth.

Prep: 15 minutes
Cook: 25 minutes

- 1 **tablespoon olive oil**
- 1½ **cups chopped onion**
- 1 **medium carrot, halved lengthwise and thinly sliced (about ¾ cup)**
- 2 **cloves garlic, minced**
- 3 **cups reduced-sodium chicken broth**
- 2 **14½-ounce cans low-sodium tomatoes, undrained and cut up**
- ¾ **cup water**
- ½ **cup long-grain rice**
- 1 **teaspoon dried Italian seasoning, crushed**
- 4 **cups shredded fresh spinach**
- 1 **15-ounce can reduced-sodium navy beans or white kidney beans, rinsed and drained**
- 1 **medium zucchini, quartered lengthwise and sliced (about 1½ cups)**
- ¼ **teaspoon freshly ground pepper**

  Grated Parmesan cheese (optional)

Exchanges: 1½ Starch 4 Vegetable ½ Fat

1 In a Dutch oven heat olive oil over medium-high heat. Cook and stir the onion, carrot, and garlic in hot oil about 3 minutes or until onion is tender. Stir in the broth, undrained tomatoes, water, uncooked rice, and Italian seasoning.

2 Bring to boiling; reduce heat. Simmer, covered, about 20 minutes or until rice is tender. Stir in the spinach, beans, zucchini, and pepper. Cook, covered, for 5 minutes more. If desired, sprinkle each serving with Parmesan cheese. Makes five 1¾-cup servings.

Nutrition facts per serving: 246 calories, **4 g** total fat (**1 g** saturated fat), **0 mg** cholesterol, **462 mg** sodium, **43 g** carbohydrate, **9 g** fiber, **11 g** protein
Daily values: 72% vit. A, 68% vit. C, 12% calcium, 32% iron

chipotle & CORN CHOWDER

The smoky flavor of the chipotle peppers (dried smoked jalapeño peppers) combines with corn to make a bordertown chowder with substance and sizzle—the Southwest at its best!

soups & stews

Start to Finish: 40 minutes

- 1 **tablespoon olive oil**
- 2 **cups thinly sliced leeks (6 medium)**
- 1 **cup chopped red or green sweet pepper**
- 3 **cups reduced-sodium chicken broth**
- 3 **cups fresh or frozen whole kernel corn**
- 2¼ **cups finely chopped red potatoes (3 medium)**
- 1 **to 3 teaspoons chopped, canned chipotle peppers in adobo sauce**
- 1 **teaspoon paprika**
- 2 **tablespoons all-purpose flour**
  Salt (optional)

Exchanges: 4 Starch 2 Vegetable

1 In a large saucepan heat olive oil over medium heat. Cook and stir leeks and sweet pepper in hot oil about 10 minutes or until tender.

2 Add 2¾ cups of the broth to the saucepan. Return to boiling. Stir in corn, potatoes, chipotle peppers, and paprika. Bring to boiling; reduce heat. Simmer, covered, for 10 to 15 minutes or until potatoes are tender.

3 Meanwhile, in a screw-top jar combine the remaining ¼ cup broth and the flour. Cover and shake until smooth; stir into potato mixture. Cook and stir until slightly thickened and bubbly. Cook and stir for 1 minute more. If desired, season with salt. Makes four 1⅔-cup servings.

Nutrition facts per serving: 362 calories, **6 g** total fat (**1 g** saturated fat), **0 mg** cholesterol, **535 mg** sodium, **74 g** carbohydrate, **12 g** fiber, **10 g** protein
Daily values: 27% vit. A, **119%** vit. C, **6%** calcium, **33%** iron

ratatouille SOUP

The French word ratatouille means to "beat with a hammer." How this came to be a stew of eggplant, tomatoes, and sweet peppers is not known, but we promise—you won't need a hammer to make this stew.

Start to Finish: 40 minutes

- 1 **small eggplant (¾ pound), cubed (4 cups)**
- 2 **medium zucchini, cut into ½-inch slices (2⅔ cups)**
- 1 **medium red sweet pepper, cut into 1-inch pieces (1 cup)**
- 1 **medium onion, thinly sliced**
- 5 **cloves garlic, sliced**
- 1 **tablespoon olive oil**
- 1 **teaspoon dried Italian seasoning, crushed**
- 2 **14½-ounce cans reduced-sodium chicken broth**
- 1 **cup dried cavatelli**
- 1 **15-ounce can reduced-sodium navy beans, rinsed and drained**
- 2 **medium tomatoes, coarsely chopped**

Exchanges: 1 Starch **3** Vegetable **½** Fat

1 In a large, shallow roasting pan combine the eggplant, zucchini, sweet pepper, onion, and garlic. In a small bowl combine the olive oil, Italian seasoning, ¼ teaspoon salt, and ¼ teaspoon pepper; drizzle over vegetables, tossing to coat. Bake in a 425° oven about 20 minutes or until vegetables are tender, stirring once.

2 Meanwhile, in a Dutch oven combine the broth and 3 cups water. Bring to boiling; add cavatelli. Return to boiling. Cook about 12 minutes or until tender. Reduce heat. Stir in the beans, tomatoes, and roasted vegetables. Heat through. Makes six 1⅔-cup servings.

Nutrition facts per serving: 186 calories, **4 g** total fat (**0 g** saturated fat), **0 mg** cholesterol, **490 mg** sodium, **32 g** carbohydrate, **7 g** fiber, **8 g** protein
Daily values: 13% vit. A, **54%** vit. C, **4%** calcium, **16%** iron

Bean Business

If you're keeping an eye on sodium, you may substitute low-sodium cooked beans for canned beans by keeping a supply in your freezer. Cook a big batch of dried beans according to package directions (add very little or no salt). Cook them until just tender, as freezing tenderizes them more. Drain, cool, and place in freezer bags or containers in 1¾-cup amounts (1¾ cups cooked beans equal a 15-ounce can of beans). Label and freeze the beans for up to 3 months. To use, place the beans (thawed or frozen) in a saucepan with ½ cup water for each 1¾ cup of beans. Simmer, covered, over low heat until heated through. Drain and use as you would canned beans.

onion & MUSHROOM SOUP

This hearty soup combines the natural sweetness of caramelized onions with the nutlike flavor of wild rice. Plus, it is high in complex carbohydrates and protein—enough to be a meal in itself.

soups & stews

Start to Finish: 40 minutes

- 1 tablespoon olive oil
- 4 large onions, cut into ¾-inch chunks (about 4 cups)
- 1 cup sliced leeks (3 medium)
- 2 teaspoons brown sugar
- 3 cups sliced fresh mushrooms, such as shiitake, button, or brown mushrooms
- 1 cup finely chopped carrots (2 medium)
- 1 14½-ounce can reduced-sodium chicken broth
- 1¾ cups water
- 1½ cups cooked wild rice or brown rice
- 2 tablespoons dry sherry (optional)
- ⅛ teaspoon pepper
- ½ cup cold water
- 2 tablespoons all-purpose flour

Exchanges: **1½** Starch **4** Vegetable **½** Fat

❶ In a large saucepan heat olive oil over medium-low heat. Cook onion and leeks in hot oil, covered, for 13 to 15 minutes or until onions and leeks are tender, stirring occasionally. Uncover; stir in brown sugar. Cook and stir over medium-high heat for 4 to 5 minutes more or until onions and leeks are golden brown.

❷ Stir mushrooms and carrots into onion mixture. Cook and stir over medium heat about 3 minutes or until mushrooms are tender. Stir in chicken broth, the 1¾ cups water, cooked rice, sherry (if desired), and pepper.

❸ In a screw-top jar combine the ½ cup cold water and flour. Cover and shake until smooth; stir into the rice mixture. Cook and stir until slightly thickened and bubbly. Cook and stir for 1 minute more. Makes four 1¾-cup servings.

Nutrition facts per serving: 234 calories, **5 g** total fat (**1 g** saturated fat), **0 mg** cholesterol, **333 mg** sodium, **44 g** carbohydrate, **8 g** fiber, **8 g** protein
Daily values: 81% vit. A, **26%** vit. C, **6%** calcium, **21%** iron

salad
MEALS

Sometimes you're just in the mood for a lighter meal. No problem. This chapter features main-dish salads that will satisfy your mood and your appetite. Each salad has a personality all its own—whether it's a distinctive homemade dressing, an interesting combination of ingredients, or specially prepared meat.

Szechwan Chicken Salad, *recipe page 130*

szechwan CHICKEN SALAD

Jicama, a crisp root vegetable, stars in this grilled chicken salad with carrot, cucumbers, and enoki mushrooms. A light sprinkling of peanuts adds crunch and flavor. (See photograph, page 129.)

Prep: 25 minutes
Marinate: 4 to 24 hours
Grill: 12 minutes

- 2 **teaspoons cooking oil**
- 1 **teaspoon toasted sesame oil**
- 3 **cloves garlic, minced**
- 2 **tablespoons grated fresh ginger**
- ⅓ **cup rice vinegar or white wine vinegar**
- 2 **tablespoons reduced-sodium soy sauce**
- 4 **skinless, boneless chicken breast halves (12 ounces total)**
- 1 **fresh jalapeño pepper, seeded and chopped**
- ½ **teaspoon sugar**
- 1 **medium carrot, cut into matchstick strips**
- 1 **cup peeled jicama cut in matchstick strips**
- 4 **lettuce leaves**
- 2 **medium cucumbers, quartered lengthwise and cut into ¼-inch slices**
- 1⅓ **cups enoki mushrooms**
- 2 **green onions, sliced**
- 2 **tablespoons chopped unsalted cocktail peanuts**

Exchanges: 2 Lean Meat 3 Vegetable

1 In a small saucepan heat cooking oil and sesame oil over medium-high heat for 1 minute. Cook and stir garlic and ginger in hot oil for 15 seconds. Remove saucepan from heat; stir in the vinegar, the soy sauce, and 3 tablespoons water. Cool completely.

2 Rinse chicken; pat dry. Place in a plastic bag set in a shallow dish. Pour half of the soy mixture over the chicken; reserve remaining soy mixture. Close bag. Marinate in the refrigerator for 4 to 24 hours.

3 Meanwhile, for dressing, in a small bowl stir together reserved soy mixture, 2 tablespoons water, the jalapeño pepper, and sugar. Cover and chill for 4 to 24 hours.

4 Drain chicken, discarding marinade. Grill chicken on the lightly greased rack of an uncovered grill directly over medium coals for 12 to 15 minutes or until chicken is tender and no longer pink, turning once. Cut chicken into bite-size strips. Combine the carrot and jicama. To serve, line 4 salad plates with the lettuce. Top with carrot mixture, cucumbers, chicken, mushrooms, green onions, and peanuts. Stir dressing; drizzle 1 tablespoon dressing over each serving. Makes 4 servings.

Nutrition facts per serving: 200 calories, **7 g** total fat (**1 g** saturated fat), **45 mg** cholesterol, **231 mg** sodium, **15 g** carbohydrate, **3 g** fiber, **20 g** protein
Daily values: 56% vit. A, **44%** vit. C, **4%** calcium, **14%** iron

salad meals

curried chicken SALAD

Curry powder, used in small doses, really perks up a recipe like this one. The celery and apples lend crunch, while the wild rice adds a satisfying chewiness to this delicious salad.

Prep: 30 minutes
Chill: 1 to 4 hours

12 ounces skinless, boneless chicken breast halves

1 cup water

¼ teaspoon salt

⅔ cup light or fat-free mayonnaise dressing or salad dressing

¼ cup fat-free milk

2 teaspoons curry powder

¼ teaspoon salt

2 cups chopped red apples

2 cups cooked wild rice, chilled

1½ cups sliced celery

½ cup golden raisins

Romaine or spinach leaves (optional)

Exchanges: 1 Starch **1** Lean Meat **1** Fruit **1½** Fat

❶ In a medium skillet combine the chicken, water, and ¼ teaspoon salt. Bring to boiling; reduce heat. Simmer, covered, for 12 to 14 minutes or the until chicken is tender and no longer pink. Drain well; let cool. Cut the chicken into bite-size pieces.

❷ Meanwhile, for the dressing, in a small bowl stir together the mayonnaise dressing or salad dressing, milk, curry powder, and ¼ teaspoon salt.

❸ In a large bowl stir together cooked chicken, apples, cooked wild rice, celery, and raisins; stir in the dressing. Cover and chill for 1 to 4 hours. If desired, serve on romaine or spinach leaves. Makes about six 1-cup servings.

Nutrition facts per serving: 281 calories, **11 g** total fat (**2 g** saturated fat), **30 mg** cholesterol, **436 mg** sodium, **33 g** carbohydrate, **3 g** fiber, **14 g** protein
Daily values: 1% vit. A, **7%** vit. C, **3%** calcium, **8%** iron

salad meals

fruit & chicken SALAD

Frozen juice concentrates are ideal ingredients for making low-fat dressings. Because concentrates deliver a lot of punch in a small amount, you don't need to use much. Here, concentrate also lends body to the dressing.

Prep: 25 minutes
Chill: 2 to 4 hours

- ½ **cup fat-free dairy sour cream**
- ½ **cup fat-free mayonnaise dressing or salad dressing**
- 1 **tablespoon frozen orange juice concentrate, thawed**
- ⅛ **teaspoon ground ginger**
  Dash ground red pepper
- 3 **green onions, sliced (⅓ cup)**
- 2 **cups thinly sliced celery**
- 1½ **cups seedless red or green grapes, halved**
- 1½ **cups chopped cooked chicken**
- ½ **cup dried apricots, cut into slivers**
- 4 **lettuce leaves**
- 2 **plum tomatoes, thinly sliced**
- 1 **cucumber, thinly sliced**

Exchanges: 2 Lean Meat **2** Vegetable **2** Fruit

❶ For dressing, stir together the sour cream, mayonnaise dressing or salad dressing, orange juice concentrate, ginger, and red pepper. Stir in green onions.

❷ In a large bowl toss together celery, grapes, chicken, and apricots; stir in the dressing. Cover and chill for 2 to 4 hours.

❸ To serve, line 4 salad plates with lettuce leaves. Arrange tomatoes and cucumber on top of lettuce. Top with chicken mixture. Makes 4 servings.

Nutrition facts per serving: 264 calories, **3 g** total fat (**1 g** saturated fat), **44 mg** cholesterol, **511 mg** sodium, **40 g** carbohydrate, **5 g** fiber, **21 g** protein
Daily values: 23% vit. A, **50%** vit. C, **9%** calcium, **15%** iron

salad meals

apricot chicken SALAD

The sweetness of dried apricots and apricot nectar contrasts tastefully with the pungency of mustard in the dressing for this grilled salad. A small amount of sugar helps to cut the sharpness of the vinegar and mustard.

Start to Finish: 30 minutes

- ½ **cup apricot nectar or peach nectar**
- 3 **tablespoons finely chopped dried apricots or peaches**
- 3 **tablespoons snipped parsley**
- 3 **tablespoons balsamic vinegar, red wine vinegar, or cider vinegar**
- 1 **tablespoon olive oil**
- 1 **tablespoon brown mustard**
- 1 **teaspoon sugar**
- 1 **clove garlic, minced**
- 4 **skinless, boneless chicken breast halves (about 12 ounces total)**
- ¼ **teaspoon onion salt**
- ¼ **teaspoon pepper**
- 4 **cups torn mixed salad greens**
- 1 **cup sliced yellow summer squash**
- 1 **cup cherry tomatoes, halved**
- 1 **cup sliced fresh mushrooms**

Exchanges: 2 Lean Meat **2** Vegetable **½** Fruit

1 For dressing, in a small mixing bowl stir together the nectar, apricots or peaches, parsley, vinegar, olive oil, brown mustard, sugar, and garlic. Cover and chill until serving time or up to 24 hours.

2 Rinse chicken; pat dry. Sprinkle the onion salt and pepper over both sides of chicken. Grill the chicken on the lightly greased rack of an uncovered grill directly over medium coals for 12 to 15 minutes or until tender and no longer pink, turning once. (Or, place the chicken on the unheated lightly greased rack of a broiler pan. Broil 4 to 5 inches from the heat for 12 to 15 minutes or until chicken is tender and no longer pink, turning once.) Cut chicken breasts into bite-size strips.

3 Meanwhile, in a large bowl toss together greens, summer squash, tomatoes, and mushrooms. Stir dressing; pour about half of the dressing over greens mixture. Toss to coat.

4 To serve, divide greens and vegetables among 4 salad plates. Top with chicken. Drizzle each serving with 1 to 2 tablespoons of the remaining dressing. Makes 4 servings.

Nutrition facts per serving: 202 calories, **6 g** total fat (**1 g** saturated fat), **45 mg** cholesterol, **207 mg** sodium, **18 g** carbohydrate, **2 g** fiber, **19 g** protein
Daily values: 16% vit. A, **54%** vit. C, **3%** calcium, **17%** iron

Shed the Skin

It's OK to leave the skin on chicken during cooking because it adds flavor and keeps moistness in, yet the meat doesn't absorb much of the fat. However, because skin contains a lot of fat, removing it before eating chicken significantly lowers the fat. Compare the difference between a 3-ounce serving of roasted chicken served with and without skin:

Light meat with skin	8 g fat	193 calories
Light meat without skin	3 g fat	142 calories

turkey-pear SALAD

Fruit, turkey, and nuts are a tasty trio, especially when combined with a tangy buttermilk dressing. This salad is a great way to use any leftover turkey or chicken.

Start to Finish: 25 minutes

- ½ **cup buttermilk**
- 2 **tablespoons light mayonnaise dressing or salad dressing**
- 1 **tablespoon frozen apple juice concentrate or frozen orange juice concentrate, thawed**
- 1 **teaspoon Dijon-style mustard**
- 6 **cups torn mixed salad greens**
- 2 **medium pears or apples, thinly sliced**
- 8 **ounces cooked turkey or chicken, cut into bite-size strips (1½ cups)**
- ¼ **cup toasted, broken walnuts (optional)**

Exchanges: 2 Lean Meat **1** Vegetable **1** Fruit **½** Fat

1 For dressing, in a small bowl stir together buttermilk, mayonnaise dressing or salad dressing, apple or orange juice concentrate, and mustard. Cover and chill for up to 24 hours.

2 To serve, divide salad greens among 4 salad plates. Arrange the pear or apple slices and turkey or chicken on the greens; drizzle each serving with about 3 tablespoons dressing. If desired, sprinkle with walnuts. Makes 4 servings.

Nutrition facts per serving: 225 calories, **9 g** total fat (**2 g** saturated fat), **47 mg** cholesterol, **121 mg** sodium, **18 g** carbohydrate, **3 g** fiber, **18 g** protein
Daily values: 4% vit. A, **21%** vit. C, **5%** calcium, **9%** iron

salad meals

pork & MANGO SALAD

Mango chutney supplies the flavor for this exotic vinaigrette, which is a natural for complementing the flavor of pork. Look for the chutney next to the jams and jellies at the supermarket.

Start to Finish: 30 minutes

- 3 tablespoons mango chutney
- 2 tablespoons white wine vinegar or rice wine vinegar
- 1 tablespoon Dijon-style mustard or brown mustard
- 1 clove garlic, minced
- ⅛ teaspoon pepper
- 1 tablespoon olive oil
- 1 tablespoon water
- 8 ounces pork tenderloin
  Nonstick spray coating
- 6 cups torn mixed salad greens
- ½ of an 8-ounce can sliced water chestnuts, drained
- 1 medium mango, peeled, seeded, and sliced; or 2 medium nectarines, sliced
- 2 tablespoons snipped chives

Exchanges: **2** Lean Meat **1** Vegetable **1** Fruit

❶ For vinaigrette, in a blender container or food processor bowl combine chutney, vinegar, mustard, garlic, and pepper. Cover and blend or process until smooth. In a small bowl combine olive oil and water. With blender or food processor running, add oil mixture in a thin steady stream to chutney mixture; blend or process for 15 seconds more.

❷ Trim any fat from the pork; cut into ¼-inch slices. Spray a large skillet with nonstick coating. Preheat the skillet over medium-high heat. Cook pork in hot skillet for 3 to 4 minutes or until pork is no longer pink, turning once. Remove pork from skillet; keep warm.

❸ In a large bowl toss together the salad greens and water chestnuts. Pour about half of the vinaigrette over the greens mixture. Toss to coat.

❹ To serve, divide greens mixture among 4 salad plates. Arrange some of the mango or nectarine slices and pork on the greens mixture. Drizzle each serving with about 1 tablespoon of the remaining vinaigrette. Sprinkle with the chives. Makes 4 servings.

Nutrition facts per serving: 192 calories, **6 g** total fat (**1 g** saturated fat), **40 mg** cholesterol, **137 mg** sodium, **21 g** carbohydrate, **2 g** fiber, **14 g** protein
Daily values: **24**% vit. A, **32**% vit. C, **2**% calcium, **9**% iron

caribbean PORK SALAD

Pork tenderloin, one of the leanest pork cuts available, works tasty wonders in this grilled salad. The marinade adds a soy-pineapple flavor to the meat, which is carried through in the dressing.

salad meals

Prep: 30 minutes
Marinate: 4 to 24 hours
Grill: 30 minutes

- 12 ounces pork tenderloin
- ½ cup unsweetened pineapple juice
- 3 tablespoons reduced-sodium soy sauce
- 3 tablespoons vinegar
- 2 cloves garlic, minced
- ½ teaspoon ground red pepper
- 1 tablespoon olive oil
- 2 medium red, yellow, or green sweet peppers, cut into 1-inch-wide strips
- 8 ½-inch-thick slices fresh or canned pineapple
- 8 romaine leaves

Exchanges: 3 Lean Meat **1** Fruit

1 Trim fat from pork. Place pork in a plastic bag set in a shallow dish. For marinade, in a screw-top jar, combine pineapple juice, soy sauce, vinegar, garlic, and ground red pepper; cover and shake well. Pour ½ cup of the marinade over pork. Close the bag. Marinate in the refrigerator for 4 to 24 hours, turning bag occasionally.

2 Meanwhile, for salad dressing, combine the remaining marinade with the olive oil. Cover and chill until serving time.

3 Drain pork, discarding marinade. In a grill with a cover arrange preheated coals around a drip pan. Test for medium heat above pan. Place meat on grill rack directly over drip pan. Cover and grill about 30 minutes or until no pink remains and juices run clear. During the last 10 minutes of grilling, place the sweet peppers and pineapple on the grill rack over the coals. Grill until sweet peppers are tender and pineapple is heated through, turning occasionally.

4 To serve, cut pork into thin slices. Line 4 salad plates with romaine. Arrange pork, sweet pepper, and pineapple on the romaine. Shake dressing; drizzle each serving with about 2 tablespoons of the dressing. Makes 4 servings.

Nutrition facts per serving: 204 calories, **7 g** total fat (**2 g** saturated fat), **60 mg** cholesterol, **446 mg** sodium, **15 g** carbohydrate, **2 g** fiber, **21 g** protein
Daily values: **57%** vit. A, **156%** vit. C, **3%** calcium, **15%** iron

spiced BEEF SALAD

This Southwestern-style salad includes a corn relish, deli roast beef, a chili-flavored dressing, and crispy, baked tortilla chips. It's a fun, out-of-the-ordinary salad.

Start to Finish: 30 minutes

Nonstick spray coating

1   **9- to 10-inch fat-free flour tortilla or jalapeño-flavored flour tortilla**

⅓   **cup bottled reduced-calorie ranch salad dressing**

2   **teaspoons chili powder**

1   **large red sweet pepper, chopped**

1   **cup frozen whole kernel corn, thawed**

4   **green onions, sliced (½ cup)**

6   **cups torn romaine**

6   **1-ounce slices lean cooked beef**

½   **of a medium red onion, thinly sliced**

1   **cup cherry tomatoes, halved**

½   **cup shredded reduced-fat Monterey Jack cheese**

Exchanges: 1 Starch **2** Lean Meat **2** Vegetable **½** Fat

❶ Spray a baking sheet with nonstick coating; set aside. Cut tortilla in half; cut each half crosswise into ¼-inch-wide strips. Arrange strips in a single layer on prepared baking sheet. Bake in 350° oven for 5 to 10 minutes or until strips are crisp and brown. Set aside to cool.

❷ Meanwhile, for dressing, in a bowl combine bottled salad dressing and chili powder; set aside. In another bowl combine the sweet pepper, corn, and green onions; pour 2 tablespoons of the dressing over the vegetable mixture. Toss to coat.

❸ To serve, divide romaine among 4 salad plates. Spoon the vegetable mixture onto the romaine. Cut beef slices in half crosswise. Roll each half-slice of beef into a cone shape; arrange 3 rolls on each plate. Arrange the onion slices and tomatoes around vegetable mixture; sprinkle with cheese. Drizzle each serving with about 1 tablespoon of the remaining dressing. Top with tortilla strips. Makes 4 servings.

Nutrition facts per serving: 281 calories, **11 g** total fat (**3 g** saturated fat), **47 mg** cholesterol, **378 mg** sodium, **26 g** carbohydrate, **4 g** fiber, **22 g** protein
Daily values: 121% vit. A, **295%** vit. C, **15%** calcium, **23%** iron

salad meals

fajita BEEF SALAD

Lime does double duty in this recipe, both in the marinade and the dressing. Its tart flavor enhances the grilled beef and honey-kissed dressing.

Prep: 35 minutes
Marinate: 24 hours
Grill: 12 minutes

½ **teaspoon finely shredded lime peel**

⅓ **cup lime juice**

3 **tablespoons water**

4 **teaspoons olive oil**

¼ **cup chopped onion**

1 **clove garlic, minced**

12 **ounces beef flank steak**

3 **tablespoons water**

2 **tablespoons powdered fruit pectin**

2 **tablespoons honey**

6 **cups torn mixed salad greens**

2 **small red and/or yellow tomatoes, cut into wedges**

1 **small avocado, halved, seeded, peeled, and chopped (optional)**

Exchanges: 2 Lean Meat **2** Vegetable **½** Fruit **½** Fat

1 In a screw-top jar combine the lime peel, lime juice, 3 tablespoons water, and olive oil. Cover and shake well. Pour half of the lime juice mixture into a small bowl; stir in onion and garlic. Reserve remaining lime juice mixture.

2 Score the beef by making shallow diagonal cuts at 1-inch intervals in a diamond pattern. Repeat on other side. Place beef in a plastic bag set in a shallow dish. Pour the lime juice-and-onion mixture over the beef. Close bag. Marinate in the refrigerator for 24 hours, turning occasionally.

3 For dressing, in a small bowl gradually stir 3 tablespoons water into fruit pectin; stir in reserved lime juice mixture and honey. Cover and chill for 24 hours.

4 Drain beef, discarding marinade. Grill beef on the rack of an uncovered grill directly over medium coals to desired doneness, turning once. Allow 12 to 14 minutes for medium. (Or, place beef on the unheated rack of a broiler pan. Broil 3 to 4 inches from the heat to desired doneness, turning once. Allow 12 to 14 minutes for medium.)

5 To serve, thinly slice beef across grain. Arrange the greens, tomatoes, and, if desired, the avocado on 4 salad plates. Top with beef. Drizzle each serving with about 2 tablespoons of the dressing. Makes 4 servings.

Nutrition facts per serving: 224 calories, **9 g** total fat (**3 g** saturated fat), **40 mg** cholesterol, **72 mg** sodium, **20 g** carbohydrate, **2 g** fiber, **18 g** protein
Daily values: 5% vit. A, **26%** vit. C, **2%** calcium, **15%** iron

salad meals

beef & PASTA SALAD

The intense flavor of blue cheese proves that a little bit goes a long way to deliver great taste. Using a medley of vegetables and beef, this do-ahead salad is ideal for a quick midweek dinner.

Prep: 30 minutes
Chill: 2 to 24 hours

- 4 **ounces dried radiatore or medium shell macaroni**
- ⅓ **cup bottled reduced-calorie creamy Italian or ranch salad dressing**
- 2 **tablespoons snipped fresh basil or 2 teaspoons dried basil, crushed**
- 2 **tablespoons crumbled blue cheese**
- ¼ **teaspoon pepper**
- 1 **small zucchini, halved lengthwise and sliced (1 cup)**
- 1 **green onion, sliced (2 tablespoons)**
- 3 **small plum tomatoes, halved and sliced**
- 4 **cups torn fresh spinach**
- 4 **ounces thinly sliced lean cooked beef, cut into strips**

Exchanges: 1½ Starch 1 Lean Meat 2 Vegetable ½ Fat

1 In a large saucepan cook the pasta according to package directions, except omit any oil or salt; drain. Rinse with cold running water; drain again.

2 Meanwhile, for dressing, in a bowl stir together salad dressing, basil, blue cheese, and pepper; set aside.

3 In a large bowl toss together pasta, zucchini, and green onion. Drizzle dressing over pasta mixture. Toss to coat. Cover and chill for 2 to 24 hours.

4 To serve, gently stir tomato into the salad. Divide the spinach among 4 salad plates. Top with pasta mixture and beef. Makes 4 servings.

Nutrition facts per serving: 237 calories, **7 g** total fat (**2 g** saturated fat), **30 mg** cholesterol, **285 mg** sodium, **29 g** carbohydrate, **3 g** fiber, **16 g** protein
Daily values: 42% vit. A, **44%** vit. C, **8%** calcium, **26%** iron

Cheese, Please

Fortunately, many cheeses, such as Monterey Jack, cheddar, mozzarella, American, Swiss, and Parmesan, are readily available in lower-fat versions. But some highly flavored cheeses, such as blue cheese, feta, and Asiago cheese, aren't. However, these cheeses have very pungent flavors. So a little goes a long way. Just use them sparingly, then you can have your favorite cheese and eat it, too.

shrimp TABBOULEH SALAD

Middle Eastern tabbouleh lends an exotic touch to this salad, which begins with a convenient packaged salad mix. Traditional tabbouleh combines bulgur wheat with tomato, onion, parsley, mint, lemon, and olive oil.

Prep: 20 minutes
Chill: 1½ hours

- 1 **5¼-ounce package tabbouleh wheat salad mix**
- 8 **ounces peeled, deveined, cooked small shrimp or cooked bay scallops**
- 1 **cup frozen peas, thawed**
- 1 **cup chopped tomatoes**
- 4 **green onions, sliced (½ cup)**
- 3 **tablespoons snipped cilantro**
- 3 **tablespoons lemon juice**
- 1 **tablespoon olive oil**
- 4 **lettuce leaves**

Exchanges: 2 Starch **2** Lean Meat

1 Prepare salad mix according to package directions; stir in the shrimp or scallops, peas, tomatoes, green onions, cilantro, lemon juice, and olive oil. Cover and chill for 1½ hours.

2 To serve, arrange lettuce leaves on 4 salad plates. Top with salad mixture. Makes 4 servings.

Nutrition facts per serving: 235 calories, **4 g** total fat (**1 g** saturated fat), **11 mg** cholesterol, **507 mg** sodium, **37 g** carbohydrate, **9 g** fiber, **18 g** protein
Daily values: 12% vit. A, **65%** vit. C, **3%** calcium, **23%** iron

salad meals

shrimp SALAD

This salad has the makings of an elegant meal and deserves to be included on a special celebration menu. The flavors of asparagus and shrimp flourish with the addition of a balsamic vinaigrette.

salad meals

Prep: 25 minutes
Chill: 4 to 24 hours

- 2 **tablespoons dried tomato pieces (not oil-packed)**
- ¼ **cup balsamic vinegar**
- 2 **tablespoons olive oil**
- 1 **tablespoon snipped fresh basil**
- 2 **teaspoons Dijon-style mustard**
- 2 **cloves garlic, minced**
- ¼ **teaspoon sugar**
- ⅛ **teaspoon pepper**
- 12 **ounces fresh or frozen peeled shrimp**
- 4 **cups water**
- 1 **clove garlic**
- 8 **ounces asparagus, cut into 2-inch lengths**
- 6 **cups torn mixed salad greens**
- 2 **medium pears, thinly sliced**

Exchanges: 2 Lean Meat **2** Vegetable **½** Fruit **½** Fat

1 In a small bowl pour boiling water over tomato pieces to cover; let stand for 2 minutes. Drain.

2 For dressing, in a screw-top jar combine tomato pieces, vinegar, the olive oil, basil, mustard, the 2 cloves garlic, sugar, and pepper. Cover and shake well. If desired, cover and chill for up to 24 hours.

3 Thaw shrimp, if frozen. In a large saucepan bring the water and the 1 clove garlic to boiling; add asparagus. Return to boiling. Simmer, uncovered, for 4 minutes. Add shrimp. Return to boiling. Simmer, uncovered, for 1 to 3 minutes more or until shrimp are opaque. Drain, discarding garlic. Rinse under cold running water; drain well. Cover and chill for 4 to 24 hours.

4 To serve, divide greens and pears among 4 salad plates. Top each with some of the shrimp and asparagus. Shake dressing; drizzle each serving with about 2 tablespoons of the dressing. Makes 4 servings.

Nutrition facts per serving: 221 calories, **8 g** total fat (**1 g** saturated fat), **131 mg** cholesterol, **260 mg** sodium, **21 g** carbohydrate, **4 g** fiber, **17 g** protein
Daily values: 11% vit. A, **37%** vit. C, **5%** calcium, **23%** iron

marinated SEAFOOD SALAD

When it's too hot to cook, a chilled seafood salad will help keep you—and the kitchen—cool. Feta cheese, the crowning touch, adds a distinctive flavor to this salad.

salad meals

Prep: 30 minutes
Marinate: 2 to 3 hours

12 **ounces fresh or frozen peeled shrimp**

8 **ounces fresh or frozen bay scallops**

6 **cups water**

½ **teaspoon salt**

3 **tablespoons lemon juice**

2 **tablespoons olive oil**

2 **teaspoons snipped fresh oregano or tarragon or ½ teaspoon dried oregano or tarragon, crushed**

¼ **teaspoon dry mustard**

¼ **teaspoon salt**

⅛ **teaspoon pepper**

6 **cups torn mixed salad greens**

¼ **cup crumbled feta cheese**

Exchanges: 2 Lean Meat **1** Vegetable **½** Fat

1 Thaw shrimp and scallops, if frozen. In a large saucepan bring water and the ½ teaspoon salt to boiling; add shrimp and scallops. Return to boiling. Simmer, uncovered, for 1 to 3 minutes or until shrimp and scallops are opaque. Drain. Rinse under cold running water; drain well. Place shrimp and scallops in a plastic bag set in a shallow dish.

2 For dressing, combine lemon juice, olive oil, oregano or tarragon, mustard, the ¼ teaspoon salt, and the pepper. Pour over shrimp and scallops in bag. Close bag. Marinate in the refrigerator for 2 to 3 hours, turning bag occasionally.

3 To serve, divide the greens among 6 salad plates. Spoon seafood and dressing over the greens. Sprinkle each serving with feta cheese. Makes 6 servings.

Nutrition facts per serving: 156 calories, **8 g** total fat (**2 g** saturated fat), **109 mg** cholesterol, **372 mg** sodium, **4 g** carbohydrate, **1 g** fiber, **18 g** protein
Daily values: 14% vit. A, **22%** vit. C, **8%** calcium, **14%** iron

salmon salad NIÇOISE

Based on the classic French niçoise salad, this salad has all the essential ingredients: red potatoes, green beans, tomato, eggs, and capers. Instead of using the traditional tuna, this version calls for salmon.

Start to Finish: 30 minutes

12 ounces fresh or frozen salmon steaks, 1 inch thick

1½ cups water

2 tablespoons lemon juice

1 pound small round red potatoes, cut into thin slices

½ pound green beans

¼ cup lemon juice

2 tablespoons olive oil

2 tablespoons water

2 teaspoons snipped dill

1 clove garlic, minced

¼ teaspoon salt

¼ teaspoon pepper

2 medium tomatoes, cut into wedges

2 hard-cooked eggs, quartered

2 teaspoons capers, rinsed and drained

Exchanges: 1½ Starch **2** Lean Meat **2** Vegetable **1** Fat

1 Thaw salmon, if frozen. Rinse salmon; pat dry. In a large skillet bring the 1½ cups water and the 2 tablespoons lemon juice to boiling; add salmon. Return to boiling; reduce heat. Simmer, covered, for 8 to 12 minutes or until salmon flakes easily when tested with a fork. Remove salmon from skillet, discarding liquid. Cover and chill salmon.

2 Meanwhile, in a large saucepan cook potatoes in boiling water about 12 minutes or until tender, adding green beans the last 6 minutes of cooking time. Drain; set aside to cool.

3 For dressing, in a small bowl stir together the ¼ cup lemon juice, the olive oil, the 2 tablespoons water, the dill, garlic, salt, and pepper.

4 To serve, cut cooked salmon into 4 equal portions; arrange on 4 salad plates. Toss about half of the dressing with the potatoes and beans. Arrange potatoes and beans, tomato wedges, and eggs on the plates. Sprinkle each serving with capers. Drizzle each serving with about 1 tablespoon of the remaining dressing. Makes 4 servings.

Nutrition facts per serving: 325 calories, **13 g** total fat (**2 g** saturated fat), **122 mg** cholesterol, **256 mg** sodium, **35 g** carbohydrate, **4 g** fiber, **20 g** protein
Daily values: **13%** vit. A, **70%** vit. C, **5%** calcium, **25%** iron

salad meals

147

salmon SALAD

This salad will remind you of a Caesar salad—without the raw eggs, anchovies, high fat, and calories. Plain yogurt adds the creamy texture to the garlic and lemon dressing.

Exchanges: 2 Lean Meat **2** Vegetable **1** Fat

Prep: 20 minutes
Chill: 30 minutes
Broil: 8 to 12 minutes

- 2 **tablespoons olive oil**
- 5 **cloves garlic, thinly sliced**
- 2 **tablespoons lemon juice**
- 1 **tablespoon Worcestershire sauce**
- 1 **tablespoon Dijon-style mustard**
- 1 **tablespoon water**
- ½ **teaspoon pepper**
- ⅓ **cup plain fat-free yogurt**
- 12 **ounces fresh or frozen skinless, boneless salmon fillets, 1 inch thick**
  Nonstick spray coating
- 10 **cups torn romaine**
- ½ **cup thinly sliced red onion**
- ¼ **cup freshly grated Parmesan cheese**
- 1 **cup cherry tomatoes, halved**
- ½ **cup pitted ripe olives, halved (optional)**

❶ In a small saucepan heat olive oil over medium-low heat. Cook and stir garlic in hot oil for 1 to 2 minutes or until garlic is lightly golden. Transfer garlic to a blender container. Add lemon juice, Worcestershire sauce, mustard, water, and pepper. Cover; blend until combined. Reserve 2 tablespoons of garlic mixture; set aside. Add yogurt to remaining garlic mixture in blender. Cover and blend until smooth. Chill until serving time.

❷ Thaw salmon, if frozen. Rinse salmon; pat dry. Brush the reserved garlic mixture evenly over salmon. Cover and chill for 30 minutes.

❸ Spray the unheated rack of a broiler pan with nonstick coating. Place the salmon on the rack. Broil 4 to 5 inches from heat for 8 to 12 minutes or until salmon flakes easily when tested with a fork, turning once.

❹ Meanwhile, in a large bowl toss romaine, onion, and Parmesan cheese with the chilled yogurt mixture. Divide romaine mixture among 4 salad plates. Place one salmon fillet on each salad. Top with tomatoes and, if desired, olives. Makes 4 servings.

Nutrition facts per serving: 234 calories, **13 g** total fat (**3 g** saturated fat), **21 mg** cholesterol, **331 mg** sodium, **12 g** carbohydrate, **4 g** fiber, **19 g** protein
Daily values: 43% vit. A, **95%** vit. C, **16%** calcium, **19%** iron

italian bread & FISH SALAD

Panzanella is a traditional Italian bread-and-tomato side salad. Here, it's transformed into a main dish by adding fish. A generous sprinkling of fresh basil enhances the flavor—don't be tempted to leave it off.

salad meals

Start to Finish: 30 minutes

- 3 slices Italian or wheat bread, cut into 1-inch cubes
- 12 ounces fresh or frozen skinless, boneless fish fillets (salmon, halibut, or swordfish), 1 inch thick
- 1½ cups water
- 3 slices lemon
- 1 bay leaf
- 3 tablespoons white wine vinegar or white balsamic vinegar
- 2 tablespoons olive oil
- 2 cloves garlic, minced
- ¼ teaspoon salt
- ⅛ teaspoon pepper
- 6 cups torn mixed salad greens
- 3 medium tomatoes, seeded and coarsely chopped
- ½ of a medium red onion, cut into thin wedges and separated
- ½ of a medium cucumber, cut into chunks
- ¼ cup shredded fresh basil

Exchanges: ½ Starch 2 Lean Meat 2 Vegetable 1 Fat

1 To dry bread cubes, spread cubes in a single layer in a shallow baking pan. Bake in 350° oven about 10 minutes or until crisp, stirring once.

2 Meanwhile, thaw fish, if frozen. Rinse fish; pat dry. To poach fish, in a large skillet bring water, lemon slices, and bay leaf to boiling; add fish fillets. Return to boiling; reduce heat. Simmer, covered, for 8 to 12 minutes or until fish flakes easily when tested with a fork. Remove fish from skillet, discarding poaching liquid. Cut fish into bite-size pieces.

3 For dressing, in a screw-top jar combine the vinegar, olive oil, garlic, salt, and pepper. Cover and shake well. In a large bowl combine dried bread cubes and salad greens; drizzle with dressing. Toss to coat.

4 To serve, divide salad greens and bread cubes among 4 salad plates. Arrange tomatoes, onion, and cucumber on top of greens. Top with fish and basil. Makes 4 servings.

Nutrition facts per serving: 240 calories, **11 g** total fat (**2 g** saturated fat), **15 mg** cholesterol, **327 mg** sodium, **21 g** carbohydrate, **3 g** fiber, **16 g** protein
Daily values: **12%** vit. A, **46%** vit. C, **5%** calcium, **15%** iron

dilled TUNA SALAD

Turn ho-hum tuna salad into something special by tossing it with a lemon-dill dressing. Serving the salad with pita chips offers an alternative to a standard tuna salad sandwich.

Start to Finish: 25 minutes

- **1** recipe Pita Crisps
- **⅓** cup bottled reduced-calorie creamy cucumber or ranch salad dressing
- **1** tablespoon Dijon-style mustard
- **1** tablespoon snipped fresh dill or 1 teaspoon dried dillweed
- **½** teaspoon finely shredded lemon peel
- **1½** cups chopped, seeded cucumber
- **6** ounces cooked tuna fillets* or one 9¼-ounce can chunk white tuna (water pack), drained and flaked
- **½** cup shredded carrot
- **4** cups torn lettuce
- **1** medium tomato, cut into wedges
- **¼** teaspoon pepper

Exchanges: 1 Starch **1** Lean Meat **2** Vegetable **1** Fat

① Prepare Pita Crisps.

② Meanwhile, for dressing, in a bowl stir together salad dressing, mustard, dill, and lemon peel; set aside.

③ In a medium bowl gently toss together cucumber, tuna, and carrot; drizzle dressing over tuna mixture. Toss to coat.

④ To serve, divide lettuce among 4 salad plates. Spoon tuna mixture on top of lettuce. Place tomato and Pita Crisps on salad. Sprinkle salad with pepper. Makes 4 servings.

Pita Crisps: Split 2 pita bread rounds horizontally. Spray the cut side of the pita rounds with butter- or olive oil-flavored nonstick coating; sprinkle with ⅛ teaspoon garlic powder. Cut each pita half into 4 wedges. Spread wedges in a single layer in a 15x10x1-inch baking pan. Bake in a 350° oven for 8 to 10 minutes or until crisp.

*Note: To cook fresh tuna, in a medium skillet bring 1 cup of water to boiling; add the tuna. Cover and simmer for 8 to 10 minutes or until fish flakes easily with a fork. Break into small chunks. Cover and chill until needed.

Nutrition facts per serving: 236 calories, **8 g** total fat (**1 g** saturated fat), **21 mg** cholesterol, **464 mg** sodium, **25 g** carbohydrate, **2 g** fiber, **17 g** protein
Daily values: 77% vit. A, **23%** vit. C, **5%** calcium, **13%** iron

salad meals

scallops & PASTA SALAD

The fat content in this seafood pasta salad is minimal because the dressing is made without any oil. Pectin provides body to the dressing. Look for it with the jelly-making supplies or baking products at the supermarket.

Prep: 30 minutes
Chill: 3 to 24 hours

- **1 teaspoon finely shredded orange peel**
- **⅓ cup orange juice**
- **¼ cup white wine vinegar**
- **2 tablespoons powdered fruit pectin**
- **1 tablespoon sugar**
- **6 ounces dried medium shell macaroni**
- **8 ounces fresh or frozen sea scallops**
- **2 cups water**
- **4 cups torn fresh spinach**
- **1 cup frozen peas**
- **½ cup coarsely chopped red onion**
- **½ cup thinly sliced celery**
- **⅓ cup chopped red sweet pepper**

Exchanges: 2 Starch **1** Lean Meat **1** Vegetable

1 For dressing, in a small bowl stir together the orange peel, orange juice, vinegar, pectin, and sugar until smooth. Cover and chill at least 3 hours or up to 24 hours.

2 Cook macaroni according to package directions; drain. Rinse with cold water; drain again.

3 Meanwhile, thaw scallops, if frozen. Cut any large scallops in half. Bring water to boiling; add scallops. Return to boiling. Simmer, uncovered, for 1 to 3 minutes or until scallops are opaque. Drain. Rinse under cold running water.

4 For salad, in a large bowl toss together cooked macaroni, cooked scallops, spinach, peas, onion, celery, and sweet pepper. Stir dressing; pour over salad. Toss to coat. Makes five 2-cup servings.

Nutrition facts per serving: 227 calories, **1 g** total fat (**0 g** saturated fat), **14 mg** cholesterol, **142 mg** sodium, **42 g** carbohydrate, **4 g** fiber, **13 g** protein
Daily values: 40% vit. A, **66%** vit. C, **98%** calcium, **26%** iron

green bean & RICE SALAD

This salad contains two types of beans: green beans and black beans. The rice and bean combo makes it hearty enough for a light main-dish salad for four. Or, if you like, it can serve 8 to 10 people as a side dish.

salad meals

Prep: 15 minutes
Cook: 10 minutes
Chill: 2 to 8 hours

1¼ **cups water**

1 **cup quick-cooking brown rice**

1 **cup fresh green beans or frozen cut green beans**

¼ **cup finely chopped onion**

2 **cloves garlic, minced**

½ **teaspoon instant chicken bouillon granules**

1 **15-ounce can light-sodium black beans, rinsed and drained**

½ **cup chopped red sweet pepper**

½ **cup chopped, seeded cucumber**

3 **tablespoons rice wine vinegar or white wine vinegar**

2 **tablespoons olive oil**

1 **tablespoon snipped fresh oregano or 1 teaspoon dried oregano, crushed**

¼ **teaspoon black pepper**

4 **lettuce leaves**

Exchanges: 1½ Starch 2 Vegetable 1 Fat

1 In a medium saucepan combine the water, uncooked rice, green beans, onion, garlic, and bouillon granules. Bring to boiling; reduce heat. Simmer, covered, about 10 minutes or until the rice and beans are tender and liquid is absorbed. Remove from heat. Transfer to a large bowl. Gently stir in black beans, sweet pepper, and cucumber.

2 Meanwhile, for dressing, in a screw-top jar combine the vinegar, olive oil, oregano, and black pepper. Cover; shake well. Drizzle over rice mixture. Toss to coat. Cover and chill for 2 to 8 hours.

3 To serve, line 4 salad plates with lettuce. Top with rice mixture. Makes about four 1¼-cup servings.

Nutrition facts per serving: 210 calories, **7 g** total fat (**1 g** saturated fat), **0 mg** cholesterol, **225 mg** sodium, **31 g** carbohydrate, **5 g** fiber, **7 g** protein
Daily values: 11% vit. A, **43%** vit. C, **3%** calcium, **11%** iron

black bean & RICE SALAD

Fiber-rich black beans help pack nutrition into this Mexican-style salad. It's great for brown bag lunches. Baked tortilla chips, fresh fruit, and milk make this salad a meal to look forward to.

Start to Finish: 30 minutes

1 **cup cooked long-grain rice, chilled**

4 **ounces Monterey Jack cheese with jalapeño peppers, cut into ¼-inch cubes**

1 **cup chopped tomatoes**

1 **cup chopped yellow or red sweet pepper**

½ **of a medium cucumber, halved lengthwise and thinly sliced**

¾ **cup canned reduced-sodium black beans, rinsed and drained**

¾ **cup frozen whole kernel corn**

2 **green onions, thinly sliced (¼ cup)**

¾ **cup picante sauce or salsa**

6 **romaine leaves**

½ **cup fat-free dairy sour cream**

Exchanges: 1 Starch 1 Vegetable 1 Medium-Fat Meat

1 In a large mixing bowl stir together the cooked rice, cheese, tomatoes, sweet pepper, cucumber, black beans, corn, and green onions; add picante sauce or salsa. Toss to coat.

2 To serve, line 6 salad plates with romaine leaves. Top with rice mixture. Serve with sour cream. Makes six 1-cup servings.

Nutrition facts per serving: 189 calories, **7 g** total fat (**4 g** saturated fat), **17 mg** cholesterol, **374 mg** sodium, **25 g** carbohydrate, **3 g** fiber, **11 g** protein
Daily values: 20% vit. A, **87%** vit. C, **17%** calcium, **11%** iron

salad meals

Good Fats?

Fats and oils have a place in every diet. Without them, we couldn't absorb vitamins A, D, E, and K. Our nervous system couldn't function without fat and the cells of our body would fall apart. Monounsaturated fats, the fats in most vegetable oils—for example, olive oil—have added benefits. They help prevent heart disease by actively raising the levels of the desirable HDL-cholesterol in the blood. Fat (or oil) is nothing to be afraid of, but remember, at 9 calories per gram—120 calories per tablespoon—enjoy it sparingly.

tortellini SALAD

Fruit pectin, the same ingredient used for making jams and jellies, provides body to the dressing without using oil. Supermarkets usually stock pectin with the baking goods.

Prep: 40 minutes
Chill: 2 to 24 hours

- 2 **tablespoons snipped fresh basil or 1 teaspoon dried basil, crushed**
- 4 **teaspoons powdered fruit pectin**
- 1 **tablespoon Dijon-style mustard**
- 2 **cloves garlic, minced**
- 1 **teaspoon sugar**
- ¼ **teaspoon pepper**
- ⅓ **cup water**
- 2 **tablespoons white wine vinegar or rice wine vinegar**
- 1 **9-ounce package refrigerated light garlic-and-cheese tortellini or one 9-ounce package light cheese ravioli**
- 3 **cups broccoli flowerets**
- 1 **cup sliced carrots**
- 2 **green onions, sliced (¼ cup)**
- 1 **large tomato, chopped**
- 1 **cup fresh pea pods, halved**
- 4 **lettuce leaves**

Exchanges: 2 Starch **1** Lean Meat **2** Vegetable

❶ For dressing, in a small mixing bowl stir together basil, pectin, mustard, garlic, sugar, and pepper. Stir in water and vinegar. Cover and chill for 30 minutes.

❷ Meanwhile, cook tortellini or ravioli according to package directions, except omit any oil or salt. Add the broccoli and carrots during the last 3 minutes of cooking. Drain. Rinse with cold running water; drain again.

❸ In a large bowl combine the pasta mixture and green onions; drizzle with dressing. Toss to coat. Cover and chill for 2 to 24 hours.

❹ To serve, gently stir tomato and pea pods into salad. Line 4 salad plates with lettuce leaves. Top with pasta mixture. Makes four 2-cup servings.

Nutrition facts per serving: 253 calories, **4 g** total fat (**2 g** saturated fat), **43 mg** cholesterol, **398 mg** sodium, **42 g** carbohydrate, **7 g** fiber, **14 g** protein
Daily values: 102% vit. A, **141%** vit. C, **10%** calcium, **17%** iron

salad meals

vegetables
& SIDES

A great side dish can make the best meal even better. This collection of sidekicks includes inspiring recipes featuring a variety of your favorite vegetables. Try the Thai-Style Asparagus, Lemony Mixed Vegetables, Beans and Caramelized Onions, Roasted Succotash, or Pesto Potatoes to jump-start your dinner.

Vegetable Primavera, *recipe page 160*

vegetable PRIMAVERA

The Italian word "primavera" refers to the use of fresh vegetables, and that is what this recipe features. Squash, carrots, red pepper, and broccoli combine to create a festival of colors. (See photograph, page 159.)

Start to Finish: 20 minutes

3 tablespoons reduced-sodium chicken broth

1 tablespoon Dijon-style mustard

1 tablespoon olive oil

2 teaspoons white wine vinegar

Nonstick spray coating

1½ cups sliced yellow summer squash

1 cup packaged, peeled baby carrots

1 cup chopped red sweet pepper

3 cups broccoli flowerets

2 tablespoons snipped parsley

Exchanges: 1 Vegetable **½** Fat

1 In a small bowl combine 1 tablespoon of the chicken broth, the mustard, olive oil, and vinegar. Set aside.

2 Spray a large nonstick skillet with nonstick coating. Preheat the skillet over medium heat. Cook and stir squash, carrots, and sweet pepper in hot skillet about 5 minutes or until nearly tender. Add broccoli and remaining chicken broth to skillet. Cook, covered, about 3 minutes or until broccoli is crisp-tender.

3 Stir in the mustard mixture; heat through. To serve, sprinkle with parsley. Makes six ¾-cup servings.

Nutrition facts per serving: 56 calories, **3 g** total fat (**0 g** saturated fat), **0 mg** cholesterol, **114 mg** sodium, **7 g** carbohydrate, **3 g** fiber, **2 g** protein
Daily values: 75% vit. A, **99%** vit. C, **3%** calcium, **5%** iron

Spray for Success

Nonstick spray coating not only eliminates the mess of greasing pans, it also saves on fat and calories. For added pizzazz, look for roasted garlic-, olive oil-, and butter-flavored sprays. Compare the difference of using nonstick spray in place of oil, margarine, or butter:

Nonstick spray coating (1-second spray)	<1 g fat	7 calories
Butter/margarine (1 teaspoon)	4 g fat	35 calories
Oil (1 teaspoon)	5 g fat	41 calories

vegetables & sides

160

beans & CARAMELIZED ONIONS

No more boring beans! In this recipe, the familiar green bean takes on an exciting new flavor. Onions, sugar, and balsamic vinegar coat the beans in a sweet, but tangy sauce.

Start to Finish: 20 minutes

1 **tablespoon margarine or butter**

1½ **cups chopped onion**

1 **teaspoon sugar**

1 **tablespoon balsamic vinegar or red wine vinegar**

½ **of a 7½-ounce jar roasted red sweet peppers, drained and finely chopped (½ cup)**

¼ **cup quartered pitted ripe olives**

2 **tablespoons snipped fresh basil**

¼ **teaspoon salt**

¼ **teaspoon black pepper**

1 **pound green beans, cut into 2-inch lengths (about 4 cups)**

Exchanges: 2 Vegetable **1** Fat

1 In a large heavy skillet heat margarine or butter over medium heat until melted. Cook and stir onion and sugar in margarine or butter about 10 minutes or until the onion is very tender and golden brown. Stir in vinegar. Cook and stir for 1 to 2 minutes more or until liquid evaporates. Stir in the roasted red peppers, olives, basil, salt, and black pepper. Remove skillet from heat; keep warm.

2 Meanwhile, in a medium saucepan cook the green beans, covered, in a small amount of boiling water about 10 minutes or until crisp-tender; drain. To serve, stir caramelized onion into green beans. Makes about five ¾-cup servings.

Nutrition facts per serving: 86 calories, **6 g** total fat (**1 g** saturated fat), **0 mg** cholesterol, **169 mg** sodium, **14 g** carbohydrate, **4 g** fiber, **2 g** protein
Daily values: 16% vit. A, **86%** vit. C, **4%** calcium, **10%** iron

vegetables & sides

lemony MIXED VEGETABLES

Be creative with seasonings! The inspired combination of coriander, oregano, and lemon peel adds character to this simple vegetable side dish.

Prep: 20 minutes
Cook: 18 minutes

1 cup reduced-sodium chicken broth

¼ teaspoon ground coriander

⅛ teaspoon salt

⅛ teaspoon black pepper

½ pound green beans, cut into 2-inch lengths (about 2 cups)

2 cups thinly bias-sliced carrots

1 cup cauliflower flowerets

½ of a medium red sweet pepper, cut into 1-inch pieces

1 tablespoon snipped fresh oregano or 1 teaspoon dried oregano, crushed

1 tablespoon cold water

1½ teaspoons cornstarch

½ teaspoon finely shredded lemon peel

4 teaspoons lemon juice

Exchanges: 2 Vegetable

1 In a large saucepan combine the chicken broth, coriander, salt, and black pepper. Bring to boiling; add green beans. Return to boiling; reduce heat. Simmer, covered, for 10 minutes. Add carrots, cauliflower, and sweet pepper. Return to boiling; reduce heat. Simmer, covered, for 4 to 5 minutes more or until vegetables are crisp-tender.

2 Using a slotted spoon, transfer vegetables to a serving bowl, reserving broth mixture in saucepan. Cover vegetables; keep warm.

3 In a small bowl stir together oregano, water, cornstarch, and lemon peel; stir into broth mixture in saucepan. Cook and stir over medium heat until slightly thickened and bubbly. Cook and stir for 2 minutes more. Stir in lemon juice. Pour thickened broth mixture over vegetables. Toss lightly to coat. Makes six ¾-cup servings.

Nutrition facts per serving: 49 calories, **0 g** total fat (**0 g** saturated fat), **0 mg** cholesterol, **184 mg** sodium, **11 g** carbohydrate, **3 g** fiber, **2 g** protein
Daily values: 121% vit. A, 48% vit. C, 3% calcium, 6% iron

vegetables & sides

roasted SUCCOTASH

Put away your saucepan! This colorful lima bean, corn, and red pepper succotash is prepared in the oven. Just combine the ingredients in the pan, bake, and finish with a light sprinkling of fresh cilantro.

Prep: 15 minutes
Bake: 25 minutes

- **1 10-ounce package frozen baby lima beans**
- **1½ cups fresh or frozen whole kernel corn**
- **1½ cups finely chopped red sweet pepper**
- **1 cup chopped onion**
- **1 tablespoon olive oil**
- **1 teaspoon ground cumin**
- **¼ teaspoon salt**
- **⅛ to ¼ teaspoon ground red pepper**
- **1 to 2 tablespoons snipped cilantro**

Exchanges: **2** Starch **1** Vegetable **½** Fat

1 In a 15×10×1-inch baking pan combine lima beans, corn, sweet pepper, onion, olive oil, cumin, salt, and red pepper.

2 Bake in a 400° oven about 25 minutes or until vegetables are tender and lightly browned, stirring after 15 minutes. To serve, sprinkle with cilantro. Makes six ½-cup servings.

Nutrition facts per serving: 210 calories, **3 g** total fat (**1 g** saturated fat), **0 mg** cholesterol, **100 mg** sodium, **37 g** carbohydrate, **5 g** fiber, **11 g** protein
Daily values: 19% vit. A, **75%** vit. C, **3%** calcium, **23%** iron

vegetables & sides

orange-ginger CARROTS

Consider keeping fresh ginger on hand to add zesty flavor to vegetables. The knobby, tan root stays fresh in the refrigerator for at least a week. It also can be frozen for up to two months.

Start to Finish: 10 minutes

- **1** **16-ounce package peeled baby carrots**
- **2** **tablespoons orange juice**
- **1** **tablespoon honey**
- **½** **teaspoon grated fresh ginger**
- **1** **tablespoon snipped parsley**
  Finely shredded orange peel (optional)

Exchanges: **2** Vegetable

1 In a large saucepan cook the carrots, covered, in a small amount of boiling water for 3 to 5 minutes or until crisp-tender. Drain well.

2 Meanwhile, in a small bowl stir together the orange juice, honey, and ginger; drizzle over warm carrots. Toss to coat. To serve, sprinkle with parsley and, if desired, orange peel. Makes four ¾-cup servings.

Nutrition facts per serving: 67 calories, **0 g** total fat (**0 g** saturated fat), **0 mg** cholesterol, **70 mg** sodium, **16 g** carbohydrate, **4 g** fiber, **1 g** protein
Daily values: 256% vit. A, **12%** vit. C, **2%** calcium, **4%** iron

orzo-broccoli PILAF

Orzo is a tiny, rice-shaped pasta, larger than a grain of rice, but slightly smaller than a pine nut. It is a great substitute for rice in this vegetable-filled pilaf.

Prep: 20 minutes
Cook: 15 minutes
Stand: 5 minutes

- **2 teaspoons olive oil**
- **1 cup sliced fresh mushrooms**
- **½ cup chopped onion**
- **⅔ cup orzo (rosamarina)**
- **1 14½-ounce can reduced-sodium chicken broth**
- **½ cup shredded carrot**
- **1 teaspoon dried marjoram, crushed**
- **⅛ teaspoon pepper**
- **2 cups small broccoli flowerets**

1 In a large saucepan heat olive oil over medium-high heat. Cook and stir the mushrooms and onion in hot oil until onion is tender. Stir in the orzo. Cook and stir about 2 minutes more or until orzo is lightly browned. Remove from heat.

2 Carefully stir in the chicken broth, carrot, marjoram, and pepper. Bring to boiling; reduce heat. Simmer, covered, about 15 minutes or until orzo is tender but still firm. Remove saucepan from heat; stir in broccoli. Let stand, covered, for 5 minutes. Makes six ⅔-cup servings.

Nutrition facts per serving: 113 calories, **2 g** total fat (**0 g** saturated fat), **0 mg** cholesterol, **209 mg** sodium, **19 g** carbohydrate, **2 g** fiber, **4 g** protein
Daily values: 30% vit. A, **37%** vit. C, **2%** calcium, **9%** iron

vegetables & sides

barley-TOMATO PILAF

Pearl barley is featured in this pilaf. Barley is said to be "pearled" after the outer husk and bran are removed, and the remaining grain is steamed and polished. This process gives barley a unique texture.

Prep: 20 minutes
Cook: 45 minutes

Nonstick spray coating

½ **cup chopped onion**

2 **cloves garlic, minced**

1 **14½-ounce can reduced-sodium chicken broth**

¼ **cup water**

1 **teaspoon dried oregano, crushed**

½ **teaspoon paprika**

¼ **teaspoon ground turmeric**

⅛ **teaspoon black pepper**

½ **cup pearl barley**

1 **medium red or green sweet pepper, cut into matchstick strips (1 cup)**

3 **medium plum tomatoes, chopped (1 cup)**

Exchanges: ½ Starch **3** Vegetable

1 Spray a large saucepan with nonstick coating. Preheat over medium heat. Cook and stir onion and garlic in hot saucepan until onion is tender. Carefully stir in chicken broth, water, oregano, paprika, turmeric, and black pepper. Bring to boiling; stir in the barley. Return to boiling; reduce heat. Simmer, covered, for 40 minutes.

2 Stir in sweet pepper. Cook, uncovered, over medium heat for 5 to 10 minutes more or until liquid is evaporated, stirring occasionally. Stir in tomatoes. Makes four ⅔-cup servings.

Nutrition facts per serving: 119 calories, **2 g** total fat (**0 g** saturated fat), **0 mg** cholesterol, **289 mg** sodium, **24 g** carbohydrate, **5 g** fiber, **5 g** protein
Daily values: 18% vit. A, **72%** vit. C, **1%** calcium, **9%** iron

vegetables & sides

santa fe VEGETABLES

In mid- and late summer, when tomatoes and zucchini are plentiful and corn is at its sweetest, be sure to try this colorful vegetable dish. Cumin, cilantro, and pepper sauce add a touch of Southwestern pizzazz.

Start to Finish: 25 minutes

- 1 **tablespoon olive oil or cooking oil**
- 2 **cups fresh or frozen whole kernel corn**
- ¾ **cup chopped onion**
- 1½ **cups finely chopped zucchini**
- 1 **teaspoon ground cumin**
- 2 **cups chopped, seeded tomatoes**
- ¼ **cup snipped cilantro**
- ¼ **teaspoon salt**

  Few dashes bottled hot pepper sauce

Exchanges: 1 Starch 1 Vegetable ½ Fat

1 In a large heavy skillet heat oil over medium-high heat. Cook and stir the corn and onion in hot oil for 5 minutes. Stir in the zucchini and cumin. Cook and stir about 3 minutes more or until the corn is just tender.

2 Remove from heat. Stir in tomatoes, cilantro, salt, and hot pepper sauce. Makes six ⅔-cup servings.

Nutrition facts per serving: 130 calories, **3 g** total fat (**0 g** saturated fat), **0 mg** cholesterol, **102 mg** sodium, **25 g** carbohydrate, **4 g** fiber, **4 g** protein
Daily values: 7% vit. A, **34%** vit. C, **1%** calcium, **9%** iron

vegetables & sides

pesto POTATOES

A surefire dinner favorite, these mashed potatoes are lightened with reduced-fat cream cheese, skim milk, and a homemade, lower-fat pesto featuring basil and spinach.

Start to Finish: 35 minutes

2 **pounds medium yellow fleshed potatoes, such as Yukon gold**

½ **of an 8-ounce package fat-free cream cheese**

Salt and pepper

2 **to 3 tablespoons skim milk**

8 **teaspoons Pesto**

Exchanges: 1½ Starch

❶ Peel and quarter potatoes. Cook, covered, in a small amount of boiling lightly salted water for 15 to 20 minutes or until tender; drain. Mash with a potato masher or an electric mixer on low speed. Add cream cheese. Season to taste with salt and pepper. Gradually beat in enough milk to make potatoes light and fluffy. Top each serving with 1 teaspoon Pesto. Makes eight ¾-cup servings.

Pesto: In a food processor bowl combine 1 cup firmly packed fresh basil leaves; ½ cup torn fresh spinach; ¼ cup grated Parmesan cheese; ¼ cup pine nuts or almonds; 2 cloves garlic, quartered; and, if desired, ¼ teaspoon salt. Cover and process with several on-off turns until a paste forms, stopping the machine several times and scraping down the sides. With machine running, gradually add 2 tablespoons olive oil or cooking oil and 2 tablespoons water. Process to the consistency of soft butter. Cover and chill for up to 2 days or freeze for up to 1 month. Makes about ½ cup.

Nutrition facts per serving: 134 calories, **2 g** total fat (**1 g** saturated fat), **3 mg** cholesterol, **45 mg** sodium, **24 g** carbohydrate, **2 g** fiber, **5 g** protein
Daily values: 6% vit. A, **14%** vit. C, **6%** calcium, **3%** iron

vegetables & sides

garlic POTATOES & CARROTS

Is convenience a priority? Then remember this recipe—it starts with a package of refrigerated mashed potatoes. Stir in shredded carrots and roasted garlic for plenty of made-from-scratch flavor.

Start to Finish: 10 minutes

- 1 20-ounce package refrigerated country-style or regular mashed potatoes
- 1 teaspoon olive oil
- 1 cup finely shredded carrots
- 2 teaspoons bottled minced roasted garlic
- ⅛ teaspoon pepper

Exchanges: 1½ Starch

❶ Prepare potatoes according to package directions, except use olive oil in place of any butter or margarine.

❷ Stir in the carrots, garlic, and pepper. Heat through. Makes four ¾-cup servings.

Nutrition facts per serving: 138 calories, **3 g** total fat (**0 g** saturated fat), **0 mg** cholesterol, **223 mg** sodium, **23 g** carbohydrate, **2 g** fiber, **4 g** protein
Daily values: 77% vit. A, **46%** vit. C, **2%** calcium, **5%** iron

vegetables & sides

Q: Are potatoes fattening?

A: Only if you load them with butter, sour cream, or other fat-filled condiments. The truth is, the humble potato by itself is virtually fat free. It is also one of the best sources of necessary complex carbohydrates, not to mention one of the tastiest. And if you've used up your fat allotment for the day before you get to the potatoes, don't sulk. Flavor mashed potatoes with snipped fresh herbs, roasted garlic, shredded lemon peel, or skinny gravy (cornstarch-thickened broth). You won't even miss the butter or sour cream!

artichokes WITH BALSAMIC SAUCE

What a treat! Tender artichoke leaves are dipped in a sauce featuring Italian balsamic vinegar. Made from white grape juice and aged in wooden barrels, this vinegar is typically dark, pungent, and sweet.

Start to Finish: 35 minutes

- 1 **lemon**
- 2 **artichokes (about 10 ounces each)**
- 6 **cups water**
- ⅓ **cup dry white wine (optional)**
- 1 **bay leaf**
- 1 **tablespoon olive oil**
- 1 **tablespoon water**
- 1 **tablespoon balsamic vinegar**
- 2 **teaspoons Dijon-style mustard**
- 1 **small clove garlic, minced**

Exchanges: 3 Vegetable 1 Fat

❶ Halve lemon; cut one half into thin slices. Set lemon half and lemon slices aside.

❷ Wash artichokes; trim stems and remove loose outer leaves. Cut off 1 inch from each top; snip off the sharp leaf tips. Rub lemon half over the cut edges of the artichoke.

❸ In a large saucepan combine the 6 cups water, the wine (if desired), bay leaf, and reserved lemon slices. Bring to boiling. Add the artichokes and return to boiling; reduce heat. Simmer, covered, for 20 to 30 minutes or until a leaf pulls out easily. Drain artichokes upside down on paper towels.

❹ Meanwhile, for the dipping sauce, stir together the olive oil, the 1 tablespoon water, the vinegar, mustard, and garlic. Serve artichokes with dipping sauce. Makes 2 servings.

Nutrition facts per serving (with 2 tablespoons dipping sauce): 137 calories, **7 g** total fat (**1 g** saturated fat), **0 mg** cholesterol, **219 mg** sodium, **16 g** carbohydrate, **4 g** fiber, **5 g** protein **Daily values: 2%** vit. A, **24%** vit. C, **5%** calcium, **12%** iron

vegetables & sides

173

pasta & FRESH TOMATO SAUCE

This pasta sauce is the essence of simplicity—chopped Roma tomatoes lightly sautéed in a little olive oil and seasoned with basil. Served on the side, it's the ideal accompaniment to beef, chicken, or seafood.

Start to Finish: 20 minutes

4   ounces dried rotini or fusilli

2   cups coarsely chopped plum tomatoes

2   teaspoons olive oil

¼   teaspoon salt

3   tablespoons shredded fresh basil

¼   cup shaved or grated Parmesan or Romano cheese

¼   teaspoon pepper

Exchanges: 1½ Starch **1** Vegetable **½** Fat

① Cook the pasta according to package directions; drain.

② Meanwhile, in a saucepan combine tomatoes, olive oil, and salt. Cook over medium-low heat until heated through and tomatoes start to juice-out slightly. Stir in the basil.

③ Divide pasta among 4 plates. Top each serving with some of the tomato mixture. Sprinkle with Parmesan cheese and pepper. Makes 4 servings.

Nutrition facts per serving (½ cup pasta and ⅜ cup sauce): 184 calories, **5 g** total fat (**2 g** saturated fat), **5 mg** cholesterol, **260 mg** sodium, **28 g** carbohydrate, **2 g** fiber, **7 g** protein **Daily values: 8%** vit. A, **35%** vit. C, **8%** calcium, **11%** iron

vegetables & sides

asparagus & ROASTED PEPPERS

If you grow your own sweet peppers, you can roast them yourself. However, convenient roasted peppers from a jar provide a jump-start on this dish. Here, they are pureed into a colorful sauce for asparagus or broccoli.

Start to Finish: 25 minutes

- ½ of a 7¼-ounce jar (about ½ cup) roasted red sweet peppers, drained
- ¼ cup water
- 1 teaspoon snipped fresh thyme or savory or ¼ teaspoon dried thyme or savory, crushed
- 1 teaspoon lemon juice
- ½ teaspoon cornstarch
- ¼ teaspoon instant chicken bouillon granules
- ⅛ teaspoon black pepper
- ¾ pound asparagus or broccoli, cut lengthwise into spears

Exchanges: 1 Vegetable

❶ For sauce, in a blender container or food processor bowl combine the sweet peppers, water, thyme or savory, lemon juice, cornstarch, bouillon granules, and black pepper. Cover and blend or process until smooth. Pour into a small saucepan. Cook and stir until thickened and bubbly. Cook and stir for 2 minutes more. Cover and keep warm.

❷ In a large saucepan cook the asparagus, covered, in a small amount of boiling water for 4 to 6 minutes or until crisp-tender. (Or, cook broccoli for 8 to 10 minutes or until crisp-tender.) Drain well. To serve, spoon the sauce over the asparagus or broccoli. Makes 4 servings.

Nutrition facts per serving (with 2 tablespoons sauce): 27 calories, **0 g** total fat (**0 g** saturated fat), **0 mg** cholesterol, **58 mg** sodium, **5 g** carbohydrate, **2 g** fiber, **2 g** protein **Daily values: 15%** vit. A, **121%** vit. C, **1%** calcium, **5%** iron

vegetables & sides

One Sweet Pepper

Roasting sweet peppers draws out their natural sweetness and flavor. To roast the peppers, cut them into quarters. Remove stems, membranes, and seeds. Place the pepper pieces, cut side down, on a foil-lined baking sheet. Bake in a 425° oven for 20 to 25 minutes or until skins are bubbly and very dark. Wrap pepper pieces tightly in foil and let stand for 10 to 15 minutes or until cool enough to handle. Using a paring knife, pull the skin off gently. Use the peppers as directed in recipes, or cut into strips and toss with salads, layer on sandwiches, or stir into vegetable dishes.

thai-style ASPARAGUS

The nutty taste of sesame oil and pungent fresh ginger—favorites for flavoring Asian foods—team perfectly with fresh asparagus and orange sections. A sprinkling of sesame seeds tops this pretty side dish.

Start to Finish: 20 minutes

- 2 **tablespoons orange juice**
- 1 **tablespoon white wine vinegar**
- 1½ **teaspoons reduced-sodium soy sauce**
- ½ **teaspoon toasted sesame oil**
- ½ **teaspoon grated fresh ginger**
- 1 **large clove garlic, minced**

  Dash to ⅛ teaspoon ground red pepper
- 1 **teaspoon cooking oil**
- 1 **pound asparagus spears**
- 2 **oranges, peeled and sectioned**
- 2 **teaspoons toasted sesame seeds (optional)**

Exchanges: 1 Vegetable **½** Fruit

1 For vinaigrette, in a screw-top jar combine orange juice, vinegar, soy sauce, sesame oil, ginger, garlic, and red pepper. Cover and shake well; set aside.

2 In a large nonstick skillet heat oil over medium-high heat. Cook asparagus in hot oil for 3 to 4 minutes or until just tender, turning asparagus occasionally.

3 Shake the vinaigrette; pour over asparagus in skillet. Cook the asparagus for 30 seconds more. Gently stir in the orange sections. To serve, if desired, sprinkle with sesame seeds. Makes 4 servings.

Nutrition facts per serving (with 2 tablespoons vinaigrette): 55 calories, **2 g** total fat (**0 g** saturated fat), **0 mg** cholesterol, **69 mg** sodium, **9 g** carbohydrate, **2 g** fiber, **3 g** protein **Daily values: 7%** vit. A, **69%** vit. C, **2%** calcium, **4%** iron

vegetables & sides

desserts
& TREATS

Unless you have been misbehaving, there's no need to go to bed without dessert. True, desserts are where moderation and temptation often come head-to-head, but with a little planning, desserts can be enjoyed as a well-deserved treat. Aim for reasonable portion sizes, and for those times you are simply seeking to satisfy a sweet tooth, remember fruit—all on its own, au naturel.

Berry-Ginger Shortcakes, *recipe page 180*

berry ginger SHORTCAKES

Like classic shortcakes, but better! These sweet biscuits are split in half, filled with low-calorie sweetened berries, and topped with sour cream-flavored whipped topping. Heavenly! (See photograph, page 179.)

Prep: 25 minutes
Bake: 8 minutes

3 cups berries (sliced strawberries, blueberries, raspberries, and/or blackberries)

   Low-calorie liquid sweetener equal to 2 tablespoons sugar (optional)

2 tablespoons finely chopped crystallized ginger

1 recipe Shortcakes

½ of an 8-ounce container frozen fat-free whipped dessert topping, thawed

¼ cup fat-free dairy sour cream

Exchanges: 1 Starch **1** Fruit **½** Fat

1 In a small mixing bowl combine the berries, the liquid sweetener (if desired), and the crystallized ginger. Set aside.

2 Meanwhile, prepare Shortcakes.

3 To serve, in a small bowl combine the whipped topping and sour cream. Split shortcakes in half. Place bottoms on dessert plates. Divide the berry mixture among bottoms. Top each with some of the whipped topping mixture. Replace the shortcake tops. Makes 10 servings.

Shortcakes: In a medium bowl stir together 1⅔ cups all-purpose flour, 1 tablespoon sugar, 2 teaspoons baking powder, and ¼ teaspoon baking soda. Using a pastry blender, cut in 3 tablespoons butter or margarine until the mixture resembles coarse crumbs. Combine ½ cup buttermilk and ¼ cup refrigerated or frozen egg product (thawed) or 1 egg. Add to the flour mixture all at once, stirring just until mixture is moistened. Spray a baking sheet with nonstick coating. On a lightly floured surface pat the dough to ½-inch thickness. Cut the dough with a floured 2½-inch star-shaped or heart-shaped cookie cutter or a round biscuit cutter, rerolling scraps as necessary. Place shortcakes on prepared baking sheet. Bake in a 425° oven for 8 to 10 minutes or until golden. Cool the shortcakes slightly on a wire rack.

Nutrition facts per serving: 166 calories, **4 g** total fat (**2 g** saturated fat), **10 mg** cholesterol, **176 mg** sodium, **28 g** carbohydrate, **2 g** fiber, **4 g** protein
Daily values: 5% vit. A, **23%** vit. C, **9%** calcium, **11%** iron

desserts & treats

cherry bread PUDDING

Leftover French bread never tasted so good! Toss the cubed bread with bits of dried cherries, saturate with a custard mixture, and bake. You'll soon be spooning into a rich-tasting bread pudding.

Prep: 20 minutes
Bake: 35 minutes

- **2 cups fat-free milk**
- **⅓ cup refrigerated or frozen egg product, thawed**
- **¼ cup packed brown sugar**
- **1 teaspoon vanilla**
- **¼ teaspoon ground cinnamon**
- **4 cups dry French bread cubes**
- **½ cup snipped dried cherries**

Exchanges: 1½ Starch ½ Fruit ½ Milk

❶ In a medium bowl beat together the milk, egg product, brown sugar, vanilla, and cinnamon. In an ungreased 1½-quart casserole toss together bread cubes and cherries; pour egg mixture evenly over bread mixture.

❷ Bake in a 350° oven for 35 to 40 minutes or until a knife inserted near the center comes out clean. Cool slightly. Serve pudding warm. Makes 6 servings.

Nutrition facts per serving: 208 calories, **2 g** total fat (**1 g** saturated fat), **6 mg** cholesterol, **264 mg** sodium, **39 g** carbohydrate, **0 g** fiber, **7 g** protein
Daily values: 17% vit. A, **1%** vit. C, **11%** calcium, **8%** iron

strawberry CREAM PIE

In the mood for an elegant dessert? Try this creamy mousse of pureed fresh strawberries, fluffy egg whites, gelatin, and whipped topping surrounded by delicate ladyfingers.

Prep: 30 minutes
Chill: 4 hours

2½ **cups strawberries**

¼ **cup sugar**

1 **envelope unflavored gelatin**

2 **tablespoons frozen limeade concentrate or frozen lemonade concentrate, thawed**

3 **slightly beaten egg whites**

1 **tablespoon tequila or orange juice**

1 **3-ounce package ladyfingers, split**

2 **tablespoons orange juice**

½ **of an 8-ounce container frozen light whipped dessert topping, thawed**

Sliced strawberries (optional)

Fresh mint (optional)

Exchanges: 1 Starch **½** Fruit **½** Fat

❶ Place the 2½ cups strawberries in a blender container or food processor bowl. Cover and blend or process until nearly smooth. Measure strawberries (you should have about 1½ cups).

❷ In a medium saucepan stir together the sugar and gelatin. Stir in the blended strawberries and limeade or lemonade concentrate. Cook and stir over medium heat until the mixture bubbles and the gelatin is dissolved. Gradually stir about half of the gelatin mixture into the egg whites. Return mixture to the saucepan. Cook, stirring constantly, over low heat about 3 minutes or until mixture is slightly thickened. Do not boil. Pour into a medium bowl; stir in tequila or orange juice. Chill until mixture mounds when spooned, stirring occasionally (about 2 hours).

❸ Meanwhile, cut half of the split ladyfingers in half crosswise; stand on end around the outside edge of a 9-inch tart pan with a removable bottom or a 9-inch springform pan. Arrange remaining split ladyfingers in the bottom of the pan. Drizzle the 2 tablespoons orange juice over the ladyfingers.

❹ Fold whipped topping into strawberry mixture. Spoon into prepared pan. Cover and chill about 2 hours or until set. If desired, garnish with the sliced strawberries and mint. Makes 8 servings.

Nutrition facts per serving: 130 calories, **3 g** total fat (**2 g** saturated fat), **39 mg** cholesterol, **48 mg** sodium, **22 g** carbohydrate, **1 g** fiber, **4 g** protein
Daily values: 3% vit. A, **49%** vit. C, **1%** calcium, **4%** iron

desserts & treats

pumpkin-maple PIE

It tastes like Grandmother's, but it's better for you! Our special lower-fat pastry is filled with a maple-flavored pumpkin mixture that is lower in calories and fat than old-fashioned recipes—but it is every bit as good!

Prep: 25 minutes
Bake: 45 minutes

- 1 recipe Lower-Fat Oil Pastry
- 1 15-ounce can pumpkin
- ⅓ cup maple-flavored syrup
- 1 tablespoon all-purpose flour
- 2 packets heat-stable sugar substitute
- 1½ teaspoons pumpkin pie spice
- ¾ cup refrigerated or frozen egg product, thawed
- 1 cup evaporated fat-free milk
- 1½ teaspoons vanilla
  Frozen light whipped dessert topping, thawed (optional)

Exchanges: 1½ Starch ½ Milk 1 Fat

① Prepare Lower-Fat Oil Pastry. On a lightly floured surface, flatten pastry. Roll into a 12-inch circle. Wrap pastry circle around the rolling pin; unroll into a 9-inch pie plate. Ease pastry into pan, being careful not to stretch pastry. Trim to ½ inch beyond edge of pie plate. Fold under extra pastry. Crimp the edge as desired. Do not prick pastry.

② For the filling, in a medium bowl combine the pumpkin, maple-flavored syrup, flour, sugar substitute, and pumpkin pie spice; add egg product. Beat lightly with a rotary beater or fork until just combined. Gradually stir in evaporated milk and vanilla; mix well.

③ Place pastry-lined pie plate on oven rack. Carefully pour filling into pastry shell. To prevent overbrowning, cover edge of pie with foil. Bake in a 375° oven for 25 minutes. Remove the foil. Bake 20 to 25 minutes more or until a knife inserted near the center comes out clean. Cool on a wire rack. Cover and refrigerate within 2 hours. If desired, serve with dessert topping. Makes 8 servings.

Lower-Fat Oil Pastry: In a medium bowl stir together 1¼ cups all-purpose flour and ¼ teaspoon salt. Combine ¼ cup fat-free milk and 3 tablespoons cooking oil; add all at once to flour mixture. Stir with a fork until dough forms. If necessary, add 1 to 2 teaspoons additional milk. Shape the dough into a ball.

Nutrition facts per serving: 216 calories, **6 g** total fat (**1 g** saturated fat), **1 mg** cholesterol, **153 mg** sodium, **32 g** carbohydrate, **2 g** fiber, **8 g** protein
Daily values: 126% vit. A, **4%** vit. C, **11%** calcium, **15%** iron

peach-berry COBBLER

Cobbler is the ultimate comfort food. You'll agree when you spoon into syrupy peaches and raspberries covered with spicy biscuit topping, served hot with a scoop of low-fat vanilla ice cream.

Prep: 30 minutes
Cook: 25 minutes

4 **cups fresh or frozen unsweetened peach slices, thawed**

¼ **cup sugar**

¼ **cup water**

4 **teaspoons cornstarch**

1 **tablespoon lemon juice**

¼ **teaspoon ground allspice or ground cardamom**

1 **recipe Biscuit Topping**

1½ **cups fresh raspberries or frozen raspberries, thawed**

Exchanges: 1 Starch **1½** Fruit **½** Fat

❶ For filling, in a medium saucepan combine the peaches, 2 tablespoons of the sugar, the water, cornstarch, lemon juice, and allspice or cardamom. Let stand for 10 minutes.

❷ Meanwhile, prepare Biscuit Topping.

❸ Cook and stir the peach mixture over medium heat until thickened and bubbly. Stir in the raspberries. Transfer the hot filling to a 2-quart square baking dish.

❹ Immediately drop the Biscuit Topping into 8 small mounds on the hot filling. Sprinkle topping with the remaining sugar.

❺ Bake in a 400° oven about 25 minutes or until a toothpick inserted into topping comes out clean. Makes 8 servings.

Biscuit Topping: In a large bowl combine 1¼ cups all-purpose flour, 2 tablespoons sugar, ¾ teaspoon baking powder, ¼ teaspoon baking soda, ¼ teaspoon ground allspice or ground cardamom, and ⅛ teaspoon salt. In a small bowl stir together ½ cup lemon or plain fat-free yogurt; ¼ cup refrigerated or frozen egg substitute, thawed, or 1 large beaten egg; and 2 tablespoons melted butter or margarine. Add egg mixture to flour mixture, stirring just to moisten.

Nutrition facts per serving: 202 calories, **4 g** total fat (**2 g** saturated fat), **8 mg** cholesterol, **159 mg** sodium, **40 g** carbohydrate, **3 g** fiber, **4 g** protein
Daily values: 9% vit. A, **20%** vit. C, **5%** calcium, **8%** iron

desserts & treats

pear-cherry CRISP

Oatmeal contributes crunchy texture, while honey and lemon peel add zesty flavor to our pear-cherry combo. This dessert also is good for breakfast, especially when topped with lemon yogurt.

Prep: 25 minutes
Bake: 35 minutes

5 cups thinly sliced, peeled, ripe pears

⅓ cup dried tart cherries, cranberries, or blueberries

2 tablespoons honey

1 teaspoon finely shredded lemon peel

½ cup regular rolled oats

3 tablespoons brown sugar plus 3 packets heat-stable sugar substitute, or ⅓ cup packed brown sugar

3 tablespoons all-purpose flour

¼ teaspoon ground ginger

2 tablespoons butter or margarine

½ cup vanilla or lemon fat-free yogurt with sweetener

Exchanges: **1** Starch **2** Fruit **1** Fat

1 For filling, in a bowl toss together the pears; cherries, cranberries, or blueberries; honey; and lemon peel. Spoon into a 2-quart square baking dish.

2 For topping, in a medium bowl stir together the oats, brown sugar plus sugar substitute or brown sugar, flour, and ginger. Cut in butter or margarine until crumbly. Sprinkle topping over the filling.

3 Bake in a 375° oven about 35 minutes or until the pears are tender. Serve with yogurt. Makes 6 servings.

Nutrition facts per serving: 231 calories, **5 g** total fat (**2 g** saturated fat), **0 mg** cholesterol **54 mg** sodium, **47 g** carbohydrate, **4 g** fiber, **3 g** protein
Daily values: 7% vit. A, **9%** vit. C, **3%** calcium, **6%** iron

Using the ⅓ cup brown sugar option: 245 calories and **50 g** carbohydrate

desserts & treats

186

peach crumble TART

The "crumble" is a British dessert in which raw fruit is topped with a crumbly pastry mixture and baked. Here, peaches star with a sprinkling of oatmeal, flour, sugar, cinnamon, and butter. Tip: It's best served warm.

Prep: 30 minutes
Cook: 45 minutes

1 recipe Lower-Fat Oil Pastry (see recipe, page 184)

½ cup rolled oats

⅓ cup all-purpose flour

¼ cup packed brown sugar

½ teaspoon ground cinnamon

2 tablespoons butter or margarine, melted

¼ cup granulated sugar

2 tablespoons all-purpose flour

1 teaspoon ground cinnamon

6 medium peaches (2 pounds), peeled, pitted, and thinly sliced (about 6 cups)

¼ cup buttermilk

Exchanges: 1½ Starch 1 Fruit 1 Fat

❶ Prepare Lower-Fat Oil Pastry. On a lightly floured surface, flatten pastry. Roll into a 12-inch circle. Wrap pastry circle around the rolling pin; unroll pastry into a 10-inch tart pan with a removable bottom. Ease pastry into pan, being careful not to stretch pastry. Press the pastry into fluted sides of tart pan and trim edges. Do not prick pastry.

❷ For crumble topping, combine the oats, the ⅓ cup flour, the brown sugar, and the ½ teaspoon cinnamon. Stir in the butter or margarine. Set aside.

❸ For filling, in a large bowl stir together the granulated sugar, the 2 tablespoons flour, and the 1 teaspoon cinnamon. Add the peaches and buttermilk. Gently toss until coated.

❹ Spread filling evenly into pastry shell. Top with crumble topping. Bake in a 375° oven 45 to 50 minutes, or until center of filling is bubbly. If necessary, to prevent overbrowning, cover loosely with foil the last 10 minutes of baking. Serve warm or at room temperature. Makes 10 servings.

Nutrition facts per serving: 210 calories, **7 g** total fat (**2 g** saturated fat), **6 mg** cholesterol, **87 mg** sodium, **35 g** carbohydrate, **3 g** fiber, **4 g** protein
Daily values: 8% vit. A, **11%** vit. C, **2%** calcium, **9%** iron

desserts & treats

187

nectarine TART

The filling in this low-fat dessert tastes deceivingly rich. Fat-free cream cheese is the key. For a pretty finish, arrange the nectarines or peaches and blueberries in a pinwheel design before glazing with the apricot spread.

Prep: 35 minutes
Bake: 12 minutes
Chill: 2 hours

- **1 cup all-purpose flour**
- **¼ teaspoon salt**
- **¼ cup margarine or butter**
- **4 to 5 tablespoons cold water**
- **1 8-ounce package fat-free cream cheese, softened**
- **Sugar substitute equal to ¼ cup sugar, or ¼ cup sugar**
- **1 teaspoon vanilla**
- **4 or 5 nectarines or peeled peaches, pitted and sliced, or one 16-ounce package frozen unsweetened peach slices, thawed and drained**
- **½ cup blueberries**
- **½ cup low-calorie apricot spread**

Exchanges: 1 Starch **½** Fruit **½** Fat

❶ For pastry, in a medium bowl combine flour and salt. Using a pastry blender, cut in margarine or butter until pieces are the size of small peas. Sprinkle 1 tablespoon of the cold water over a portion of the mixture. Toss with a fork. Push to side of bowl. Repeat until mixture is moistened. Form into a ball.

❷ On a lightly floured surface, flatten pastry. Roll pastry into a 12-inch circle. Ease pastry into a 10-inch tart pan with a removable bottom, being careful not to stretch pastry. Press pastry about ½ inch up the sides of pan. Prick the bottom well with the tines of a fork. Bake in a 450° oven for 12 to 15 minutes or until golden. Cool on a wire rack. Remove sides of tart pan.

❸ Meanwhile, in a medium bowl combine the cream cheese, sugar substitute or sugar, and vanilla. Beat with an electric mixer until smooth; spread over the cooled pastry. Arrange the nectarines or peaches over cream cheese layer. Sprinkle with the blueberries.

❹ In a small saucepan heat apricot spread until melted; cut up any large pieces. Spoon melted spread over fruit. Chill for at least 2 hours or up to 3 hours. Makes 12 servings.

Nutrition facts per serving: 140 calories, **4 g** total fat (**1 g** saturated fat), **3 mg** cholesterol, **90 mg** sodium, **23 g** carbohydrate, **1 g** fiber, **4 g** protein
Daily values: 14% vit. A, **5%** vit. C, **5%** calcium, **3%** iron

Using the ¼ cup sugar option: 156 calories and **27 g** carbohydrate

desserts & treats

188

fruit PARFAIT

Parfait, in French, means "perfect," which is what you'll think of this dessert. Served in tall parfait glasses, the layers of fruit and cream look striking, especially when sprinkled with grated chocolate.

Prep: 20 minutes

½ **cup fat-free dairy sour cream**

Low-calorie powdered sweetener equal to 1½ teaspoons sugar, or 1 tablespoon powdered sugar

1 **tablespoon orange liqueur, raspberry liqueur, melon liqueur, or orange juice**

¼ **of an 8-ounce container frozen light whipped dessert topping, thawed**

1½ **cups sliced, peeled peaches**

1 **cup raspberries**

1 **cup blueberries**

Grated chocolate (optional)

Exchanges: 2 Fruit **½** Fat

1 In a medium bowl stir together the sour cream, powdered sweetener or powdered sugar, and liqueur or orange juice. Gently fold in dessert topping.

2 In 4 parfait glasses, layer half of the peaches, raspberries, blueberries, and sour cream mixture. Repeat layering. If desired, sprinkle grated chocolate over each serving. Serve parfaits immediately or cover and chill for up to 2 hours. Makes 4 servings.

Nutrition facts per serving: 134 calories, **2 g** total fat (**2 g** saturated fat), **0 mg** cholesterol, **33 mg** sodium, **25 g** carbohydrate, **3 g** fiber, **3 g** protein
Daily values: 10% vit. A, **27%** vit. C, **5%** calcium, **2%** iron

Using the 1 tablespoon powdered sugar option: 142 calories and **27 g** carbohydrate

Whipped Wonders

Whipped topping for dessert is a luxury we all appreciate. Which is best? Compare the differences of the various types (per tablespoon) to determine the one that's best for you.

Topping	Fat (g)	Sat. Fat (g)	Calories
Whipped cream	6	4	52
Frozen whipped dessert topping	2	2	25
Light frozen whipped dessert topping	1	1	20
Nonfat frozen whipped dessert topping	0	0	15
Reduced-calorie whipped topping	1	0	7

berry cheesecake DESSERT

Fat-free cream cheese and low-fat ricotta cheese lend rich taste to this cheesecake. Serve it when fresh berries are in season, as a tempting finale to a festive dinner.

Prep: 20 minutes
Chill: 4 to 24 hours

½ **of an 8-ounce tub (about ½ cup) fat-free cream cheese**

½ **cup low-fat ricotta cheese**

   Low-calorie powdered sweetener equal to 3 tablespoons sugar, or 3 tablespoons sugar

½ **teaspoon finely shredded orange peel or lemon peel**

1 **tablespoon orange juice**

3 **cups sliced strawberries, raspberries, and/or blueberries**

4 **gingersnaps or chocolate wafers, broken**

Exchanges: 1 Lean Meat 1 Fruit

1 In a blender container or food processor bowl combine cream cheese, ricotta cheese, powdered sweetener or sugar, orange or lemon peel, and orange juice. Cover and blend or process until smooth. Cover and chill for 4 to 24 hours.

2 To serve, divide the fruit among dessert dishes. Top each serving with the cream cheese mixture and sprinkle with the broken cookies. Makes 4 servings.

Nutrition facts per serving: 115 calories, **2 g** total fat (**1 g** saturated fat), **9 mg** cholesterol, **61 mg** sodium, **17 g** carbohydrate, **2 g** fiber, **8 g** protein
Daily values: 11% vit. A, **109%** vit. C, **12%** calcium, **4%** iron

Using sugar option: 152 calories and **26 g** carbohydrate

country APRICOT TART

The flavor of this cornmeal crust is outstanding and—better yet—it's great for those who haven't mastered the art of making beautifully crimped pie edges. You simply fold the crust over the filling.

Prep: 30 minutes
Bake: 40 minutes
Cool: 30 minutes

1   recipe Cornmeal Crust

3   tablespoons sugar plus
     3 packets heat-stable sugar
     substitute, or ⅓ cup sugar

3   tablespoons all-purpose flour

¼   teaspoon ground nutmeg or
     ground cinnamon

3   cups sliced, pitted apricots or
     3 cups frozen, unsweetened
     peach slices, thawed (do not
     drain)

1   tablespoon lemon juice

2   teaspoons fat-free milk

Exchanges: 1 Starch **1** Fruit **1** Fat

1 Grease and lightly flour a large baking sheet. Prepare Cornmeal Crust. On the baking sheet, flatten dough. Roll into a 12-inch circle. Set aside.

2 For filling, in a bowl stir together sugar plus sugar substitute or sugar, the flour, and the nutmeg or cinnamon. Stir in the apricots or peaches and lemon juice. Mound the filling in center of crust, leaving a 2-inch border. Fold border up over filling. Brush top and sides of crust with the 2 teaspoons milk.

3 Bake in a 375° oven about 40 minutes or until crust is golden and filling is bubbly. To prevent overbrowning, cover the edge of crust with foil the last 10 to 15 minutes of baking. Cool tart for 30 minutes on the baking sheet on a wire rack. Makes 8 servings.

Cornmeal Crust: In a medium bowl stir together ¾ cup flour, ⅓ cup cornmeal, 2 tablespoons sugar, 1 teaspoon baking powder, and ⅛ teaspoon salt. Cut in 3 tablespoons butter or margarine until the size of small peas. Sprinkle 1 tablespoon of cold fat-free milk over mixture; gently toss with a fork. Add 3 to 4 tablespoons more fat-free milk, 1 tablespoon at a time, until the dough is moistened (dough will be crumbly). Turn out onto a lightly floured surface and knead 7 to 8 times or just until dough clings together. Form into a ball.

Nutrition facts per serving: **176** calories, **5 g** total fat (**3 g** saturated fat), **12 mg** cholesterol, **128 mg** sodium, **32 g** carbohydrate, **2 g** fiber, **3 g** protein
Daily value: **23%** vit. A, **13%** vit. C, **5%** calcium, **8%** iron

Using ⅓ cup sugar option: **190** calories and **35 g** carbohydrate

desserts & treats

honey-ginger COMPOTE

Imagine the impression this spicy fruit compote will make when you bring it to the table in tall, stemmed glasses! Add a sprig of fresh mint to each serving for a cool summertime accent.

Prep: 20 minutes
Chill: 4 to 48 hours

½ **cup apple juice or unsweetened pineapple juice**

2 **tablespoons honey**

1 **tablespoon finely chopped crystallized ginger**

1 **tablespoon lemon juice**

2 **cups cubed cantaloupe, sliced starfruit, and/or chopped pineapple**

1 **cup blueberries or quartered strawberries**

Exchanges: 1½ Fruit

1 In a small saucepan combine apple juice or pineapple juice, honey, crystallized ginger, and lemon juice. Cook and stir over medium heat until boiling. Remove from heat; cool slightly. Cover and chill for 4 to 48 hours.

2 To serve, toss together the cantaloupe, starfruit, and/or pineapple and blueberries or strawberries; spoon into 4 tall stemmed glasses or dessert dishes. Pour apple juice mixture over fruit. Makes 4 servings.

Nutrition facts per serving: 102 calories, **0 g** total fat (**0 g** saturated fat), **0 mg** cholesterol, **12 mg** sodium, **26 g** carbohydrate, **2 g** fiber, **1 g** protein
Daily values: 26% vit. A, **68%** vit. C, **1%** calcium, **5%** iron

desserts & treats

194

gingered sauce & FRUIT

It's hard to believe this custard sauce is low in fat and calories because it looks and tastes so rich. Prepare the custard ahead and store it in the refrigerator for up to 24 hours. Spoon over the fruit just before serving.

Prep: 25 minutes
Chill: 1 to 24 hours

⅓ **cup fat-free milk**

2 **tablespoons sugar**

1 **tablespoon chopped crystallized ginger**

1 **beaten egg**

⅓ **cup fat-free milk**

½ **teaspoon vanilla**

3 **cups sliced fresh strawberries, kiwifruit, peaches, or pears**

2 **tablespoons slivered almonds, toasted**

Exchanges: 1 Fruit **½** Fat

① In a blender container combine the ½ cup milk, the sugar, and crystallized ginger. Cover; blend until mixture is smooth.

② For sauce, in a small heavy saucepan combine the egg and the ⅓ cup milk. Add blended mixture. Cook and stir over medium heat about 10 minutes or until mixture just coats a metal spoon. Remove saucepan from heat. Stir in vanilla.

③ Quickly cool custard sauce by placing the saucepan in a sink of ice water for 1 to 2 minutes, stirring constantly. Pour custard sauce into a bowl. Cover the surface with plastic wrap. Refrigerate for at least 1 hour or up to 24 hours.

④ Place fruit in 6 dessert dishes. Spoon custard sauce over fruit. Sprinkle with almonds. Makes 6 servings.

Nutrition facts per serving: 83 calories, **3 g** total fat (**0 g** saturated fat), **36 mg** cholesterol, **48 mg** sodium, **13 g** carbohydrate, **2 g** fiber, **3 g** protein
Daily values: 3% vit. A, **71%** vit. C, **4%** calcium, **5%** iron

Ending on a Sweet Note

When preparing desserts, experiment using the minimum amount of sweetener possible to get the desired results and the flavor you crave. Make the sweetness of sugar work harder by magnifying it with vanilla or spices, such as cinnamon and cloves. And you don't always have to use bar chocolate, either. When a recipe calls for unsweetened chocolate and when it is feasible, substitute unsweetened cocoa powder, a lower-fat alternative to bar chocolate. For each ounce of bar chocolate, stir together 3 tablespoons of cocoa powder and 1 tablespoon water.

cranberry TART

Tissue-thin layers of phyllo pastry form the crispy crust of this tart. Packaged frozen phyllo dough is readily available in supermarkets, and is easy to use.

Prep: 55 minutes
Bake: 20 minutes
Cool: 1 hour
Chill: 4 to 24 hours

1 **cup cranberries**

¼ **cup sugar**

1 **tablespoon orange juice**

1 **8-ounce package light cream cheese**

¼ **cup sugar**

1 **egg**

1 **egg white**

1 **teaspoon vanilla**

  Butter-flavored nonstick spray coating

4 **sheets frozen phyllo dough, thawed**

1 **ounce white chocolate, melted (optional)**

Exchanges: **1** Starch ½ Fruit **1** Fat

1 In a small saucepan combine the cranberries, ¼ cup sugar, and the orange juice. Cook, uncovered, over medium heat until the cranberries pop and the mixture thickens slightly, stirring frequently. Set aside.

2 In a food processor bowl combine the cream cheese, ¼ cup sugar, the egg, egg white, and vanilla. Process until smooth, scraping the side of bowl as necessary. Set aside.

3 Spray a 9-inch tart pan or pie plate with nonstick coating. Spray 1 phyllo sheet with nonstick coating. Fold the sheet in half crosswise to form a rectangle (about 13×9 inches). Gently press the folded sheet of phyllo into the prepared tart pan, allowing ends to extend over edge of pan. Spray with nonstick coating. Spray and fold another sheet of phyllo; place across first sheet in a crisscross fashion. Spray with nonstick coating. Repeat with remaining 2 sheets of phyllo. (If desired, turn under edges of phyllo to form a crust.) Bake in a 350° oven for 5 minutes.

4 Spoon cream cheese mixture into phyllo crust, spreading evenly. Spoon cranberry mixture over cream cheese mixture. Use a knife to marble mixture slightly.

5 Bake 20 to 25 minutes or until phyllo is lightly browned and filling is set. Let cool on a wire rack for 1 hour. Cover and chill 4 to 24 hours. If desired, before serving, drizzle edges of phyllo with melted white chocolate. Makes 10 servings.

Nutrition facts per serving: 192 calories, **7 g** total fat (**4 g** saturated fat), **40 mg** cholesterol, **142 mg** sodium, **18 g** carbohydrate, **1 g** fiber, **4 g** protein
Daily values: 8% vit. A, **3%** vit. C, **2%** calcium, **2%** iron

mango MOUSSE

How do you tell if a mango is ripe? Look for fruit that has a colorful green or gold skin with a blush of red or purple. Mangoes are ready to eat when they are soft enough to yield to gentle pressure.

Prep: 20 minutes
Freeze: 45 minutes
Chill: 2 hours

2 ripe mangoes, peeled, seeded, and chopped

2 tablespoons sugar

1 envelope unflavored gelatin

2 teaspoons lemon juice

1 8-ounce container frozen light whipped dessert topping, thawed

Exchanges: ½ Starch **1** Fruit **1** Fat

1 Place mangoes in a food processor bowl or blender container. Cover and process or blend until smooth. Add enough water to make 2 cups total. Transfer the mango mixture to a medium saucepan. Bring to boiling.

2 Meanwhile, in a large bowl stir together sugar and gelatin. Pour mango mixture over gelatin mixture; stir until gelatin dissolves. Stir in lemon juice. Cover; freeze for 45 to 60 minutes or until mixture mounds, stirring occasionally. Beat mango mixture with an electric mixer for 2 to 3 minutes or until thick and light. Fold in whipped topping.

3 Spoon or pipe mango mixture into 6 dessert dishes or parfait glasses. Cover and refrigerate for 2 hours or until set. Makes 6 servings.

Nutrition facts per serving: 149 calories, **5 g** total fat (**0 g** saturated fat), **1 mg** cholesterol, **31 mg** sodium, **25 g** carbohydrate, **2 g** fiber, **1 g** protein
Daily values: **31%** vit. A, **34%** vit. C, **2%** calcium, **1%** iron

Managing a Mango

Removing the large seed of a mango takes a little cutting know-how. Place the fruit on its blossom end and align a sharp knife slightly off-center of the stemmed end of the fruit. Slice down through the peel and flesh, next to the pit. Repeat on other side. Cut off the remaining flesh around the seed. Cut off the peel; cut the mango into pieces as directed.

mint chocolate CREAM PUFFS

These cream puffs are hard to resist! The small, hollow puffed pastries are filled with reduced-calorie chocolate pudding that's dressed up with a dash of peppermint extract.

Prep: 25 minutes
Bake: 30 minutes
Cool: 1 hour
Chill: 2 to 24 hours

Nonstick spray coating

½ **cup water**

2 **tablespoons margarine or butter**

½ **cup all-purpose flour**

2 **eggs**

1 **4-serving-size package reduced-calorie regular chocolate pudding mix**

⅛ **teaspoon peppermint extract**

1 **cup sliced strawberries**

Exchanges: 1½ Starch **½** Fat

❶ Spray a baking sheet with nonstick coating; set aside.

❷ In a small saucepan combine the water and margarine or butter. Bring to boiling. Add the flour all at once, stirring vigorously. Cook and stir until mixture forms a ball that doesn't separate. Remove from heat. Cool for 5 minutes. Add eggs, one at a time, beating after each addition until mixture is shiny and smooth. Drop dough in 8 mounds 3 inches apart on the prepared baking sheet.

❸ Bake in a 400° oven about 30 minutes or until golden brown. Cool completely on a wire rack. Split puffs; remove any soft dough from inside.

❹ Meanwhile, for the filling, prepare pudding mix according to package directions. Stir in the peppermint extract. Cover surface with plastic wrap. Chill for 2 to 24 hours.

❺ To serve, spoon about ¼ cup of the filling into the bottom half of each cream puff. Top with strawberries. Replace tops. Makes 8 servings.

Nutrition facts per serving: 126 calories, **4 g** total fat (**1 g** saturated fat), **53 mg** cholesterol, **225 mg** sodium, **20 g** carbohydrate, **1 g** fiber, **2 g** protein
Daily values: 5% vit. A, **17%** vit. C, **0%** calcium, **5%** iron

berry dessert NACHOS

Nachos for dessert? Sure! The homemade cinnamon and sugar crisps are layered with fresh berries, fat-free whipped topping, almonds, and grated chocolate.

Prep: 20 minutes
Bake: 5 minutes
Cool: 15 minutes

½ cup fat-free dairy sour cream

½ cup frozen fat-free whipped dessert topping, thawed

Low-calorie liquid sweetener equal to 2 tablespoons sugar

⅛ teaspoon ground cinnamon

6 7- to 8-inch fat-free flour tortillas

Butter-flavor nonstick spray coating

1 tablespoon sugar

⅛ teaspoon ground cinnamon

3 cups raspberries and/or blackberries

2 tablespoons sliced toasted almonds

1½ teaspoons grated semisweet chocolate

Exchanges: 1½ Starch 1 Fruit

① In a small bowl stir together sour cream, dessert topping, liquid sweetener, and ⅛ teaspoon cinnamon; cover and chill.

② Meanwhile, cut each tortilla into 8 wedges. Arrange wedges on 2 baking sheets. Lightly spray wedges with nonstick coating. In a small bowl stir together sugar and ⅛ teaspoon cinnamon; sprinkle over tortilla wedges. Bake in a 400° oven about 5 minutes or until crisp. Cool completely on a wire rack.

③ To serve, place 8 tortilla wedges on each of 6 dessert plates. Top with raspberries and/or blackberries and sour cream mixture. Sprinkle with almonds and grated chocolate. Makes 6 servings.

Nutrition facts per serving: 195 calories, **2 g** total fat (**0 g** saturated fat), **0 mg** cholesterol, **358 mg** sodium, **38 g** carbohydrate, **3 g** fiber, **5 g** protein
Daily values: 2% vit. A, **70%** vit. C, **4%** calcium, **9%** iron

melon ICE

Summer is synonymous with fresh melons. This honeydew melon ice will be a welcome treat when the temperature soars. It will satisfy your sweet tooth with a mere 47 calories and zero grams fat.

Prep: 25 minutes
Freeze: 8 hours
Stand: 5 minutes

1 **large ripe honeydew melon, seeded, peeled, and chopped (about 8 cups)**

2 **cups water**

⅓ **cup powdered fructose or 23 packets powdered fructose**

1 **teaspoon ground ginger**

Exchanges: 1 Fruit

1 In a large bowl combine melon, water, fructose, and ginger. Place melon mixture, a portion at a time, in a food processor bowl or blender container. Cover and process or blend until smooth.

2 Pour melon mixture into a 13×9×2-inch baking pan; cover with foil. Freeze about 4 hours or until almost firm. Break the mixture into small chunks; transfer to a chilled, large bowl. Beat with an electric mixer until slushy. Return mixture to pan. Cover; freeze at least 4 hours more.

3 Before serving, let stand at room temperature about 5 minutes. Makes sixteen ½-cup servings.

Nutrition facts per serving: 47 calories, **0 g** total fat (**0 g** saturated fat), **0 mg** cholesterol, **9 mg** sodium, **12 g** carbohydrate, **1 g** fiber, **0 g** protein
Daily values: 0% vit. A, **35%** vit. C, **0%** calcium, **0%** iron

lemon-BLUEBERRY FREEZE

Give yogurt a whirl! Place a blend of lemonade drink mix, blueberries, and vanilla yogurt in the freezer container of an ice cream freezer, and churn it into flavorful frozen yogurt. Simple, but tasty.

Prep: 10 minutes
Freeze: 25 minutes
Ripen: 4 hours

3 **cups prepared lemonade from sugar-free lemonade mix**

2 **cups fresh or frozen blueberries**

3 **tablespoons sugar**

2 **8-ounce cartons vanilla low-fat yogurt**

Exchanges: 1 Fruit

1 In a blender container or food processor bowl combine 1½ cups of the lemonade, the blueberries, and sugar. Cover and blend or process until smooth.

2 Place the yogurt in the freezer container of a 4-quart ice-cream freezer. Stir in berry mixture and remaining 1½ cups lemonade. Freeze mixture according to the manufacturer's directions. Ripen 4 hours. Makes twelve ½-cup servings.

Nutrition facts per serving: 62 calories, **1 g** total fat (**0 g** saturated fat), **2 mg** cholesterol, **25 mg** sodium, **13 g** carbohydrate, **1 g** fiber, **2 g** protein
Daily values: 1% vit. A, **5%** vit. C, **5%** calcium, **0%** iron

Fructose Facts

Found in fruits and honey, fructose is sweeter than any other type of sugar in an equal amount. It often is called high-fructose syrup or high-fructose corn syrup on food labels. These are very concentrated forms of fructose. Fructose can be purchased in a crystalline form or in individual packets. Fructose causes a lower rise in blood glucose than sucrose (table sugar) or starches. It is best to limit your intake of large amounts of this sweetener in the form of fructose-sweetened foods. If eaten often, fructose been shown to increase total cholesterol, triglycerides, and LDL cholesterol ("bad" cholesterol) levels. Moderation, as with regular sugar, is key.

lemon CREAM

This light, airy lemon cream is the ultimate in elegant desserts and is surprisingly easy to make. This tangy lemon dessert holds its shape with the help of gelatin, eggs, and light whipped topping.

Prep: 20 minutes
Ice bath: 35 minutes
Chill: 2 to 24 hours

¼ **cup sugar**

1 **envelope unflavored gelatin**

1½ **cups water**

2 **slightly beaten eggs**

1 **tablespoon finely shredded lemon peel**

⅓ **cup lemon juice**

½ **of an 8-ounce container frozen light whipped dessert topping, thawed**

Lemon peel strips (optional)

Exchanges: 1 Starch ½ Fat

1 In a medium saucepan combine the sugar and gelatin; stir in water. Cook and stir over medium heat until mixture bubbles and gelatin is dissolved. Gradually stir about half of the gelatin mixture into the slightly beaten eggs. Return the mixture to the saucepan. Cook, stirring constantly, over low heat for 2 to 3 minutes or until slightly thickened.

2 Transfer to a medium bowl. Stir in the shredded lemon peel and lemon juice. Chill in ice water about 20 minutes or just until the mixture thickens slightly, stirring occasionally.

3 Fold the whipped topping into the lemon mixture. Chill again in ice water about 15 minutes or just until mixture mounds, stirring occasionally.

4 Spoon into individual dessert dishes or soufflé dishes. Cover and chill at least 2 hours or until set. If desired, garnish with lemon peel strips. Makes six ½-cup servings.

Nutrition facts per serving: 107 calories, **4 g** total fat (**3 g** saturated fat), **71 mg** cholesterol, **37 mg** sodium, **15 g** carbohydrate, **0 g** fiber, **3 g** protein
Daily values: 5% vit. A, **13%** vit. C, **2%** calcium, **2%** iron

chocolate-CHERRY BISCOTTI

These Italian cookies are made by first baking the dough in a loaf, then slicing the loaf and baking the slices. The result is an ultra-crunchy cookie that is perfect for dipping into coffee.

Prep: 25 minutes
Bake: 18 minutes/16 minutes
Cool: 1 hour

Nonstick spray coating

¼ **cup margarine or butter**

½ **cup sugar**

1 **teaspoon baking powder**

¼ **teaspoon baking soda**

½ **cup refrigerated or frozen egg product, thawed**

½ **teaspoon vanilla**

2 **cups all-purpose flour**

¼ **cup unsweetened cocoa powder**

⅓ **cup finely chopped dried tart cherries**

Exchanges: ½ Starch

1 Spray a cookie sheet with nonstick coating; set aside.

2 In a medium bowl beat margarine or butter on medium speed with an electric mixer for 30 seconds. Add sugar, baking powder, and baking soda; beat until combined. Beat in egg product and vanilla. In a small bowl stir together flour and cocoa powder; beat as much of the flour mixture as you can into the margarine mixture. Stir in the remaining flour mixture and cherries.

3 On waxed paper, shape dough into two 12-inch-long logs. Place on prepared cookie sheet; flatten the logs slightly to 1½-inch width. Bake in a 375° oven for 18 to 20 minutes or until firm and a wooden toothpick inserted near the center of each log comes out clean. Cool on sheet for 1 hour.

4 Cut each log into ½-inch slices. Arrange the slices, cut sides down, on the cookie sheet. Bake in a 325° oven for 8 minutes; turn and bake for 8 minutes more or until crisp. Transfer cookies to a wire rack; cool. Makes 40 cookies.

Nutrition facts per cookie: 48 calories, **1 g** total fat (**0 g** saturated fat), **0 mg** cholesterol, **35 mg** sodium, **8 g** carbohydrate, **0 g** fiber, **1 g** protein
Daily values: **3**% vit. A, **0**% vit. C, **1**% calcium, **2**% iron

desserts & treats

206

spiced CORNMEAL COOKIES

These finger-shaped cookies contain cornmeal, which adds a bit of toasty crunch. Cinnamon and hazelnuts contribute spicy, sweet flavor, making these cookies the ultimate treat.

Prep: 30 minutes
Bake: 10 minutes

¼ **cup margarine or butter**

¾ **cup all-purpose flour**

¼ **cup yellow cornmeal**

¼ **cup sugar**

1 **egg white**

¼ **teaspoon finely shredded lemon peel**

¼ **teaspoon vanilla**

⅛ **teaspoon salt**

⅛ **teaspoon ground cinnamon**

2 **tablespoons finely chopped hazelnuts or almonds**

Exchanges: ½ Starch

1 In a large bowl beat the margarine or butter with an electric mixer on medium to high speed for 30 seconds. Add about half of the flour, the cornmeal, sugar, egg white, lemon peel, vanilla, salt, and cinnamon. Beat until combined. Beat or stir in remaining flour. Stir in hazelnuts or almonds.

2 Shape the dough into 24 fingers, about 2½ inches long. Place on an ungreased baking sheet. Bake in a 375° oven about 10 minutes or until the bottoms are golden. Transfer to a wire rack; cool. Makes 24 cookies.

Nutrition facts per cookie: 48 calories, **2 g** total fat (**0 g** saturated fat), **0 mg** cholesterol, **36 mg** sodium, **6 g** carbohydrate, **0 g** fiber, **1 g** protein
Daily values: 2% vit. A, **0%** vit. C, **0%** calcium, **1%** iron

How Sweet It Is

Each of the sugar substitutes on the market reacts differently in a recipe because of its unique chemical makeup. Sugar substitutes are concentrated in sweetness and best used in amounts smaller than the real thing. Some sugar replacers don't work well in baking because you use so much less than regular sugar, the replacer can't provide sufficient bulk. In these cases you can use them in place of part of the sugar.

Aspartame, one of the most popular sugar substitutes, isn't stable when heated and can't be used for cooking and baking, while acesulfame K is stable when heated (see page 220). For all sugar alternatives, read the labels to be sure you'll get the sweet reward you seek—with success.

desserts & treats

207

the basics

For anyone with diabetes, it is reassuring to know that the future gets brighter every day for managing the disease. Ongoing research provides people with the most up-to-date and effective treatment plans possible.

buying a book such as this one is a significant step in managing your health. It shows that you realize your own role in treating your disease. *You* are the star player on your diabetes treatment team. In fact, you have the most important role in managing your diabetes to live a long, healthy, and productive life.

To help you feel confident in managing diabetes, these pages bring you the latest basics about the disease—what it is, who is at risk, how it's diagnosed, and how it's treated. But the main focus is on eating well with diabetes. You will learn the role of food in managing your blood sugar levels. You'll also get the latest nutrition advice; tips for shopping, cooking, and eating out; and the basics of building a meal plan using the Exchange Lists for Meal Planning from the American Diabetes Association and The American Dietetic Association.

The recipes in this book prove that you can still eat great-tasting food. Best of all, the recipes are healthful, everyday family fare. There's no need to make separate meals for yourself or someone in your family who has diabetes. Main dishes, side dishes, snacks, desserts, and more—there are recipes for all tastes and all occasions.

diabetes BASICS

Diabetes Defined

To manage diabetes, it helps to understand how it affects your body. In all healthy people, the body turns food into glucose (blood sugar) to use for energy. Insulin, produced by the pancreas, is the hormone responsible for shuttling glucose into the body's cells where it is either used right away or stored for later use. With diabetes, however, high levels of glucose build up in the blood because either the pancreas doesn't produce enough insulin or the body can't use the insulin it does produce. Your treatment will depend on which problem you have. Diabetes is broken down into two categories: type 1 or type 2.

Type 1 Diabetes

Type 1 diabetes occurs when the body's immune system destroys the insulin-producing cells in the pancreas, usually leading to a total halt in insulin production. People with type 1 diabetes must take insulin shots daily or use an insulin pump (programmable pumps that automatically infuse insulin) to keep the blood glucose within normal range. Without insulin, blood glucose rises to dangerously high levels, which, if left untreated, can lead to coma or death. Type 1 most often occurs in children or young adults. Until recently, type 1 diabetes was called insulin-dependent or juvenile diabetes.

Type 1 diabetes often appears suddenly. Symptoms can include the following:

- high levels of sugar in the blood
- high levels of sugar in the urine
- frequent urination
- extreme hunger
- extreme thirst
- extreme weight loss
- weakness and fatigue
- moodiness and irritability
- nausea and vomiting

Type 2 Diabetes

In type 2, the pancreas produces some insulin, but a condition called insulin resistance causes the body's cells to "resist" insulin's message to let blood glucose inside the cells. This leads to high levels of glucose in the blood. Because people with type 2 diabetes often are overweight, treatment usually includes weight loss. Until recently, type 2 diabetes was called non-insulin dependent or adult-onset diabetes.

Often, type 2 diabetes develops slowly, and symptoms are mild. Symptoms include the following:

- increased thirst
- more frequent urination
- edginess, fatigue, and nausea
- increased appetite accompanied by weight loss
- repeated or hard-to-heal infections (for example, skin, gum, vaginal, or bladder)
- blurred vision
- tingling or numbness in the hands or feet
- dry, itchy skin

Who's at Risk for Diabetes?

People who are at risk for diabetes may:

- be 45 years old or older
- be overweight
- have a close relative with diabetes, such as a father, mother, sister, or brother
- be of African-American, Latino, Native American, or Asian descent
- have delivered a baby weighing more than 9 pounds or had gestational diabetes during pregnancy
- have high blood pressure
- have "good" (HDL) cholesterol that is too low (less than 35 mg/dl), and triglycerides (another type of fat in the blood) that are too high (greater than 250 mg/dl)
- have had a past blood sugar test that was above normal, but not high enough to result in a diagnosis of diabetes

Diagnosing Diabetes

In 1997, the American Diabetes Association released new guidelines for diabetes screening. The goal of these guidelines is to detect the disease as early as possible so that the onset of serious complications can be prevented or postponed. Left untreated, diabetes can lead to serious complications such as heart disease, stroke, high blood pressure, blindness, kidney disease, and nerve damage.

The 1997 guidelines recommended diabetes screening for everyone aged 45 and older. However, a 1998 study by the Center for Disease Control suggests that screening all adults aged 25 and older would help in diagnosing diabetes almost six years earlier. In any case, if test results are normal, screening should be repeated every three years. If you're at high risk for diabetes, your doctor may begin testing you at a younger age or more often than every three years.

Three tests are used to screen for diabetes. Your doctor will determine which test is best for you. Diabetes is present when your blood glucose is greater than or equal to the levels described below after receiving one of these tests on two different days:

- a fasting blood glucose test result of 126 milligrams per deciliter (mg/dl)—the amount of glucose in 100 milliliters of blood. (Previously, a test result of 140 mg/dl indicated diabetes.) Fasting means you can't eat any food or drink calorie-containing beverages at least 8 hours before the test.

- a blood glucose test result of 200 mg/dl taken at any time of day, regardless of when you last ate, along with common diabetes symptoms such as increased urination and thirst, and unexplained weight loss.

- an oral glucose tolerance test result of 200 mg/dl in a blood sample taken two hours after you drink glucose.

There is no cure for diabetes, but keeping blood glucose near normal can help reduce the risk of eye problems by up to 76 percent, nerve damage by 60 percent, and severe kidney problems by 54 percent.

Treating Diabetes—You Are in Control

If you have diabetes, you can take positive steps to keep your blood glucose as normal as possible, which will help you feel good and delay or prevent complications. Your health care team will work with you to develop a treatment plan—consisting of a healthful diet, physical activity, and, if necessary, medication—that's right for you, your lifestyle, and your type of diabetes. Though your treatment plan will be customized for you, treating each type of diabetes generally involves the following:

Type 1 Diabetes. As previously noted, in type 1 diabetes, the pancreas does not produce insulin, which makes it challenging to control blood sugar. Typically, a treatment plan includes a carefully designed diet of three meals and at least two snacks

Gestational Diabetes—A Temporary Condition

Gestational diabetes occurs when blood glucose levels rise above normal during pregnancy. After delivery, blood glucose usually returns to normal, though women who have gestational diabetes are at greater risk for developing type 2 diabetes later in life. Women most at risk for gestational diabetes are those who are overweight or have a family history of the disease. Left uncontrolled, gestational diabetes can lead to high blood pressure or a large baby that may complicate delivery. Most pregnant women are routinely tested for the condition. If you test positive, your doctor and registered dietitian will work closely with you to keep your blood glucose under control.

daily, planned physical activity, home blood glucose testing several times a day, and multiple daily insulin injections. Meals and snacks are timed to match the effect of the insulin at its strongest level.

Type 2 Diabetes. Many people with type 2 diabetes can control it without medication by following a specially designed meal plan and engaging in routine physical activity. Because 9 out of 10 people newly

medication, need to lose weight, or have other health problems, such as heart disease or high blood pressure. Best of all, your meal plan will suit your lifestyle and include the foods you like. There's no need for special foods or "diabetic" food products.

The dietary guidelines for people with diabetes are excellent for anyone interested in healthful eating. They are based on a plan that:

Blood Glucose Monitoring

Whether you have type 1 or type 2 diabetes, it's important to test your blood glucose, especially if you are taking insulin shots or oral medication. Usually, you test your blood glucose before each meal to determine whether it is in the high, low, or normal range. Your health care practitioner will teach you how to measure your blood glucose with a simple finger-prick test, and how to adjust your food intake, physical activity, or medication when your blood glucose is too high or low. Good diabetes control means keeping your blood glucose level as close to normal as possible. The normal range before eating is 70 to110 mg/dl. Your doctor will discuss the best goals for you.

- helps you achieve and maintain a healthful weight. If you have type 2 diabetes and are overweight, losing even 10 or 20 pounds can help bring your blood glucose into the normal range and lower your blood cholesterol and blood pressure. If you are taking insulin or oral diabetes medication, losing weight may allow you to decrease your medication.

diagnosed with type 2 diabetes are overweight, the meal plan may be designed to help in weight loss. It also will help achieve or maintain healthy blood cholesterol and blood pressure levels. Home blood glucose testing and sometimes oral medication and/or insulin also are part of treating type 2 diabetes.

food FACTOR

A More Flexible Approach

Following a healthful meal plan is one of the most important steps you can take to keep your blood glucose under control. In years past, people with diabetes were expected to follow a strict diet regimen with little regard for individual food likes and dislikes. Today, experts on diabetes know that a "one-size-fits-all" diet doesn't work—and, fortunately, isn't necessary.

A registered dietitian will custom-design a meal plan that's just right for you. The plan will reflect whether you are taking insulin shots or oral diabetes

- includes a wide variety of foods. Your body needs more than 40 different nutrients for good health, but it's difficult to get them if you eat the same few foods all the time. Besides, eating many different foods is enjoyable!
- includes plenty of grains, vegetables, and fruits. These foods supply important vitamins, minerals, and fiber, and, when eaten as part of a low-fat diet, may help reduce the risk of heart disease and cancer.
- is low in fat, saturated fat, and cholesterol. To reduce the risk of heart disease, health experts

recommend following an eating plan that averages no more than 30 percent of total daily calories from fat, less than 10 percent of calories from saturated fat, and no more than 300 milligrams of cholesterol. This guideline is very important for people with diabetes, who have a greater risk for heart disease.

- is moderate in salt and sodium. Eating too much sodium (one of the components that makes up salt) increases blood pressure in some people. Health experts recommend limiting sodium to 2,400 mg per day. Your dietitian will determine a daily sodium level based on your needs.
- is moderate in sugar. Surprised? Some sugar can be part of a healthful diabetes meal plan. Read more about sugar and diabetes in the box above.

The chart below shows the recommended breakdown of the major nutrients and how they should be distributed in the diet. The calories per gram of weight for each nutrient are in parentheses.

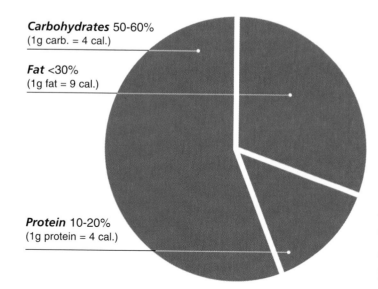

Carbohydrates 50-60%
(1g carb. = 4 cal.)

Fat <30%
(1g fat = 9 cal.)

Protein 10-20%
(1g protein = 4 cal.)

The Sweet Truth About Sugar

Not long ago, people with diabetes were cautioned to avoid table sugar (sucrose) because this simple carbohydrate was thought to cause a greater rise in blood glucose than the complex carbohydrates found in starchy foods such as potatoes and bread.

But the sugar bowl is no longer off limits. Several research studies have shown that simple carbohydrates like sugar don't raise blood glucose any higher or faster than other types of carbohydrates. The American Diabetes Association now says that you can include some sugar in your meal plan as long as you count it as part of your total carbohydrates for the day.

Keep in mind, though, that sugar contains calories but few vitamins, minerals, or other nutrients. Many sugary desserts such as ice cream, cake, and pie also contain large amounts of fat (and calories), which can increase your risk for heart disease. Talk to your dietitian for more specifics on occasionally including sugar in your diabetes meal plan.

Putting Together a Meal Plan

Many people with diabetes follow a diet that uses the Exchange Lists for Meal Planning, a system designed by the American Diabetes Association and The American Dietetic Association. If you decide to follow this system, your registered dietitian will work with you to develop a "pattern" of exchanges—or meal plan—that is right for you and your particular needs.

Your individualized meal plan will help you know what, how much, and when to eat. It also will be nutritionally balanced to provide the vitamins, minerals, and fiber you need. It will limit the amount of fat, saturated fat, cholesterol, and sodium. If you need to lose weight, it will contain the right number of calories to help you lose at a safe pace. If your weight is appropriate for your height and build, the calories will be based on maintaining that weight.

Your meal plan also will guide you in eating the right amounts of three major nutrients found in foods—carbohydrates, protein, and fat. The calories from all three nutrients affect your blood glucose level, but carbohydrates affect it most. Generally, your breakdown for the day will look like the chart at left.

Food Exchanges 101

If using food exchanges is new to you, this section will introduce you to the basics. If you're an "exchange pro," consider this a refresher course. With the exchange system, foods are divided into these general categories:

- the Carbohydrate Group, which contains the starch, fruit, milk, other carbohydrates, and vegetable lists.
- the Meat and Meat Substitutes Group (protein), which is divided into very lean, lean, medium-fat, and high-fat lists.
- the Fat Group, which divides the fats into monounsaturated, polyunsaturated, and saturated.

Each list includes foods that have about the same number of calories and amounts of carbohydrate, protein, and fat. One serving of a food is called an "exchange" because you can swap it for one serving of any other food or beverage on that list. For example, from the starch list, you could exchange a small dinner roll for ⅓ cup of cooked brown rice or a small baked potato. Each food exchange list contains many choices so you can enjoy a variety of foods each day.

You'll also find a free foods list, which shows foods that contain few calories when eaten in the amounts

One starch exchange is

1 ounce of a bread product, such as 1 slice of bread or ½ of a small bagel;

½ cup of cooked cereal, grain, pasta, or starchy vegetable such as corn; or

¾ to 1 ounce of most snack foods.

For good health, eat at least 6 exchanges daily from the starch list.

Starch Exchange Tips

- Most foods from the starch list provide B vitamins and iron. Whole grains and beans, peas, and lentils are good sources of fiber.
- Choose starches made with little or no added fat most often.
- Count one serving of starchy vegetables (such as corn, potatoes, and peas) made with fat as 1 starch exchange and 1 fat exchange.
- Use the "Starchy Foods Prepared with Fat" section of the starch list (see page 225) to select foods such as French-fried potatoes, microwave popcorn, and muffins. A serving of these foods counts as 1 starch exchange and 1 fat exchange.

About 95 percent (15.3 million people) of Americans with diabetes have type 2. Just under 800,000 new diabetes cases are diagnosed each year.

indicated, and a combination foods list, which helps you fit foods composed of more than one type of food exchange into your meal plan.

General serving sizes and tips on using each food exchange list follows. Detailed serving sizes for each list are located on pages 224 to 231.

Starch List

Foods in the starch list include bread, cereals, grains, pasta, starchy vegetables, crackers, snacks, and cooked dried beans, peas, and lentils. One serving of foods from this list contains about 80 calories, 15 grams of carbohydrate, 3 grams of protein, and 0 to 1 gram of fat.

- One serving of beans, peas, and lentils counts as 1 starch exchange and 1 very lean meat exchange. These foods also are found on the meat and meat substitutes list.

Fruit List

Fruit is the perfect choice when your sweet tooth strikes. Fruit supplies you with vitamins A and C, potassium, and fiber, all wrapped up in a handy, fat-free package. Fruits (and grains and vegetables) also contain phytochemicals—plant compounds that may protect against heart disease and cancer.

One fruit exchange supplies about 60 calories and 15 grams of carbohydrate. The fruit list includes fresh, frozen, canned, and dried fruits, as well as fruit juices.

One fruit exchanges is

1 small to medium piece of fresh fruit, such as an apple or orange;

½ cup of canned or fresh fruit or fruit juice; or

¼ cup of dried fruit.

For good health, eat 2 to 4 exchanges daily from the fruit list.

Fruit Exchange Tips

- Frequently select deep yellow or orange fruits (cantaloupe, apricots, peaches, or mangoes) and "high C" options (oranges, grapefruits, strawberries, or kiwi).
- Exchanges for canned fruit are based on fruits labeled "no added sugar" or fruit packed in juice or extra light syrup. All these contain about the same amount of carbohydrate per serving.
- Serving sizes for canned fruit include the fruit and a small amount of juice.
- Count ½ cup of cranberries or rhubarb sweetened with sugar substitute as free foods.
- Boost fiber by opting for whole fruit more often than juice.

Milk List

Milk and yogurt are excellent sources of calcium, the nutrient you need for strong, healthy bones. Milk products also provide protein, phosphorous, magnesium, and vitamins A, D, B-12, and riboflavin. Because the fat and calorie content of milk products varies, the exchanges on this list are divided into the three groups shown below:

	Carbohydrate	Protein	Fat	Calories
Fat-Free/Low-Fat	12g	8g	0-3g	90
Reduced-Fat	12g	8g	5g	120
Whole	12g	8g	8g	150

One milk exchange is

1 cup of milk; or

¾ cup of plain yogurt or 1 cup of yogurt sweetened with sugar substitute.

For good health, eat or drink 2 to 3 exchanges daily from the milk list.

Milk Exchange Tips

- Keep calories, fat, and saturated fat at a minimum by selecting from the fat-free/low-fat milk group most often.
- Cheeses are found on the meat list; cream, half-and-half, and cream cheese are found on the fat list; non-dairy creamers are found on the free foods list.
- Rice milk is on the starch list; soy milk is on the medium-fat meat list.
- Chocolate milk, low-fat yogurt with fruit, ice cream, and frozen yogurt are on the other carbohydrates list.

Other Carbohydrates List

Can desserts and snack foods be part of your diabetes meal plan? Yes, with some careful planning and smart substitutions. The other carbohydrates list helps you fit occasional sweet treats such as cakes, cookies, ice cream, and pie, as well as higher-fat snacks such as potato chips and tortilla chips, into your meal plan. One exchange from this list contains about 15 grams of carbohydrate.

Other Carbohydrates Exchange Tips

- You may occasionally substitute foods from the other carbohydrates list for a starch, fruit, or milk exchange on your meal plan.
- Foods on this list are not nutrient dense foods; practice moderation when choosing from this list.

Vegetable List

Vegetables are low in calories and contain a minimal amount of fat. They are also loaded with vitamins A and C, folic acid, iron, magnesium, and fiber. One vegetable exchange contains about 5 grams of carbohydrate, 2 grams of protein, and 25 calories.

One teaspoon of sugar contains 16 calories and 4 grams of carbohydrate. About 4 teaspoons of sugar equal one carbohydrate exchange.

- Note serving sizes for foods on this list. They contain added sugars or fat so serving sizes are often small.
- Some choices count as 1 or more carbohydrate and fat exchanges. Adjust your meal plan accordingly.
- Smaller servings of fat-free salad dressings are found on the free foods list.

One vegetable exchange is

1 cup of raw vegetables such as lettuce, spinach, or broccoli flowerets; or

½ cup of cooked vegetables or vegetable juice.

For good health, eat 3 to 5 vegetable exchanges daily.

Carbohydrate Counting

People with either type 1 or type 2 diabetes may use carbohydrate counting to manage what they eat and control their blood glucose. Simply put, you keep track of the number of carbohydrate grams you eat each day. This method is based on the fact that carbohydrates have a profound affect on blood glucose.

You and a registered dietitian will start out by designing a meal plan that shows you how many grams of carbohydrate to eat at each meal and snack to keep your blood glucose close to normal. You then choose foods that total the specified number of carbohydrates for each meal and snack.

How do you know how many grams of carbohydrate are in foods? The exchange lists (see pages 224 to 231) show the average amount of carbohydrates for a serving of each food on the lists. The "nutrition facts" panel on packaged foods also lists the grams of carbohydrates in a serving. In addition, books listing carbohydrate counts for foods are available in bookstores. The recipes in this book lists grams of carbohydrate in one serving.

Many people with diabetes find carbohydrate counting simpler to use than the exchange system and say it allows more food choices and better blood glucose control. However, strictly monitoring blood glucose, measuring portion sizes, and eating a nutritious, balanced diet with the appropriate number of calories and amount of fat and other nutrients are just some of the essential steps to making carbohydrate counting work. Talk to a registered dietitian to see if it's right for you.

Vegetable Exchange Tips

- The vegetable exchanges on this list contain only small amounts of calories and carbohydrates, so you can eat 1 or 2 exchanges at a meal or snack without counting them. If you eat 3 or more vegetable exchanges at a time, count them as 1 carbohydrate choice (15 grams carbohydrate).
- Several times weekly choose dark green, leafy vegetables such as spinach, romaine lettuce, broccoli, and cabbage, and deep yellow and orange varieties such as carrots and red peppers (also, sweet potatoes and acorn squash from the starch list).
- For vitamin C, select tomatoes, Brussels sprouts, greens, sweet or hot peppers, broccoli, and cauliflower.
- One vegetable exchange contains 1 to 4 grams of fiber.

Meat and Meat Substitutes List

Meat, poultry, fish, eggs, cheese, peanut butter, and tofu belong on the meat and meat substitutes list because they are excellent sources of protein, B vitamins, iron, and zinc. Because the fat and calorie content of meat products varies, the exchanges on this list are divided into four groups. One exchange (one ounce) from each group includes:

	Carbohydrate	Protein	Fat	Calories
Very lean	—	7g	0-1g	35
Lean	—	7g	3g	55
Medium fat	—	7g	5g	75
High fat	—	7g	8g	100

One meat exchange is

1 ounce cooked meat, poultry, or fish;

1 ounce cheese;

1 egg;

½ cup cooked dried beans, peas, or lentils;

2 tablespoons peanut butter; or

3 slices bacon.

For good health, eat 4 to 6 exchanges daily from the meat and meat substitutes list.

Meat Exchange Tips

• One ounce of cooked lean meat, poultry, or fish is about the size of a matchbox; 3 ounces is the size of a deck of cards. One ounce of cheese is about the size of a 1-inch cube.

• A small chicken leg or thigh, or ½ cup cottage cheese or tuna equals 2 meat exchanges.

• A small hamburger, ½ of a whole chicken breast, a medium pork chop, or one unbreaded fish fillet equals 3 meat exchanges.

• Choose from selections on the high-fat meat list no more than three times per week.

• An exchange of dried beans, peas, or lentils counts as 1 very lean meat exchange and 1 starch exchange.

• Two tablespoons of peanut butter or a hot dog counts as 1 high-fat meat exchange.

Smaller serving sizes of peanut butter and bacon are counted as fat exchanges instead of meat exchanges (see Fat list).

Fat List

Fat can fool you: It packs a big calorie punch in a small package. Often hidden in foods, calorie-dense fats can add extra pounds quickly or foil your weight loss efforts if you aren't careful. Eating too much fat, especially saturated fat, can also increase your risk for heart disease and some cancers. Each fat exchange provides about 5 grams of fat and 45 calories.

One fat exchange is

1 teaspoon vegetable oil, regular margarine, butter, or mayonnaise;

1 tablespoon regular salad dressing;

10 peanuts, 6 almonds or cashews, or 4 pecan or walnut halves;

2 teaspoons peanut butter; or

1 slice bacon.

Your dietitian will determine the best number of fat exchanges to include in your daily meal plan.

Fat Exchange Tips

• Foods in the fat list are divided into monounsaturated, polyunsaturated, and saturated fats. Eating small amounts of monounsaturated and polyunsaturated fats may help protect against heart disease, so spend your fat exchanges on these fats most often.

• Measure fat list foods carefully to avoid extra calories.

• Avocados, olives, and coconut are on the fat list.

Exchange Essentials

- Serving sizes for foods on the exchange lists are usually given for the cooked measure.
- Be accurate with portion sizes. Misjudging portions can impact your blood glucose and your weight. Carefully note the serving sizes on the exchange lists and on food labels. Weigh and measure your food until you can accurately "eyeball" portions, especially when you add a new food to your meal plan.
- Each exchange list contains a wide array of choices. Vary your selections to make sure you get a variety of nutrients—and to please your palate!
- Because exchanges from the starch, fruit, and milk lists contain about the same amount of carbohydrates, you may exchange choices from these groups within your meal plan. But be careful about missing out on nutrients. For instance, if you often trade your milk exchanges for starches or fruits, you may fall short on calcium.
- Foods such as beans, peas, lentils, bacon, and peanut butter are on two lists so you can enjoy more flexibility when planning meals.

- Cream, half-and-half, and cream cheese also are on this list.
- Larger serving sizes of peanut butter and bacon are counted as high-fat meat exchanges instead of fat exchanges (see meat list).
- Fat-free versions of margarine, salad dressing, mayonnaise, sour cream, and cream cheese are on the free foods list.
- Nonstick cooking spray, nondairy creamers, and whipped topping are also on the free foods list.

free foods listed with a serving size. Be sure to eat them throughout the day, rather than all at once, or they could affect your blood glucose. Eat all you like of foods listed without a serving size.

Combination Foods List

"Mixed" foods such as casseroles, soups, pizza, and many of the recipes from this book combine foods from two or more of the food exchange lists. For recipes in this book, food exchanges are calculated for you and appear above each recipe.

You will find exchanges for several mixed foods on the combination foods list. Many food manufacturers list exchanges right on the package.

For foods not on this list or for your own recipes, estimate exchanges by determining what portion of an exchange each ingredient represents. For example, a serving of stew may contain 2 ounces of cooked lean beef (2 lean meat exchanges), ½ cup of potato (1 starch exchange), and ½ cup of carrots (1 vegetable exchange).

The chart on page 218 helps you plan meals by showing the amount of carbohydrate, protein, fat, and calories for one exchange from each list.

Nearly 16 million Americans have diabetes. Of these, one-half—8 million people—don't know they have diabetes. About 5 percent of Americans with diabetes have type 1 (700,000 people).

The Free Foods List

Some things in life are free! The free foods list contains dozens of foods and drinks that contain less than 20 calories or less than 5 grams of carbohydrate per serving. Feel free to enjoy up to three daily servings of

food selection TIPS

Eating right with diabetes can be easy and enjoyable when you take advantage of the following tips. They'll help you choose foods that are low in fat and sodium, yet high in fiber, without sacrificing good taste. If you need to lose weight, they'll help you trim calories, too.

At the Supermarket

- Learn to read labels. The "nutrition facts" label helps you track how much fat, saturated fat, cholesterol, sodium, fiber, and important nutrients you eat. The label also lists the number of calories and grams of carbohydrate, protein, and fat in a serving of food. You can use these numbers to calculate the exchanges in a serving of food. Some food manufacturers list the exchanges on the package. (The nutrition facts per serving also are listed for every recipe in this book.) Supermarkets often show nutrition information for fresh meat, poultry, seafood, vegetables, and fruits on posters or take-home brochures in each department.
- Think "lean." Choose cuts of meat with the words "round" or "loin" in the name (for example, ground round or pork tenderloin), skinless poultry, fish, and dry beans, peas, and lentils.
- Buy fat-free and low-fat milk and yogurt. Taste-test different types of reduced-fat cheese to find ones you like.
- Stock up on tasty low-fat snacks such as pretzels, air-popped popcorn, flavored rice cakes, and baked bagel chips.
- Choose soft-style margarines with liquid vegetable oil as the first ingredient. Tub or liquid margarines have less saturated fat than stick margarines.
- Get big fat savings! Try reduced-fat or fat-free sour cream, cream cheese, mayonnaise, salad dressing, margarine, and tartar sauce. Experiment to find the best-tasting brands.
- Select frozen vegetables made without butter or sauces.
- Look for reduced-sodium Worcestershire and soy sauce; canned broth, beans, and soups; bouillon cubes; luncheon meats; bacon; and ham.
- Choose whole-grain breads and crackers to boost fiber. The first ingredient should be whole wheat or another type of whole-grain flour.
- Choose a high-fiber cereal.

In the Kitchen

- Trim all visible fat from meat or poultry. Use tuna packed in water, not oil.
- Sauté foods in cooking spray, low-sodium broth, or fruit juice.
- Bake, broil, grill, poach, steam, or microwave foods instead of frying.
- Cook and bake with a monounsaturated oil such as olive, canola, or peanut oil.

Exchange List for Meal Planning

	Carbohydrate	Protein	Fat	Calories
Carbohydrate Group				
Starch	15g	3g	0 to 1g	80
Fruit	15g	—	—	60
Milk				
Fat free	12g	8g	0 to 3g	90
Reduced fat	12g	8g	5g	120
Whole	12g	8g	8g	150
Other carbohydrates	15g	varies	varies	varies
Vegetables	5g	2g	—	25
Meat and Meat Substitute Group				
Very lean	—	7g	0 to 1g	35
Lean	—	7g	3g	55
Medium fat	—	7g	5g	75
High fat	—	7g	8g	100
Fat Group	—	—	5g	45

- Use evaporated fat-free milk in place of whole milk or cream in sauces, soups, and baked goods.
- Omit the butter, margarine, or cooking oil called for in package directions for rice or pasta.
- Cut cholesterol by substituting two egg whites or ¼ cup egg substitute for one whole egg in recipes.
- Serve bean-based dishes such as vegetable chili or a hearty bean soup once or twice a week for a meal that is low in fat, saturated fat, and cholesterol (hold the high-fat cheeses or sour cream), and high in fiber.

- about their menu items. Ask for it.
- Enjoy French fries, but order the smallest size or split them with a friend.
- Minimize calories and fat by choosing fast-food items such as grilled chicken sandwiches and small burgers.
- Look for healthy choices. Some fast-food restaurants offer baked potatoes and salads with reduced- or low-calorie dressing.
- Order foods that are baked, broiled, grilled, or steamed instead of fried.
- Ask to have your food prepared without added fat or added salt.
- Request salad dressings, sauces, and gravies on the side.
- Squeeze fresh lemon on chicken, fish, and vegetables for a tangy flavor.
- Ask for sugar substitutes and diet drinks.

The exact causes of diabetes are not known, but it is known that it runs in families that have a history of the disease.

- Replace high-fat ingredients in soups, sauces, and dips such as sour cream, yogurt, and mayonnaise, with reduced-fat counterparts.
- Substitute whole wheat flour for up to half of the all-purpose flour called for in a recipe to add fiber to baked goods.
- Add salt either during cooking or at the table—not both. Either way, measure the amount you use.
- Reduce the salt in canned vegetables by draining them in a colander, then rinsing with tap water.

At Restaurants

- Choose wisely at fast-food restaurants. Fast foods can occasionally be part of your meal plan. Many fast-food restaurants provide a brochure listing food exchanges and other nutrition information

- Order the fruit cup or melon wedge from the appetizer list for dessert.
- Beware of gigantic portions. Eat about the same amount you usually eat at home and bring the rest home to enjoy tomorrow.

How Sugar Substitutes Measure Up

Though some sugar can be part of a healthful diabetes meal plan, as discussed, you may still choose to use sugar substitutes (artificial sweeteners) and the many foods that contain them such as yogurt, ice cream, and soft drinks. When appropriate, many of the dessert recipes in this cookbook give you the option to use a sugar substitute.

Sugar substitutes can add flexibility to your meal plan because they sweeten foods without adding calories and don't affect your blood glucose level. Sugar substitutes are "free" foods, so they don't use up any of your daily carbohydrate allotment, making more room for other carbohydrate-containing foods. Here are the facts on four sugar substitutes.

Saccharin is found in soft drinks, chewing gum, and several brands of tabletop sweeteners including Sweet 'n' Low, Sweet 10, Sugar Twin, and SweetMate. Saccharin can be used to sweeten both hot and cold foods. Some studies suggest that large amounts of saccharin cause cancer in laboratory animals, though no evidence shows this same effect in humans. The American Diabetes Association recommends that

Sugar By Any Other Name...

... is just as sweet! Sugar is found naturally in grains, legumes, milk, vegetables, and fruits, but is best known for the pleasing sweetness it provides when added to goodies such as cakes, cookies, and candy. Surprise! Sugar also is added to such savory foods as salad dressings and tomato products. In fact, bread just isn't the same without the addition of some sugar.

The names below are all types of sugar. The ingredients listed on food packages are shown in descending order by weight, from the highest to the least amount. A food may be high in sugar if one of these names is the first or second ingredient or if several types appear on the list.

- high-fructose corn syrup
- fruit juice concentrate
- glucose (dextrose)
- sugar (sucrose)
- corn sweetener
- honey
- invert sugar
- molasses
- corn syrup
- brown sugar
- lactose
- raw sugar
- fructose
- syrup
- maltose

foods at the end of cooking. People with the rare genetic disorder phenylketonuria (PKU) should avoid products made with aspartame.

Acesulfame K is used to sweeten desserts, candy, gum, and beverages, and in the tabletop sweetener Sweet One. You can use Acesulfame K in cooking and baking, but it won't provide the same texture, volume, or browning as sugar.

Sucralose is a new heat-resistant sweetener that should be widely available in the year 2000. Look for it in foods such as desserts, beverages, and tabletop sweeteners. Sucralose can be used in cooking and baking.

A single packet of some sugar substitutes contains the sweetening power of two teaspoons of sugar. Check the package for specifics.

pregnant women avoid heavy use of saccharin.

Aspartame (often listed as NutraSweet on ingredients lists) is used in more than 6,000 food and beverage products, as well as in the tabletop sweetener Equal. Aspartame loses its sweetness when heated for a long time, although you can add it to

The Physical Activity Factor

Many good things can be said about physical activity. In fact, it is as important as any component of your overall treatment. Physical activity leads to better blood glucose control by helping your body use insulin efficiently and burn calories, making it easier to achieve or maintain a healthful weight. In addition, it reduces risk for heart disease, high blood pressure, and colon cancer; improves circulation; strengthens bones, muscles, and joints; increases energy; and enhances your sense of well-being. With all those benefits, it's clear why physical activity is an essential—and enjoyable—part of a diabetes treatment plan.

If you've been a couch potato for quite some time, hold on before donning your running shoes and dashing out the door. People with diabetes must take some special steps before beginning a physical activity routine.

Get an "activity prescription" from your doctor. This plan will get you started on a regular plan that includes the best type and amount of physical activity for you. Your plan takes into account your current fitness level, the timing of your meal plan and diabetes medication, and any special health concerns. For instance, if you have eye or blood vessel problems, your doctor will advise you on which activities are safe.

What types of activities are best? You don't have to huff and puff at the gym to benefit. The best activity for you is one you like doing and will stick with. Many people enjoy walking, bicycling, golfing, or swimming. As you become more fit, you might try

If you haven't been active for a while, start out slowly. For instance, taking a 10-minute walk after dinner a few nights a week is a good way to start. But even such everyday activities as gardening, mowing the lawn, washing windows, and vigorous housecleaning count toward your 30-minute total.

Weight Loss and Activity

If your doctor advises you to lose weight, regular physical activity can help you reach that goal faster than dieting alone. As discussed, 30 minutes of activity on most—and preferably all—days is the key. The list below shows how long it takes to burn 100 calories. Variety helps keep your motivation high. So, try to vary the types of activities you do daily.

Activity	Minutes to Burn 100 Calories*
Aerobic dancing	14
Bicycling (10 mph)	14
Brisk walking (3½ mph)	21
Gardening	17
Golf, pulling clubs	17
Running (6 mph)	8½
Swimming laps	10½

*Based on 150-pound person.

To Keep Blood Glucose Steady

- Eat meals and snacks at about the same time each day.
- Eat about the same amount of food each day.
- Don't skip meals or snacks.
- See a registered dietitian often to see if your meal plan needs adjusting.

more challenging activities such as rollerblading, step aerobics, or cross-country skiing. Always talk with your doctor before changing your routine.

How much physical activity is enough? Health experts agree that you can reap benefits from as little as 30 minutes of moderate activity on most—and preferably all—days. You don't even have to get your "daily 30" all at one time—you can accumulate it in 10-minute chunks of activity throughout the day.

diabetes DIALOGUE

Q I have high blood pressure and need to limit the sodium in my diet. Do I have to give up foods that are high in sodium such as pickles or canned soup?

A No, not if you're a savvy meal planner. Following a low-sodium diet doesn't mean every food you eat has to be low in sodium. What's important is how much sodium you consume for the whole day.

If you include a serving of a high-sodium food in your meal plan, you can balance it by making the rest of your food choices low in sodium so you don't exceed your total for the day. You can use this method to balance high-fat or high-cholesterol foods in your meal plan, too. The nutrition facts label is a great tool to help you follow the nutrition guidelines in your meal plan. The recipes in this book also include reduced-sodium products to help keep you within your guidelines.

Q I heard that chromium picolinate supplements can bring down blood glucose levels in people with diabetes? Should I take them?

A Chromium works with insulin to help your body use blood glucose for energy. A recent study of people with type 2 diabetes in China showed that taking large amounts (1,000 micrograms daily) of chromium picolinate resulted in significant reductions in blood glucose levels. But don't rush out and buy those supplements yet! More research is needed before definite conclusions are drawn.

The Chinese eat and live differently from North Americans and could have different levels of chromium in their bodies. Americans may not experience the same results. In fact, similar studies conducted in the United States and Canada generally do not show the same favorable results. Bottom line? The safety of taking chromium picolinate supplements over extended periods of time is not known.

For Americans, 50 to 200 micrograms of chromium daily are considered safe and adequate, and deficiencies are rare. Eating a variety of foods, including chromium-rich foods such as whole grains, peas, meat, cheese, and eggs, helps you get enough of this mineral.

Q Can I drink alcohol if I have diabetes?

A Talk with your doctor to see whether drinking alcohol is OK for you. Generally, people with diabetes can enjoy an occasional drink if their blood glucose is well controlled and they don't have other medical conditions that prohibit drinking.

If you get the "all clear" from your doctor, drink only in moderation. That means no more than one drink a day for women and two drinks a day for men (one drink = 12 ounces beer, 5 ounces wine, or 1½ ounces 80-proof distilled spirits). People who take insulin should not omit any foods to accommodate alcohol. It should be regarded as an addition to the meal plan. People who don't take insulin and are watching their weight usually are instructed to substitute one alcoholic drink for two

Because the onset of type 2 diabetes often is gradual, people may have it several years before they're diagnosed, meaning that high blood sugar levels are causing damage to blood vessels before treatment ever begins.

fat exchanges or an equal amount of fat calories. Never drink alcohol on an empty stomach—your blood glucose can go too low. Your registered dietitian will help you safely include alcohol in your meal plan.

Q I know fiber is important. But how much fiber do I need each day?

A The recommendation for people with diabetes is the same as for the general population—20 to 35 grams of fiber each day. Fiber comes in two forms: insoluble and soluble. Try to eat both types each day.

Insoluble fiber helps keep your bowels regular and may protect against colon cancer. Good sources of insoluble fiber are whole wheat bread, bran cereals, and many vegetables and fruits.

Soluble fiber may help reduce heart disease when included in a low-fat diet. Though not conclusive, some research suggests that eating soluble fiber-rich foods may help control blood glucose in people with diabetes, possibly by slowing down digestion so glucose from food is absorbed more slowly. Good sources of soluble fiber are oatmeal, oat bran, psyllium-containing cereals, dried beans and peas, lentils, barley, carrots, and apples.

Q I have type 2 diabetes and my doctor says losing a few pounds might bring down my blood glucose. What's the best way to lose weight?

A Going on a strict, low-calorie diet or skipping meals isn't recommended for losing weight. Skipping meals can be dangerous if you're taking insulin or oral medication for diabetes. The best way to lose weight is to take small steps to eat less and become more active. To lose at the safest rate—about 1 pound per week—and ensure a more permanent loss, you must create a 500-calorie deficit each day. For instance, you could eat 250 fewer calories by trimming portion sizes and substituting low-calorie foods for high-calorie ones and burn off 250 more calories by taking a brisk 50-minute walk. Making gradual changes helps you stick with your new habits—and keep weight off. Your registered dietitian and doctor will advise you on the best weight-loss plan for you.

Sources for More Information

Contact any one of these organizations for more information about diabetes.

The American Diabetes Association
1660 Duke Street
Alexandria, VA 22314
Phone: 800/342-2383

The American Dietetic Association National Center for Nutrition and Dietetics
216 W. Jackson Blvd.
Chicago, IL 60606-6995
Phone: 800/877-1600

American Association of Diabetes Educators
100 W. Monroe
Fourth Floor
Chicago, IL 60603
Phone: 800/832-6874

Canadian Diabetes Association
Suite 800
15 Toronto Street
Toronto, ON Canada M5C 2E3
Phone: 416/363-3373

International Diabetes Center
3800 Park Nicollet Blvd.
Minneapolis, MN 55416
Phone: 800/898-4322

International Diabetic Athletes Association
1647-B W. Bethany Home Road
Phoenix, AZ 85015
Phone: 602/433-2113

Joslin Diabetes Center
1 Joslin Place
Boston, MA 02215
Phone: 617/732-2400

Internet Resources
www.diabetes.com
www.aadenet.org
www.diabetesmonitor.com
www.joslin.org
www.diabetes.org

exchange
LISTS

Diet plays an important role in the management of diabetes, as discussed in the basics section pages 208 to 223. The exchange system helps you monitor your carbohydrate intake easier.

t the exchange system takes the guesswork out of keeping track of how many carbohydrates you're eating. To use exchanges correctly, it's important to talk to your doctor and dietitian. They will determine your calorie needs and teach you how to use the exchanges. Based on your individual needs, such as height, weight, and activity, your dietitian will provide you with a daily meal plan. The meal plan indicates the number of servings from each food list that you are allowed per meal each day. Carry your meal plan with you at all times by making a copy of page 237 and writing in the exchanges your

dietitian has determined for you. If your plan changes, make a copy of page 237 and fill in your new exchanges.

The meal plan should be designed to fit your individual needs. If you find the plan too difficult to follow (for example, it includes more milk than you usually drink), ask your dietitian to change the plan. You can monitor your food choices easier if your plan fits your needs. The following pages list the serving amounts for various foods. The lists include Starch, Fruit, Milk, Other Carbohydrates, Vegetables, Meat and Meat Substitutes, Fat, Fast foods, Combination Foods, and Free Foods.

starch list

One Starch Exchange equals 15 grams carbohydrate, 3 grams protein, 0-1 grams fat, and 80 calories.

Bread / Count as 1 Starch Exchange

Bagel	½ (1 oz.)
Bread, reduced-calorie	2 slices (1½ oz.)
Bread (pumpernickel, rye, white, whole wheat)	1 slice (1 oz.)
Breadsticks, crisp, 4" long x ½"	2 (⅔ oz.)
English muffin	½
Hot dog or hamburger bun	½ (1 oz.)
Pita, 6" across	½
Raisin bread, unfrosted	1 slice (1 oz.)
Roll, plain, small	1 (1 oz.)
Tortilla (corn), 6" across	1
Tortilla (flour), 7–8" across	1
Waffle, 4½" square, reduced-fat	1

Cereals and Grains / Count as 1 Starch Exchange

Bran cereals	½ cup
Bulgur	½ cup
Cereals, sugar-frosted	½ cup
Cereals, unsweetened, ready-to-eat	¾ cup
Cornmeal (dry)	3 Tbsp.
Couscous	⅓ cup
Flour (dry)	3 Tbsp.
Granola, low-fat	¼ cup
Grape Nuts	¼ cup
Grits	½ cup
Kasha	½ cup
Millet	¼ cup
Muesli	¼ cup
Oats	½ cup
Pasta	½ cup
Puffed cereal	1½ cups
Rice (brown or white)	⅓ cup
Rice milk	½ cup
Shredded wheat	½ cup
Wheat germ	3 Tbsp.

Crackers and Snacks / Count as 1 Starch Exchange

Animal crackers	8
Graham crackers, 2½" square	3
Matzoh	¾ oz.
Melba toast	4 slices
Oyster crackers	24
Popcorn (popped, no fat added or low-fat microwave)	3 cups
Pretzels	¾ oz.
Rice cakes, 4" across	2
Saltine-type crackers	6
Snack chips, fat-free (potato, tortilla)	15–20 (¾ oz.)
Whole wheat crackers, no fat added	2–5 (¾ oz.)

* 400 mg or more sodium per exchange

Starchy Vegetables / Count as 1 Starch Exchange

Baked beans	⅓ cup
Corn	½ cup
Corn on cob, medium	1 (5 oz.)
Mixed vegetables with corn, peas, or pasta	1 cup
Peas, green	½ cup
Plantain	½ cup
Potato, baked or boiled	1 small (3 oz.)
Potato, mashed	½ cup
Squash, winter (acorn, butternut)	1 cup
Yam, sweet potato, plain	½ cup

Dried Beans, Peas, and Lentils

Count as 1 Starch Exchange, plus 1 Very Lean Meat Exchange

Beans and peas (black-eyed, garbanzo, kidney, pinto, split, white)	½ cup
Lentils	½ cup
Lima beans	⅔ cup

Starchy Foods Prepared with Fat

Count as 1 Starch Exchange, plus 1 Fat Exchange

Biscuit, 2½" across	1
Chow mein noodles	½ cup
Corn bread, 2" cube	1 (2 oz.)
Crackers, round butter type	6
Croutons	1 cup
French-fried potatoes	16 to 25 (3 oz.)
Granola	¼ cup
Muffin, small	1 (1½ oz.)
Pancake, 4" across	2
Popcorn, microwave	3 cups
Sandwich crackers (cheese or peanut butter filling)	3
Stuffing, bread, prepared	⅓ cup
Taco shell, 6" across	2
Waffle, 4½" square	1
Whole wheat crackers, fat added	4 to 6 (1 oz.)

Some foods purchased uncooked will weigh less after it is cooked. Starches often swell in cooking so a small amount of uncooked starch will become a much larger amount of cooked food. The following table shows these changes.

Food (Starch Group)	Uncooked	Cooked
Cream of Wheat	2 Tbsp.	½ cup
Dried beans	¼ cup	½ cup
Dried peas	¼ cup	½ cup
Grits	3 Tbsp.	½ cup
Lentils	3 Tbsp.	½ cup
Macaroni	¼ cup	½ cup
Noodles	⅓ cup	½ cup
Oatmeal	3 Tbsp.	½ cup
Rice	2 Tbsp.	⅓ cup
Spaghetti	¼ cup	½ cup

fruit list

One Fruit Exchange equals 15 grams carbohydrate and 60 calories.
Weights include skin, core, seeds, and rind.

Fruit / Count as 1 Fruit Exchange

Apple, small, unpeeled	1 (4 oz.)
Apples, dried	4 rings
Applesauce, unsweetened	½ cup
Apricots, canned	½ cup
Apricots, dried	8 halves
Apricots, fresh	4 whole (5½ oz.)
Banana, small	1 (4 oz.)
Blackberries	¾ cup
Blueberries	¾ cup
Cantaloupe, small	⅓ melon (11 oz.) or 1 cup cubes
Cherries, sweet, canned	½ cup
Cherries, sweet, fresh	12 (3 oz.)
Dates	3
Figs, dried	1½
Figs, fresh	1½ large or 2 medium (3½ oz.)
Fruit cocktail	½ cup
Grapefruit, large	½ (11 oz.)
Grapefruit sections, canned	¾ cup
Grapes, small	17 (3 oz.)
Honeydew melon	1 slice (10 oz.) or 1 cup cubes
Kiwifruit	1 (3½ oz.)
Mandarin oranges, canned	¾ cup
Mango, small	½ fruit (5½ oz.) or ½ cup
Nectarine, small	1 (5 oz.)
Orange, small	1 (6½ oz.)

Papaya	½ fruit (8 oz.) or 1 cup cubes
Peach, medium, fresh	1 (6 oz.)
Peaches, canned	½ cup
Pear, large, fresh	½ (4 oz.)
Pears, canned	½ cup
Pineapple, canned	½ cup
Pineapple, fresh	¾ cup
Plums, canned	½ cup
Plums, small	2 (5 oz.)
Prunes, dried	3
Raisins	2 Tbsp.
Raspberries	1 cup
Strawberries	1¼ cup whole berries
Tangerines, small	2 (8 oz.)
Watermelon	1 slice (13½ oz.) or 1¼ cup cubes

Fruit Juice / Count as 1 Fruit Exchange

Apple juice/cider	½ cup
Cranberry juice cocktail	⅓ cup
Cranberry juice cocktail, reduced-calorie	1 cup
Fruit juice blends, 100% juice	⅓ cup
Grapefruit juice	½ cup
Grape juice	⅓ cup
Orange juice	½ cup
Pineapple juice	½ cup
Prune juice	⅓ cup

milk list

One Milk Exchange equals 12 grams carbohydrate and 8 grams protein.

Fat-Free & Low-Fat Milk (0-3 g fat/serving)
Count as 1 Milk Exchange

Fat-free milk	1 cup
½% milk	1 cup
1% milk	1 cup
Fat-free or low-fat buttermilk	1 cup
Evaporated fat-free milk	½ cup
Fat-free dry milk	⅓ cup dry
Plain nonfat yogurt	¾ cup
Nonfat or low-fat fruit-flavored yogurt sweetened with aspartame or with a non-nutritive sweetener	1 cup

Reduced-Fat (5 g fat/serving) / Count as 1 Milk Exchange

2% milk	1 cup
Plain low-fat yogurt	¾ cup
Sweet acidophilus milk	1 cup

Whole Milk (8 g fat/serving) / Count as 1 Milk Exchange

Evaporated whole milk	½ cup
Goat's milk	1 cup
Whole milk	1 cup

other carbohydrates list

One Exchange equals 15 grams carbohydrate, or 1 starch, or 1 fruit, or 1 milk

Food / Count as 1 Carbohydrate Exchange	Serving Size	Exchanges Per serving
Angel food cake, unfrosted	¹⁄₁₂ cake	2 carbohydrates
Brownie, small, unfrosted	2 in. square	1 carbohydrate, 1 fat
Cake, unfrosted	2 in. square	1 carbohydrate, 1 fat
Cake, frosted	2 in. square	2 carbohydrates, 1 fat
Chocolate milk, whole	1 cup	2 carbohydrates, 1 fat
Cookie, fat-free	2 small	1 carbohydrate
Cookie or sandwich cookie with creme filling	2 small	1 carbohydrate, 1 fat
Cranberry sauce, jellied	¼ cup	2 carbohydrates
Cupcake, frosted	1 small	2 carbohydrates, 1 fat
Doughnut, plain cake	1 medium (1½ oz)	1½ carbohydrates, 2 fats
Doughnut, glazed	3¾ in. across (2 oz.)	2 carbohydrates, 2 fats
Fruit juice bars, frozen, 100% juice	1 bar (3 oz.)	1 carbohydrate
Fruit snacks, chewy (pureed fruit concentrate)	1 Tbsp.	1 carbohydrate
Fruit spreads, 100% fruit	1 Tbsp.	1 carbohydrate
Gelatin, regular	½ cup	1 carbohydrate
Gingersnaps	3	1 carbohydrate
Granola bar	1 bar	1 carbohydrate, 1 fat
Granola bar, fat-free	1 bar	2 carbohydrates
Honey	1 Tbsp.	1 carbohydrate
Hummus	⅓ cup	1 carbohydrate, 1 fat
Ice cream	½ cup	1 carbohydrate, 2 fats
Ice cream, light	½ cup	1 carbohydrate, 1 fat
Ice cream, fat-free, no sugar added	½ cup	1 carbohydrate
Jam or jelly, regular	1 Tbsp.	1 carbohydrate
Pie, fruit, 2 crusts	⅙ pie	3 carbohydrate, 2 fats
Pie pumpkin or custard	⅛ pie	1 carbohydrate, 2 fats
Potato chips	12-18 (1 oz.)	1 carbohydrate, 2 fats
Pudding, regular (made with low-fat milk)	½ cup	2 carbohydrates
Pudding, sugar-free (made with low-fat milk)	½ cup	1 carbohydrate
Salad dressing, fat-free*	¼ cup	1 carbohydrate
Sherbet, sorbet	½ cup	2 carbohydrates
Spaghetti or pasta sauce, canned*	½ cup	1 carbohydrate, 1 fat
Sugar	1 Tbsp.	1 carbohydrate
Sweet roll or Danish	1 (2½ oz.)	2½ carbohydrates, 2 fats
Syrup, light	2 Tbsp.	1 carbohydrate
Syrup, regular	1 Tbsp.	1 carbohydrate
Syrup, regular	¼ cup	4 carbohydrates
Tortilla chips	6-12 (1 oz.)	1 carbohydrate, 2 fats
Vanilla wafers	5	1 carbohydrate, 1 fat
Yogurt, frozen, low-fat, fat-free	⅓ cup	1 carbohydrate, 0-1 fat
Yogurt, frozen, fat-free, no sugar added	½ cup	1 carbohydrate
Yogurt, low-fat with fruit	1 cup	3 carbohydrates, 0-1 fat

* 400 mg or more sodium per exchange

vegetables list

One Vegetable Exchange equals 5 grams carbohydrate, 2 grams protein, 0 grams fat, and 25 calories.

Food	Uncooked	Cooked or Juice
Artichoke	1 cup	½ cup
Artichoke hearts	1 cup	½ cup
Asparagus	1 cup	½ cup
Beans (green, Italian, wax)	1 cup	½ cup
Bean sprouts	1 cup	½ cup
Beets	1 cup	½ cup
Broccoli	1 cup	½ cup
Brussels sprouts	1 cup	½ cup
Cabbage	1 cup	½ cup
Carrots	1 cup	½ cup
Cauliflower	1 cup	½ cup
Celery	1 cup	½ cup
Cucumber	1 cup	½ cup
Eggplant	1 cup	½ cup
Green onions or scallions	1 cup	½ cup
Greens (collard, kale, mustard, turnip)	1 cup	½ cup
Kohlrabi	1 cup	½ cup
Leeks	1 cup	½ cup
Mixed vegetables (without corn, peas, or pasta)	1 cup	½ cup

Food	Uncooked	Cooked or Juice
Mushrooms	1 cup	½ cup
Okra	1 cup	½ cup
Onions	1 cup	½ cup
Pea pods	1 cup	½ cup
Peppers (all varieties)	1 cup	½ cup
Radishes	1 cup	½ cup
Salad greens (endive, escarole, lettuce, romaine)	1 cup	½ cup
Sauerkraut*	1 cup	½ cup
Spinach	1 cup	½ cup
Summer squash	1 cup	½ cup
Tomato	1 cup	½ cup
Tomatoes, canned	1 cup	½ cup
Tomato sauce*	1 cup	½ cup
Tomato/vegetable juice*	1 cup	½ cup
Turnips	1 cup	½ cup
Water chestnuts	1 cup	½ cup
Watercress	1 cup	½ cup
Zucchini	1 cup	½ cup

* 400 mg or more sodium per exchange

meat & meat substitutes list

Very Lean Meat and Substitutes

One exchange equals 0 grams carbohydrate, 7 grams protein, grams fat, and 35 calories.

Count as 1 Very Lean Meat Exchange

Fat-free cheese (≤1g fat/oz.)	1 oz.
Nonfat or low-fat cottage cheese (≤1g fat/oz.)	¼ cup
Fresh or frozen cod, flounder, haddock, halibut, trout, tuna (fresh or canned in water)	1 oz.
Buffalo, duck, or pheasant (no skin), ostrich, venison	1 oz.
Chicken or turkey (white meat, no skin), Cornish hen (no skin)	1 oz.
Clams, crab, imitation shellfish, lobster, scallops, shrimp	1 oz.
Egg substitutes, plain	¼ cup
Egg whites	2
Hot dogs with ≤ 1 g fat per ounce*	1 oz.
Kidney (high in cholesterol)	1 oz.
Processed sandwich meats with 1 gram or less fat per ounce such as chipped beef,* deli thin shaved meats, turkey ham	1 oz.
Sausage with ≤ 1g fat per ounce	1 oz.

Count as 1 Very Lean Meat Exchange and 1 Starch Exchange

Dried beans, lentils, peas, (cooked)	½ cup

Lean Meat and Substitutes

One exchange equals 0 grams carbohydrate, 7 grams protein, 3 grams fat, and 55 calories.

Count as 1 Lean Meat Exchange

USDA Select or Choice grades of lean beef trimmed of fat, such as flank, round, and sirloin steak; ground round; roast (chuck, rib, rump); steak (cubed, porterhouse, T-bone); tenderloin	1 oz.
Cheeses (≤3g fat/oz.)	1 oz.
Chicken and turkey (dark meat, no skin), chicken white meat (with skin), domestic duck or goose (well-drained of fat, no skin)	1 oz.
Cottage cheese (4.5% fat)	¼ cup
Game: Goose (no skin), rabbit	1 oz.
Herring (uncreamed or smoked)	1 oz.
Hot dogs (≤3g fat/oz.*)	1½ oz.
Lamb: Chop, leg, roast	1 oz.
Liver, heart (high in cholesterol)	1 oz.
Oysters	6 medium
Parmesan, grated	2 Tbsp.
Pork (lean), such as boiled, canned, or cured ham; Canadian-style bacon*; center loin chop; fresh ham; tenderloin	1 oz.
Processed sandwich meat with (≤3g fat/oz.) such as kielbasa or turkey pastrami	1 oz.
Salmon (fresh or canned), catfish	1 oz.
Sardines (canned)	2 medium
Tuna (canned in oil, drained)	1 oz.
Veal, lean chop, roast	1 oz.

* 400 mg or more sodium per exchange

Medium-Fat Meat and Substitutes

One exchange equals 0 grams carbohydrate, 7 grams protein, 5 grams fat, and 75 calories.

Count as 1 Medium-Fat Meat Exchange	
Most beef products fall into this category (corned beef; ground beef; meatloaf; Prime grades of meat trimmed of fat, such as prime rib; short ribs)	1 oz.
Chicken dark meat (with skin), fried chicken (with skin), ground turkey or ground chicken	1 oz.
Egg (high in cholesterol, limit to 3 per week)	1
Feta Cheese (≤5g fat/oz.)	1 oz.
Fish (Any fried fish product)	1 oz.
Lamb (ground, rib roast)	1 oz.
Mozzarella Cheese (≤5g fat/oz.)	1 oz.
Pork (Boston butt, chop, cutlet, top loin)	1 oz.
Ricotta Cheese (≤5g fat/oz.)	2 oz. (¼ cup)
Sausage (≤5g fat/oz.)	1 oz.
Soy milk	1 cup
Tofu	4 oz. (½ cup)
Veal Cutlet (cubed or ground, unbreaded)	1 oz.

High-Fat Meat and Substitutes

One exchange equals 0 grams carbohydrate, 7 grams protein, 8 grams fat, and 100 calories.

These items are high in saturated fat, cholesterol, and calories and may raise blood cholesterol levels if eaten regularly.

Count as 1 High-Fat Meat Exchange	
Bacon	3 slices (20 slices/lb.)
Cheese (All regular cheeses, such as American,* cheddar, Monterey Jack, Swiss)	1 oz.
Hot dog (chicken or turkey)*	1 (10/lb.)
Pork (Ground pork, pork sausage, spareribs)	1 oz.
Processed sandwich meat such as bologna, pimiento loaf, salami (≤5g fat/oz.)	1 oz.
Sausage, such as bratwurst, Italian, knockwurst, Polish, smoked	1 oz.

Count as 1 High-Fat Meat plus 1 Fat Exchange	
Hot dog (beef, pork, or combination)*	1 (10/lb.)
Peanut butter (contains unsaturated fat)	2 Tbsp.

* 400 mg or more sodium per exchange

fat list

One Fat Exchange equals 5 grams fat and 45 calories.

Monounsaturated Fats List / Count as 1 Fat Exchange

Almonds, cashews	6 nuts
Avocado, medium	⅛ (1 oz.)
Green Olives, stuffed*	10 large
Mixed Nuts (50% peanuts)	6 nuts
Oil (canola, olive, peanut)	1 tsp.
Peanut butter, smooth or crunchy	2 tsp.
Peanuts	10 nuts
Pecans	4 halves
Ripe (black) Olives	8 large
Sesame seeds	1 Tbsp.
Tahini paste	2 tsp.

Polyunsaturated Fats List / Count as 1 Fat Exchange

Margarine Lower-fat (30% to 50% vegetable oil)	1 Tbsp.
Margarine Stick, tub, or squeeze	1 tsp.
Mayonaise (Reduced-fat)	1 Tbsp.
Mayonaise (Regular)	1 tsp.
Miracle Whip Salad Dressing (Reduced fat)	1 Tbsp.
Miracle Whip Salad Dressing (Regular)	2 tsp.
Oil (corn, safflower, soybean)	1 tsp.

Salad dressing (Reduced-fat)	2 Tbsp.
Salad dressing (Regular)*	1 Tbsp.
Seeds (pumpkin, sunflower)	1 Tbsp.
Walnuts	4 halves

Saturated Fats List** / Count as 1 Fat Exchange

Bacon, cooked	1 slice (20 slices/lb.)
Bacon grease	1 tsp.
Butter (Reduced-fat)	1 Tbsp.
Butter (Stick)	1 tsp.
Butter (Whipped)	2 tsp.
Coconut, sweetened, shredded	2 Tbsp.
Cream, half-and-half	2 Tbsp.
Cream Cheese (Reduced-fat)	2 Tbsp. (1 oz.)
Cream Cheese (Regular)	1 Tbsp. (½ oz.)
Shortening or lard	1 tsp.
Sour Cream (Reduced-fat)	3 Tbsp.
Sour Cream (Regular)	2 Tbsp.

*= 400 mg or more sodium per exchange
** Saturated fats can raise blood cholesterol levels if eaten regularly.

combination foods list

Entrees / Count as 1 Combination Food Exchange

Entrees / Count as 1 Combination Food Exchange	Serving size	Exchanges per serving
Tuna noodle casserole, chili with beans, lasagna, macaroni, and cheese, spaghetti with meatballs*	1 cup (8 oz.)	2 carbohydrates, 2 medium-fat meats
Chow mein (without noodles or rice)*	2 cups (16 oz.)	1 carbohydrate, 2 lean meat
Pizza, cheese, thin crust*	¼ of 10 in. (5 oz.)	2 carbohydrates, 2 medium-fat meats, 1 fat
Pizza, meat topping, thin*	¼ of 10 in. (5 oz.)	2 carbohydrates, 2 medium-fat meats, 2 fats
Potpie*	1 (7 oz.)	2 carbohydrates, 1 medium-fat meat, 4 fats

Frozen entrees / Count as 1 Combination Food Exchange	Serving size	Exchanges per serving
Entrée with less than 300	1 (8 oz.)	2 carbohydrates, 3 lean meats
Salisbury steak with gravy mashed potato*	1 (11 oz.)	2 carbohydrates, 3 medium-fat meats, 3-4 fats
Turkey with gravy, mashed potato, dressing*	1 (11 oz.)	2 carbohydrates, 2 medium-fat meats, 2 fats

Soup / Count as 1 Combination Food Exchange	Serving size	Exchanges per serving
Bean*	1 cup (8 oz.)	1 carbohydrate, 1 very lean meat
Cream (made with water)*	1 cup (8 oz.)	1 carbohydrate, 1 fat
Split pea (made with water)*	½ cup (4 oz.)	1 carbohydrate
Tomato (made with water)*	1 cup (8 oz.)	1 carbohydrate
Vegetable beef, chicken noodle or other broth-type*	1 cup (8 oz.)	1 carbohydrate

fast foods

Food	Serving size	Exchanges per serving
Burritos with beef*	2	4 carbohydrates, 2 medium-fat meats, 2 fats
Chicken nuggets*	6	1 carbohydrate, 2 medium-fat meats, 1 fat
Chicken breast and wing, breaded and fried*	1 each	1 carbohydrate, 4 medium-fat meats, 2 fats
Fish sandwich/tartar sauce*	1	3 carbohydrates, 1 medium-fat meat, 3 fats
French fries, thin*	20-25	2 carbohydrates, 2 fats
Hamburger, regular	1	2 carbohydrates, 2 medium-fat meats
Hamburger, large*	1	2 carbohydrates, 3 medium-fat meats, 1 fat
Hot dog with bun*	1	1 carbohydrate, 1 high-fat meat, 1 fat
Individual pan pizza*	1	5 carbohydrates, 3 medium-fat meats, 3 fats
Soft-serve cone	1 medium	2 carbohydrates, 1 fat
Submarine sandwich*	1 sub (6 in.)	3 carbohydrates, 1 vegetable, 2 medium-fat meats, 1 fat
Taco, hard shell*	1 (6 oz.)	2 carbohydrates, 2 medium-fat meats, 2 fats
Taco, soft shell*	1 (3 oz.)	1 carbohydrate, 1 medium-fat meat, 1 fat

free foods list

A free food is any food or drink that contains less than 5 grams carbohydrate and less than 20 calories per serving.

Fat-Free or Reduced-Fat Foods

Cream cheese, fat-free	1 Tbsp.
Creamers, nondairy, liquid	1 Tbsp.
Creamers, nondairy, powdered	2 tsp.
Margarine, fat-free	4 Tbsp.
Margarine, reduced-fat	1 tsp.
Mayonnaise, fat-free	1 Tbsp.
Mayonnaise, reduced-fat	1 tsp.
Miracle Whip, nonfat	1 Tbsp.
Miracle Whip, reduced-fat	1 tsp.
Nonstick cooking spray	
Salad dressing, fat-free	1 Tbsp.
Salad dressing, fat-free, Italian	2 Tbsp.
Salsa	¼ cup
Sour cream, fat-free, reduced-fat	1 Tbsp.
Whipped topping, regular or light	2 Tbsp.

Sugar-Free or Low-Sugar Foods

Candy, hard, sugar-free	1 candy
Gelatin, unflavored	
Gelatin dessert, sugar-free	
Gum, sugar-free	
Jam or jelly, low-sugar or light	2 tsp.
Sugar substitutes†	
Syrup, sugar-free	2 Tbsp.

†Sugar substitutes, alternatives, or replacements that are approved by the Food and Drug Administration (FDA) are considered to be safe to use.
Common brand names include: Equal (aspartame), Sprinkle Sweet (saccharin), Sugar Twin (saccharin), Sweet One (acesulfame K), Sweet 'n' Low (saccharin), Sweet-10 (saccharin).

Drinks

Bouillon, broth, consommé*	
Carbonated or mineral water	
Club soda or tonic water, sugar-free	
Cocoa powder, unsweetened	1 Tbsp.
Coffee and tea	
Diet soft drinks, sugar-free	
Drink mixes, sugar-free	

Condiments

Catsup	1 Tbsp.
Horseradish	
Lemon or lime juice	
Mustard	
Pickles, dill*	1½ large
Soy sauce, regular or light*	
Taco sauce	1 Tbsp.
Vinegar	

Seasonings**

Flavoring extracts
Garlic
Herbs, fresh or dried
Pimiento
Spices
Tabasco or hot pepper sauce
Wine, used in cooking
Worcestershire sauce

*400 mg or more sodium per exchange

**Use seasonings sparingly that contain sodium or seasonings that are salts, such as garlic or celery salt and lemon pepper.

glossary OF TERMS

Calorie A term that describes the heat or energy value of food. In the diet, calories come from carbohydrates, protein, fat, and alcohol.

Carbohydrate A major nutrient or source of energy in foods. Sugars and starches are the most common carbohydrates. Food sources include sugars, breads, cereals, vegetables, fruit, and milk. One gram of carbohydrate equals 4 calories.

Certified Diabetes Educator (CDE) A health educator who specializes in diabetes and has passed the Certification Examination for Diabetes Educators and is certified by the American Association of Diabetes Educators. The initials CDE are listed after a person's name if he or she has this certification. CDEs must complete continuing education to remain certified.

Cholesterol This is a fat-like substance made in the liver. It is found in the blood and all foods from animals, such as milk, meats, eggs, and butter. A high level in the blood is a major risk factor for developing heart disease. Eating foods high in dietary cholesterol has been shown to raise blood cholesterol levels.

Diabetes Mellitus A disease that is indicated when the body cells fail to use carbohydrates because of an inadequate production or use of the hormone called insulin. Insulin is produced by the pancreas.

Dietitian A registered dietitian (RD) is recognized by the medical community as the primary provider of nutritional care, education, and counseling. The initials RD after a person's name ensures that he or she has met the standards set by the American Dietetic Association. An RD is required to take an exam to become registered and must take continuing nutrition education to remain registered.

Exchange Foods that are grouped together on a list according to the similarities of the foods. Measured amounts of foods within the group can be exchanged or traded in planning meals. A single exchange contains approximately the same amounts of carbohydrate, protein, fat, and calories.

Free foods A food or drink that has less than 20 calories or less than 5 grams of carbohydrates per serving and do not need to be counted as exchanges. These foods should be limited to three servings per day and spread throughout the day to avoid affecting blood sugar levels. Foods listed without a serving size can be eaten as often as desired.

Fat A major energy source and nutrient found in food. Fat is a more concentrated source of calories than protein or carbohydrate with 9 calories per gram of weight. Fat is found in the fat and meat lists. Some types of milk and foods from the starch list also contain fat.

Monounsaturated fat This type of fat is liquid at room temperature and is found in vegetable oils, such as canola and olive oils. These types of fats have been found to help lower high blood cholesterol levels when they are included in a lower fat diet.

Polyunsaturated fat This type of fat is usually liquid at room temperature and is found in vegetable oils, such as safflower, sunflower, corn, and soybean oils. Polyunsaturated fats have been found to help lower high blood cholesterol levels when they are part of a lower fat diet.

Saturated fat This type of fat has been shown to raise blood cholesterol levels. It is found in animal foods and is usually hard at room temperature. Examples include butter, lard, meat fat, solid shortening, palm oil, and coconut oil.

Fiber An indigestible part of foods that adds bulk but no calories to the diet. It is most notably found in foods from the Starch, Vegetable, and Fruit lists.

Fructose A simple carbohydrate, fructose naturally is found in fruit. It also is added to various foods in the form of crystalline fructose or high-fructose corn syrup. It is 1½ times sweeter than table sugar (sucrose).

Glucose A simple sugar found in the blood. It is made either by the digestion of food or from other carbohydrate and protein sources in the body.

Gram A unit of mass and weight in the metric system. This unit of measure is used for the three major nutrients found in foods—protein, carbohydrate, and fat. Thirty grams equal one ounce.

HDL (high-density lipoproteins) Often called the "good cholesterol" because these substances carry cholesterol out of the body. These lipoproteins are not actually cholesterol but substances made up of fat and protein.

Hyperglycemia High blood glucose (sugar) levels.

Hypoglycemia Low blood glucose (sugar) levels.

Insulin A hormone produced by the pancreas that is necessary in utilizing carbohydrates in the body.

Insulin reaction A rapid decline in the blood glucose level resulting from the action of injected insulin.

LDL (low-density lipoproteins) Often called the "bad cholesterol" because these substances carry cholesterol from the liver into the body cells and often deposits the cholesterol on the arterial walls, where it can eventually build up. These lipoproteins are not actually cholesterol but substances made up of fat and protein.

Meal plan A guide that shows the number of exchanges to eat at each meal based on an individual's calorie needs and activity level.

Protein One of the three major nutrients found in food. Protein provides approximately 4 calories per gram of weight. Protein is predominately found in foods from the Milk and Meat exchange lists. It is found in smaller amounts in foods from the Vegetable and Starch lists.

Sodium This mineral is essential to the body to maintain life. It is found mainly as a component of salt. The reduction of sodium (and salt) in the diet can help in lowering high blood pressure.

Starch One of the two major types of carbohydrates. Those foods that contain mostly starches are found in the Starch list.

Sugar alcohols These alcohols, such as sorbitol, mannitol, and xylitol, often are used in foods instead of sugar. These sugars do not contain ethanol, as in alcoholic beverages. They are found naturally in many fruits and vegetables and often are used to sweeten sugarless gums, candies, jams, and jellies. In some people, sorbitol and mannitol may cause a laxative effect when eaten in large amounts. It is best to eat them in moderation.

Sugars One of the two major types of carbohydrates. The main food groups that contain naturally occurring sugars include those from the Milk, Vegetable, and Fruit lists. Added sugars include table sugar and the sugar alcohols (see "sugar alcohols" above.)

Tryglycerides A type of fat that is normally found in the blood. These fats are made from the foods eaten. Being overweight or consuming too much fat, alcohol, or sugar can increase blood tryglycerides.

index

tips

exchanges

Use these abbreviated lists as general guides to serving amounts (see full Exchange Lists located on the inside covers of front and back of book):

One Starch Exchange Is:

1 ounce of a bread product, such as 1 slice of bread

1 ounce cheese

1 egg

½ cup cooked dried beans, peas, lentils

2 tablespoons peanut butter

3 slices bacon

½ cup cooked cereal, grain, pasta, or starchy vegetable such as corn

¾ to 1 ounce of most snack foods

One Meat Exchange Is:

1 ounce cooked meat, poultry, or fish

1 ounce cheese

1 egg

½ cup cooked dried beans, peas, lentils

2 tablespoons peanut butter

3 slices bacon

One Vegetable Exchange Is:

1 cup raw vegetables such as lettuce, spinach, or broccoli flowerets

½ cup cooked vegetables or vegetable juice

One Fruit Exchange Is:

1 small to medium piece of fresh fruit such as an apple or orange

½ cup canned or fresh fruit or fruit juice

¼ cup dried fruit

One Milk Exchange Is:

1 cup milk

1 cup yogurt

One Fat Exchange Is:

1 teaspoon vegetable oil, regular margarine, butter, or mayonnaise

1 tablespoon regular salad dressing

6 almonds or cashews, or 4 pecan or walnut halves

2 teaspoons peanut butter

1 slice bacon

One Free Food is:

1 tablespoon fat-free cream cheese

1 tablespoon fat-free mayonnaise

4 tablespoons fat-free margarine

1 tablespoon fat-free salad dressing

¼ cup salsa

1 tablespoon fat-free or reduced-fat sour cream

your meal plan

See your doctor and dietitian for your personal meal plan. Record your exchange totals on a photocopy of this page.

Fold the photocopy on the dotted lines and carry it with you to work and restaurants. (This page also includes a simplified breakdown of the Exchanges.)

If your meal plan changes, simply photocopy this page again and write in your new exchanges.

Write the number of exchanges from each food group into the spaces provided on the table below.

	Breakfast	Snack	Lunch	Snack	Dinner	Snack
Calories						
Starch ( )						
Meat ( )						
Fruit ( )						
Vegetable ( )						
Milk (Skim) ( )						
Fat ( )						

combination foods

Entrées

Count as 2 Carbohydrates, 2 Medium-Fat Meat

1 cup tuna noodle casserole, lasagna, spaghetti with meatballs, chili with beans, macaroni and cheese

Count as 2 Carbohydrates, 2 Medium-Fat Meats, 2 Fats

¼ of a 10-inch pizza with meat topping, thin crust

Frozen entrées

Count as 2 Carbohydrates, 2 Medium-Fat Meats, 2 Fats

1 Turkey with gravy, mashed potato, dressing (11 ounces)

Count as 2 Carbohydrates, 3 Lean Meats

Entrée with less than 300 calories (8 ounces)

Soups

Count as 1 Carbohydrate

½ cup split pea (made with water)

1 cup tomato (made with water)

1 cup vegetable beef, chicken noodle, or other broth-type

metric cooking hints

By making a few conversions, cooks in Australia, Canada, and the United Kingdom can use these recipes with confidence. The charts on this page provide a guide for converting measurements from the U.S. customary system, which is used throughout this book, to the imperial and metric systems. There also is a conversion table for oven temperatures to accommodate the differences in oven calibrations.

Product Differences: Most of the ingredients called for in the recipes in this book are available in English-speaking countries. However, some are known by different names. Here are some common American ingredients and their possible counterparts:

- Sugar is granulated or castor sugar.
- Powdered sugar is icing sugar.
- All-purpose flour is plain household flour or white flour. When self-rising flour is used in place of all-purpose flour in a recipe that calls for leavening, omit the leavening agent (baking soda or baking powder) and salt.
- Light-colored corn syrup is golden syrup.
- Cornstarch is cornflour.
- Baking soda is bicarbonate of soda.
- Vanilla is vanilla essence.
- Green, red, or yellow sweet peppers are capsicums.
- Golden raisins are sultanas.

Volume and Weight: Americans traditionally use cup measures for liquid and solid ingredients. The chart, below, shows the approximate imperial and metric equivalents. If you are accustomed to weighing solid ingredients, the following approximate equivalents will be helpful.

- 1 cup butter, castor sugar, or rice = 8 ounces = about 250 grams
- 1 cup flour = 4 ounces = about 125 grams
- 1 cup icing sugar = 5 ounces = about 150 grams
  Spoon measures are used for smaller amounts of ingredients. Although the size of the tablespoon varies slightly in different countries, for practical purposes and for recipes in this book, a straight substitution is all that is necessary.

  Measurements made using cups or spoons always should be level unless stated otherwise.

equivalents: U.S.=Australia/U.K.

⅛ teaspoon = 0.5 ml
¼ teaspoon = 1 ml
½ teaspoon = 2 ml
1 teaspoon = 5 ml
1 tablespoon = 1 tablespoon
¼ cup = 2 tablespoons = 2 fluid ounces = 60 ml
⅓ cup = ¼ cup = 3 fluid ounces = 90 ml
½ cup = ⅓ cup = 4 fluid ounces = 120 ml
⅔ cup = ½ cup = 5 fluid ounces = 150 ml
¾ cup = ⅔ cup = 6 fluid ounces = 180 ml
1 cup = ¾ cup = 8 fluid ounces = 240 ml
1¼ cups = 1 cup
2 cups = 1 pint
1 quart = 1 liter
½ inch =1.27 cm
1 inch = 2.54 cm

baking pan sizes

American	Metric
8×1½-inch round baking pan	20×4-cm cake tin
9×1½-inch round baking pan	23×3.5-cm cake tin
11×7×1½-inch baking pan	28×18×4-cm baking tin
13×9×2-inch baking pan	30×20×3-cm baking tin
2-quart rectangular baking dish	30×20×3-cm baking tin
15×10×1-inch baking pan	30×25×2-cm baking tin (Swiss roll tin)
9-inch pie plate	22×4- or 23×4-cm pie plate
7- or 8-inch springform pan	18- or 20-cm springform or loose-bottom cake tin
9×5×3-inch loaf pan	23×13×7-cm or 2-pound narrow loaf tin or pâté tin
1½-quart casserole	1.5-liter casserole
2-quart casserole	2-liter casserole

oven temperature equivalents

Fahrenheit Setting	Celsius Setting*	Gas Setting
300°F	150°C	Gas Mark 2 (slow)
325°F	160°C	Gas Mark 3 (moderately slow)
350°F	180°C	Gas Mark 4 (moderate)
375°F	190°C	Gas Mark 5 (moderately hot)
400°F	200°C	Gas Mark 6 (hot)
425°F	220°C	Gas Mark 7
450°F	230°C	Gas Mark 8 (very hot)
Broil		Grill

*Electric and gas ovens may be calibrated using Celsius. However, for an electric oven, increase the Celsius setting 10 to 20 degrees when cooking above 160°C. For convection or forced-air ovens (gas or electric), lower the temperature setting 10°C when cooking at all heat levels.